PASSING THE TEST

PASSING THE TEST | The false promises of standardized testing

Edited by Marita Moll

National Library of Canada Cataloguing in Publication

National Library of Canada Cataloguing in Publication
Passing the test : the false promises of standardizing testing
/ edited by Marita Moll.
Includes bibliographical references.
ISBN 0-88627-334-X
1. Educational tests and measurements—Canada. 2. Education—Standards—
Canada. I. Moll, Marita II. Canadian Centre for Policy Alternatives.
LB3054.C3P38 2004   371.26'2'09717   C2003-906548-0

Cover design by Chris Moll

Book layout by Nadene Rehnby www.handsonpublications.com

Printed in Canada

Canadian Centre for Policy Alternatives
Suite 410, 75 Albert Street
Ottawa, ON K1P 5E7
Tel 613-563-1341 Fax 613-233-1458
www.policyalternatives.ca
ccpa@policyalternatives.ca

Friend and well-known educational testing expert, David Ireland, died suddenly September 12th, 2003. David's enlightened perspective on educational testing, described here by his colleague Peter Moskos, was a lasting gift to the educational community and one for which we shall remember him.

When David started a research project, he would always ask the client three questions:

- What do you want to know?

- Why do you want to know it?

- And what would you do if you did know it?

It was really important to David that research mattered, that it would have an impact on peoples' lives, an impact that would make their lives better.

The work of which he was proudest in his career was the work he did in the Carleton Board on board-wide exams. The project was David's brainchild. He conceived it. He had the vision. The Board told David it wanted board-wide exams. But David had the brilliance to do it in a way that gave it over to teachers in math and English and let them carry it out. He trusted teachers and he believed that they had the experience and ability to execute the project. When we designed exams, it was class-room teachers, not Board consultants who did it. And every teacher had a role to play, whether it was in writing questions, marking papers or figuring out what the results meant. The project worked brilliantly because teachers carried it out. It was there to help them and support them and to help and support students. And when we had school and board-wide results, what mattered to David most was what we were going to do about them. How were we going to change our teaching so that students' performances and their knowledge and abilities improved?

TABLE OF CONTENTS

PART 1 | Opening salvos and soundbytes

PART 2 | A whirlwind tour of world-wide testing

PART 3 | Soap, SAIP or standardized test: What is the PCAP?

PART 4 | Cornering the market on HB pencils: Provincial achievement tests

PART 5 | Can't take it anymore? Join the resistance!

PART 6 | Beyond standardized testing: Meaningful school accountability

LIST OF ABBREVIATIONS

CLI	Canadian Learning Institute
CMEC	Council of Ministers of Education, Canada
CTBS	Canadian Test of Basic Skills
HRDC	Human Resources Development Canada
ICT	Information and Communication Technology
IEA	International Association for the Evaluation of Educational Achievement
NCLB	No Child Left Behind
NLSCY	National Longitudinal Survey of Children and Youth
OECD	Organisation for Economic Co-operation and Development
PCAP	Pan-Canadian Assessment Program
PISA	Programme for International Student Assessment
PIRLS	Progress in International Reading Literacy Study
SAIP	School Achievement Indicators Program
SAT	Scholastic Aptitude Tests
SITES	Second Information Technology in Education Study
TIMSS	Third International Mathematics and Science Study
YITS	Youth in Transition Survey

Passing the test
The false promises of standardized testing

In recent years, large-scale testing projects have become firmly established in Canada and around the world. Students in many provinces are inundated with regional tests, provincial tests, national tests and international tests. Appropriating resources from already cash-starved systems, these tests are now self-perpetuating industries with considerable public monies being spent on their design, production, implementation, analysis, and promotion. In Ontario alone, $57 million will be spent annually to push students through a battery of 20 provincial tests by the time they reach Grade 12. The tests have become increasingly politicized, with schools ranked publicly in local newspapers, and high school graduation (in Ontario) hinging on the outcome of a single literacy test.

While opposition to these large-scale testing programs is mounting, it is difficult for the public to enter into the debate when presented with tables, pie charts, and graphs derived from processes that are not fully explained to them and little contextual information within which to interpret the results.

The articles and essays in this book will extend the information usually provided about standardized testing by documenting concerns of researchers, teachers, parents and students to current processes, their impacts, and the use of results. The prospect of a public education system driven by the demands of standardized testing does not sit well with parents or the general public. This collection will help explain why that is so and what can be done about it.

The editor wishes to thank all who made this collection possible by contributing their papers and articles, and the staff at CCPA for the work that goes into preparing a manuscript for publication. The assistance of Dietrich Gunther, who, as part of field work activities as a teacher education student at Queen's University, did some of the early research for the testing tables, is also appreciated.

The support of Susan Ohanian and John P. Fox, who contributed artwork, is gratefully acknowledged.

For further information on standardized testing in Canada, including updated tables and e-copies of selected articles, please see www.maritamoll.ca

— Marita Moll

Large scale educational assessment

The new face of testing

by Marita Moll

"Wherever you can, count," said Francis Galton, founder of the late 19th century Eugenics Society and one of the fathers of "mental measurement."[1] A hundred years later, this thinking has taken firm hold in the educational establishment, both in Canada and internationally. The standardized testing movement now consumes millions of dollars and hundreds of hours that could be better spent on educational resources known to improve learning—like text-books, teachers, and adequate support services. All these things are still necessary, it seems, as no one has yet shown that testing, by itself, can improve learning.

Testing has become so highly valued that educational organizations now boast about how much testing takes place in their jurisdictions. The Council of Ministers of Education, Canada (CMEC), which plays a major role in testing in Canada, says:

> How well are our schools preparing students for a global economy and for lifelong learning? Attempting to answer this question, ministries of education have participated, since the mid-eighties, in a variety of studies. At the international level, through the Council of Ministers of Education Canada (CMEC), they took part in the International Educational Indicators Program of the Organization for Economic

Cooperation and Development (OECD); individually, they participated in various achievement studies such as those of the International Assessment of Educational Progress (IAEP) and the International Association for the Evaluation of Educational Achievement (IEA). In addition, in most jurisdictions, the ministries undertook or enhanced measures to assess students at different stages in their schooling.[2]

It's interesting to note that the word "test" does not appear in the above quote. It's also rarely used in the websites associated with the testing projects mentioned. As far as test developers are concerned, these data- gathering activities are studies, surveys, assessments, and indicators. Call them anything, but don't call them tests.

Unfortunately, to the students writing them, the teachers preparing for them, and concerned parents dealing with the increasing fallout that surrounds them, these are still tests. They are administered in addition to, not in lieu of, normal course work and classroom-based testing activities. They are stressful, time-consuming, and expensive. As they become increasingly integrated and cross-tabulated, they are starting to cast long shadows over education systems, nationally and internationally.

What is standardized testing?

Ross Traub, in *Standardized Testing in Canada*,[3] defines standardized testing as follows:

> *Generically, an* achievement test *is designed to assess the knowledge and understanding a student has acquired of a school subject. A* standardized achievement test *is further defined by its being given and scored in the same way, whenever and whereever it is used. Standardization means that the scores of all students tested can be fairly compared, one against the other. Very often we think of standardized tests as consisting of multiple-choice questions, the answers to which can be scored by machine. But so-called performance tests—essays in language or social studies, laboratory assignments in science, problem solving exercises in mathematics, and so forth—can also be standardized; the essential requirements are that the conditions of administration and scoring be the same for all the students who are tested so that their scores can be compared.[4] (emphasis in original)*

Traub also distinguishes between two kinds of standardized achievement tests—examinations and assessments:

- *[Examinations] are tests used in certifying the degree to which a student has mastered the syllabus for a course… They occur at the end of courses at the highest academic level and performance on an examination makes up a portion…of the final mark for the course.*

- *Assessments involve the use of tests for purposes other than certifying a student's achievement. [They] can be administered at any time during the school year, and they are not necessarily given to every student qualified by grade level and prior instruction to take them… In such a case, the objective is to estimate the general level of…achievement in the population of students from which the sample was drawn, just as an opinion pollster attempts to read the public mood on an issue by interviewing a very few randomly chosen members of the general population.[5]*

The context of testing, however, has changed dramatically since this definition was presented in 1994. No longer just a tool for program review or curriculum evaluation, modern testing enables much wider comparisons. While the sampling method of assessment is still used, increasingly, all students in the target grades are tested. These scores are then published to create competition in education by publicly ranking schools according to test results. Both examinations and assessments are now used for "purposes other than certifying a student's achievement." In today's context, they function more like product research for target marketing than "opinion polling to read the public mood."

> Large-scale provincial, national, and international testing is not designed to improve learning. It is designed to collect data from the system, and to catalogue, classify, and rank that data.

Large-scale provincial, national, and international testing is not designed to improve learning. It is designed to collect data from the system, and to catalogue, classify, and rank that data. Testing is a multi-million dollar industry with spin-offs in all directions—including pre-tests, re-tests, test analysis, test development, and tutoring for tests. Promoting the ever-expanding testing regimes is essential to this industry, and governments are listening. Until recently, the government of Ontario was planning to extend its already extensive testing program to include assessments in two core subjects per year in every grade from 3 to 11. Test-weary Ontario directors of education asked for a three-year moratorium on this expansion plan.[6]

Wherever you can, count

Educational data gathering is no longer restricted to information about how much Jimmy learned about science last year. Surveys have become regular testing companions—seeking to extract as much information as possible about Jimmy. What kind of a home does he come from? Are there any books there? Does he have a computer? How much money do his parents earn? Some of the data-gathering starts even before Jimmy goes to school, and some of it continues to reflect what he does after he leaves school. Some of the surveys target teachers, parents, and administrators, as well as students. All these data enable the creation of databanks about individuals and groups that are well beyond the mandate of any school system or any single government body.

Trading personal information for potentially better decisions on educational policy is a tricky business. We have indicated that we are not comfortable with government databases that place too much personal information in the hands of single agencies. Not long ago, there was a massive protest when the public learned about a system of interconnected databases that had quietly been built in the federal Department of Human Resources Development Canada. Under siege for weeks, the department was finally forced to delink the databases in response to privacy concerns. The current emphasis on cradle-to-grave data gathering through the education system could well dwarf the previous attempts at government recordkeeping.

In a brand new development, the Canadian government announced, in spring 2003, its intention to create a special agency to serve as a clearing house for all the educational and personal information gathered by activities like standardized testing and surveying activities. The *Canadian Learning Institute* is to be a pan-Canadian, independent organization. It is envisioned as a multi-stakeholder effort whose key objective is to broaden and deepen data and information on education and learning.[7] Serious questions need to be asked about this initiative. Will data gathering become even more entrenched with a new home to accommodate it all? Will it lead to even more data gathering? Will more information really lead to better decision-making? Some people think we already have lots of information and not nearly enough political will to act on information that suggests reduced class size, improved access to early childhood programs, or other programs that would require more funding.

Count me out!

Everyone would like to see educational policy that would better serve the needs of Canadian children. But there's plenty of evidence that relevant data and good advice have not stopped governments in the past from ignoring the facts. The key piece of information that is constantly revealed by test scores is already a well-known fact: high test scores usually match up pretty closely with students from high-income families or schools serving high-income areas.

Eminent Canadian scientist and social activist Ursula Franklin made some astute observations about data gathering at a speech to a community group in 1994:

> There is an enormous amount of information that has nothing to do with anything. There is a sort of civic landfill and you ought not to get into the business of civic landfill. If your aim is to change conditions, then there is a certain amount of information needed, but not more. After that, one needs to address the questions, "Why does nothing happen? Why do some proposals that seem fairly reasonable, workable, and sensible never get beyond the lip service stage?" That requires a very different sort of knowledge. That is the knowledge of the structure of power.[8]

Large-scale educational assessments are not about learning. They represent a power shift in education, taking decision-making power from parents and the local community and redirecting it to central organizations and institutions that are disconnected from the local context. The reality behind the numbers becomes a problem for local authorities who, in many areas, are left to take the blame for whatever "deficiencies" the tests reveal but who have lost much of their ability to make local decisions that would improve the situation. The battle between local and centralized decision-making in education is a continuous one, but the profusion of standardized testing definitely gives the upper hand to central authorities who are now in a position to match service delivery and testing of services delivered. This leaves little room for addressing local needs with locally designed programs.

However, an informal "count me out" movement against excessive testing is gathering momentum around the globe. Hundreds of teachers in Britain have recently voted to boycott the tests. Hundreds of parents in Alberta have requested that their children be exempted from the tests. A U.S. group is even suggesting that all politicians take all the tests. If this were successful, it could be the final blow to Francis Galton's dream.

That could probably be "counted" as progress.

Marita Moll is an educational researcher and freelance writer.
An edited version of this article appeared in the Toronto Star, May 23,
2003: "Where are school tests taking us?"

Notes

[1] According to "A brief history of testing" posted at nomoretests.com, "the often overlooked roots of testing date back to the eugenics movement of the late 19th century. This movement was spearheaded by two men, Frances Galton and Charles Spearman. As founder of the Eugenics Society, Galton was known as the father of mental measurement and is famed for saying 'wherever you can, count.' Spearman's work defined a 'general mental ability,' or G force, which was passed on from gene to gene. ... The cause was next taken up by Alfred Binet of France, who was the Minister of Public Instruction in 1904. . . . who created the original version of today's common IQ tests, known as the Binet-Simon Scale."

[2] Council of Ministers of Education, Canada. *Report on Mathematics Assessment 1997: Introduction.* http://www.cmec.ca/saip/math97/Pages/intro1E.html 06 Mar 02.

[3] Traub, Ross. *Standardized Testing in Canada; A Survey of Standardized Achievement Testing by Ministries of Education and School Boards.* Toronto: Canadian Education Association, 1994.

[4] Ibid

[5] Ibid.

[6] Lindgren, April. "2nd chance for literacy failures." *Ottawa Citizen* Friday, Feb. 21, 2003. A1-2.

[7] Canada. Government of Canada. Department of Finance. Budget 2003. P. 134. Available online: http://www.fin.gc.ca/budget03/pdf/bp2003e.pdf

[8] Franklin, Ursula M. *Every Tool Shapes the Task; Communities and the Information Highway.* Vancouver: Lazara Press, 1996. p. 9.

[9] Traub, Ross. *Standardized Testing in Canada; A Survey of Standardized Achievement Testing by Ministries of Education and School Boards.* Toronto: Canadian Education Association, 1994 provides the general definition of exams used above. Proficiency tests have been added to this list because, where they exist, they are prerequisites for graduation at the high school/secondary school level.

[10] Traub, Ross. *Standardized Testing in Canada; A Survey of Standardized Achievement Testing by Ministries of Education and School Boards.* Toronto: Canadian Education Association, 1994 provides the general definition of provincial assessments.

What's so standard about standardized testing?

Where high-stakes testing has become common practice, there is evidence of low-achieving students being dismissed on test days, students with low test scores being placed in special education programs to avoid having their scores reflected in school reports, students being refused admission on the basis of low scores, and students with low test scores even being encouraged to drop out of school.

Froese-Germain, B. (2001). "Standardized testing + high stakes decisions = educational inequity," Interchange, 32(2), 111-30.

United States

Although in common parlance, the National Assessment of Educational Progress (NAEP) achievement levels have been rejected by everyone who has ever studied them: UCLA's Center for Research on Evaluation, Student Standards and Testing (CRESST), the General Accounting Office and the National Academy of Sciences, as well as by individual psychometricians such as Lyle Jones of the University of North Carolina. The studies agree that the methods used are flawed and, more importantly, the results don't accord with any other data.

Bracey, Gerald W. "No Child Left Behind (NCLB) - A Plan for the destruction of public education: Just say 'NO!'" in Moll, Marita (ed) Passing the Test; The False Promises of Standardized Testing. Ottawa: Canadian Centre for Policy Alternatives, 2003.

Texas

Every year, the Texas board of education establishes a "cut grade" — the number of questions a student must answer correctly to pass a test. Between 1998 and 2002, the cut grade for tests has decreased by as many as 11 points, including in the math tests for Grades 4, 8 and 10. The board says the fluctuations simply reflect the varying level of difficulty of each test and are necessary to maintain equivalent passing standards. Others worry politics are muddying the results in Texas.

"Once you start digging, its amazing how these scores can be manipulated for political purposes."

Schmidt, Sarah. "Texas: miracle of mirage?" National Post, November 19, 2002. p. A12.

Great Britain

In the summer of 2001, a grade fixing scandal erupted when it was discovered that up to 20,000 students received artificially deflated marks, part of an apparent campaign to quiet critics about slipping standards.

Schmidt, Sarah. "The A-level debacle." National Post, November 20, 2002. P. A11.

Canada

In 1998 CMEC decided that SAIP results would be reported in relationship to "public expectations of student performance." Claiming to be too resource-strapped to use any other method, CMEC developed a short-cut process of chatting up focus groups to generate numbers that are then represented as public opinion. CMEC now reports all SAIP results by comparing them to expectations set in this haphazard way.

The media duly reported that, in the most recent tests, Canadian students had failed to live up to the public's expectations, but no reporter questioned how these expectations were set. The public might have been interested to learn that its views were generated by 85 people invited by their respective ministers of education to guess how well students should perform on tests that these judges weren't even allowed to see.

Robertson, Heather-jane. "Bogus points" in Moll, Marita (ed) Passing the Test; The False Promises of Standardized Testing. Ottawa: Canadian Centre for Policy Alternatives, 2003.

Ontario

In the 1996 Third International Mathematics and Science exam, the Grade 8 test results, presented in graph form in a mailout to every household, showed math and science results for the top seven of 40 countries, followed by the scores for Canada and Ontario, indicating the province ranked "the lowest of the low in lowly Canada." In reality, Canada ranked above average in both subjects when compared with all 40 countries. Ontario's math score was one percentage point below the international average. Its science score was two percentage points *over* the international mean.

Froese-Germain, B. (2001). "Standardized testing + high stakes decisions = educational inequity," Interchange, 32(2), 111-30.

In the 2002 Grade 10 literacy test, the provincial improvement of 8% pass rate [over the trial run administered in 2001] was a travesty given that students knew the test would count and tried hard, and many schools had been drilling students on sample questions. The passing grade was probably lower as well, but the EQAO method of establishing the pass rate caused so much confusion that no one was sure.

Lipman, Peter. "The Ontario Grade 10 literacy test and the neo-conservative agenda." in Moll, Marita (ed) Passing the Test; The False Promises of Standardized Testing. Ottawa: Canadian Centre for Policy Alternatives, 2003.

Alberta

. . . the standards (acceptable & excellence) are determined after the tests are scored. For example, in 2002, the standard of excellence in Grade 6 math was set at 91%, with 15% of our Grade 6 students achieving at or above that level. However, if we use the traditionally accepted 80% mark for the standard of excellence, which is used for the Grade 12 diploma exams, 47% of our students achieved excellence. This seems to indicate that the results are being manipulated to make sure the government achieves its 15% (excellence) and 85% (acceptable) standards, as well as to ensure that there were no drastic swings in results from year-to-year.

Hampton, Wayne. "Challenging the testing regime in Alberta." in Moll, Marita (ed). Passing the Test: The False Promises of Standardized Testing. Ottawa: Canadian Centre for Policy Alternatives, 2003.

Table 1:   Summary of international test and survey instruments administered to Canadian elementary/secondary students

PIRLS (Progress in International Reading Literacy Study)

SUBJECT: reading

LEVEL: 9/10-year-olds

INTERNATIONAL SPONSORING AGENCY:
   IEA (International Association for the Evaluation of Educational Achievement)

CANADIAN PARTICIPANTS:
   Statistics Canada
   CMEC (Council of Ministers of Education Canada)

PIRLS is an international comparative study of the reading literacy of young students. It focuses on the achievement and reading experiences of children in 35 countries in grades equivalent to fourth grade (9- and 10-year-olds) in the United States. PIRLS consists of a test assessing a range of reading comprehension strategies for two major reading purposes—literary and informational. PIRLS collects extensive information about home, school, and national influences on how well students learn to read. Parents and caregivers also completed questionnaires about their children's early literacy activities.

Thirty-five countries participated in PIRLS 2001. With 150,000 students tested, PIRLS 2001 was the first in a planned 5-year cycle of international trend studies in reading literacy.

Students in Ontario and Quebec were part of the 2003 PIRLS cycle.

Source: http://timss.bc.edu/pirls2001.html

PISA (Programme for International Student Assessment)

SUBJECT: reading, math, science

LEVEL: 15-year-olds

INTERNATIONAL SPONSORING AGENCY:
   OECD (Organisation for Economic Co-operation and Development)

CANADIAN PARTICIPANTS:
   HRDC (Human Resources Development Canada)
   CMEC (Council of Ministers of Education Canada) Statistics Canada
   Provincial Ministries and Departments of Labour and Education

PISA is a 3-year survey of the knowledge and skills of 15-year-olds in the principal industrialized countries. It is designed to assess literacy in reading, mathematics and science. The PISA life cycle will consist of three writings of the test, each one containing elements of each subject, but with over half the assessment on one specific subject. The 2000 writing focused on reading, 2003 will focus on mathematics and 2006 on science. As it assesses literacy, 'passing' should not hinge on following a specific curriculum.

About 265,000 students from 32 countries participated in PISA 2000 (4 - 10,000 in each country except Canada). In Canada, approximately 30,000 15-year-olds from more than 1,000 schools participated in PISA in order to collect information at the provincial level and to allow for data from both official language groups. In addition to the assessment portion, students and their principals answered a survey about themselves.

According to the PISA Canada web site: "PISA aims to assess to what degree students approaching the end of their compulsory education have acquired some of the knowledge and skills that are essential for full participation in society:

- How well are young adults prepared to meet the challenges of the future?
- Are they able to analyse, reason and communicate their ideas effectively?
- Do they have the capacity to continue learning throughout life?
- Are some kinds of teaching and school organisation more effective than others?

Sources: PISA International: http://www.pisa.oecd.org/index.htm; OECD: http://www.oecd.org ; PISA Canada: http://www.pisa.gc.ca/

SITES (Second Information Technology in Education Study)

SUBJECT: Information technology survey
INTERNATIONAL SPONSORING AGENCY:
             IEA (International Association for the
             Evaluation of Educational Achievement)
             Module 2 co-ordinated with a similar OECD survey
CANADIAN PARTICIPANTS:
             Statistics Canada
             CMEC (Council of Ministers of Education Canada)

SITES is a survey divided into three modules. Module 1 (1997-99) surveyed principals and information technology co-ordinators at a sample of schools in 26 countries. Questions in the survey included summaries of information and communication technology (ICT) resources, access and utilization of these resources, and indicators of their integration into instructional processes.

Module 2 (2000-02) was co-ordinated with a complementary study of technology-based innovative schools sponsored by the OECD. Approximately 25 countries subscribed to the study, with each country conducting from 4 to 12 case studies, depending on the grade level(s) included. It is expected that the cross-national study will be based on approximately 250 case studies. Two Canadian researchers are listed among the leaders of Module 2: Ron Owston, York University, and Richard Jones, EQAO.

The goals of SITES Module 2 are:

- To identify and provide rich descriptions for innovative, technology-based pedagogical practices that are considered valuable by each country and that might be considered for large-scale implementation or adoption by schools in other countries.
- To provide information to national and local policy-makers that they can

use to make decisions related to ICT and the role it might play in advancing their country's educational goals and addressing educational needs and problems.

- To provide teachers and other practitioners with new ideas about how they can use ICT to improve classroom practices.
- To add to the body of research knowledge and theory about the contexts and factors within and across countries that contribute to the successful and sustained use of innovative technology-based pedagogical practices.
- To investigate the measurement quality of Module 1 indicators and contribute to the development of Module 3 assessments.

Module 3 is a planned survey of teachers to determine their attitudes, training and past experiences with technology, and their classroom practices. The optional student survey will include indicators of knowledge, attitudes, exposure to different learning applications, and the use of ICT in the home. SITES information page: http://SITESM2.org/SITES_Research_Projects/sites_research_projects.html

TIMSS (Third International Mathematics and Science Study)

SUBJECT: math, science

LEVEL: Original sample from Grade 3, 4, 7, 8 and last year of high school
Followups: Grade 8

INTERNATIONAL SPONSORING AGENCY:
IEA (International Association for the Evaluation of Educational Achievement)

CANADIAN PARTICIPANTS:
Statistics Canada
CMEC (Council of Ministers of Education Canada)

TIMSS compares the teaching and learning of mathematics and science at the elementary and secondary school levels with the aim of informing educators around the world about exemplary practices and outcomes.

TIMSS was conducted in 1995 at five grade levels: third, fourth, seventh, and eighth grades as well as the final year of secondary school. In total, about 500,000 students from 50 countries participated in the study, though not all countries participated in all parts of the study. In Canada, Statistics Canada was responsible for choosing a national representative sample of Canadian schools. There was a second sitting of the study in 1999 of only Grade 8 students and there will be another sitting for Grade 8 students in 2003. Subsequent sittings are intended to provide trend data to those who participated in the first TIMSS in 1995.

Students also completed a questionnaire about their opinions, attitudes, and interests. Teachers were asked about their academic and professional preparation, their teaching approaches, and the material they taught. Principals provided information about schools, students, and teachers.

Sources: International TIMSS site: http://timss.bc.edu/; Canadian TIMSS page: http://www.curricstudies.educ.ubc.ca/wprojects/TIMSS/; IEA Home Page: http://www.iea.nl/Home/home.html

Table 2: Summary of national tests and survey instruments

PCAP (Pan-Canadian Assessment Program)

Proposed to replace SAIP in 2007

SUBJECT: reading and writing, mathematics, science. Others to be added.

SPONSORING AND FUNDING AGENCIES:
     CMEC (Council of Ministers of Education Canada)
     Other participants yet to be announced

PCAP is a proposed new pan-Canadian indicator system that would allow comparison with international results over time. It will initially assess student performance in the core subjects of reading, mathematics and science. It is designed so that other subjects, such as second languages, information and communications technologies, and the arts, can be added as the need arises. PCAP will replace the School Achievement Indicators Program (SAIP), which has been in place for 10 years, and will preserve the wealth of data gathered through SAIP.

"The beauty of PCAP is that it enables us to assess the performance of our education systems here in Canada but also dove-tails with the important international assessments we are doing through the OECD. By integrating existing testing programs, PCAP greatly eases the testing burden on schools."

Source: CMEC press release, Apr. 3, 2003 http://www.cmec.ca/releases/2003-04-02.en.asp

SAIP (Student Achievement Indicators Program)

To be replaced in 2007 by Pan-Canadian Assessment Program (PCAP)

SUBJECT: mathematics, reading and writing, science

LEVEL: 13 and 16-year-olds

SPONSORING AND FUNDING AGENCIES:
     CMEC (Council of Ministers of Education Canada)
     HRDC (Human Resources Development Canada)

SAIP is a wholly Canadian endeavour designed to measure how well school systems across the country meet the needs of students and society. SAIP endeavours to answer the following question: "How well are our schools preparing students for a global economy and for lifelong learning?"

SAIP is administered to a random sample of over 35,000 13- and 16-year-olds across Canada. The program, like PISA (Program for International Student Assessment), measures skills in mathematics (content and problem solving), science, and reading and writing. A complete SAIP life cycle is three assessments, but unlike PISA each assessment measures only one skill—mathematics—1993, 97, 01; reading & writing—1994, 98, 02, 05; science—1996,99,04

According to the SAIP web site "[the] information, together with the review mechanisms of individual jurisdictions, will give each minister of education a basis for examining the curriculum and other aspects of the school system."

"The total yearly expenditure to prepare and administer SAIP is approximately $3 million. Half of these costs are covered by a direct contribution on the part of HRDC; the other half comes from the provinces and territories in the form of human and material resources assuring the ongoing development and administration of the assessments in their respective schools."

Sources: SAIP: http://www.cmec.ca/saip/indexe.stm; CMEC: http://www.cmec.ca/indexe.stm

YITS (Youth in Transition Survey)

SPONSORING AND FUNDING AGENCIES:
> HRDC (Human Resources Development Canada)
> CMEC (Council of Ministers of Education Canada)
> Statistics Canada
> Provincial Ministries and Departments of Labour and Education

YITS is a longitudinal survey given to Canadian youth. It was first distributed at the same time as PISA, to the same group of 15-year-olds in May-Apr 2000. A telephone survey was also conducted with a group of 18-20-year-olds. Parents of the 15-year-old group were also interviewed by telephone. The same groups that were interviewed in 2000 will be interviewed every two years for several years (next in 2002).

For the 15-year-old group (approximately 30,000), information was gathered in the first survey about their school experiences, achievements, expectations, and initial employment experiences (if any). Information gathered from the 18-20- year-old group (approximately 23,000) included transitions to post-secondary education and to the labour market.

The YITS web site lists the following 10 objectives:

1. To examine key transitions in the lives of youth (transition from high school to post-secondary schooling, initial transition from schooling to the labour market).

2. To better understand educational and labour market pathways and the factors influencing these pathways.

3. To identify educational and occupational pathways that provide a smoother transition to the labour market.

4. To examine the incidence, characteristics, factors, and effects of leaving school.

5. To understand the impact of school effects on educational and occupational outcomes.

6. To examine the contribution of work experience programs, part-time jobs, and volunteer activities to skill development and transition to the labour market.

7. To study the attitudes, behaviours, and skills of young people entering the labour market.

8. To gain a better understanding of the determinants of post-secondary entry and post-secondary retention, including education financing.

9. To better understand the role of educational and labour market aspirations and expectations in investment in further education and career choice.

10. To explore the educational and occupational pathways of various sub-groups, particularly "youth at risk."

Sources: http://www.pisa.gc.ca/yits.shtml

NLSCY (National Longitudinal Survey of Children and Youth)

SPONSORING AND FUNDING AGENCIES:
> HRDC (Human Resources Development Canada)
> Statistics Canada.

NLSCY is meant to measure and track the development and well-being of Canada's children and youth over time. This survey is distinctly different from YITS in that it is designed to follow a group from birth to adulthood (or in this case 0-25 years old). The initial cohort of 15,000 subjects were aged 0-11 years in 1994, the first year of the study. There will be new surveys to answer every two years until individual participants reach the age of 25.

The need for a greater understanding of learning and development in children's early years has prompted a second cohort of younger children to be added to the sample as the initial cohort ages. This second cohort, which will eventually number approximately 20,000, are to be followed through the transition into elementary school.

"The primary objective of the NLSCY is to fill an information gap by establishing a national database on the characteristics and life experiences of children and youth in Canada as they grow up. The data supports research on outcomes at each stage of development, and the research in turn informs the development of policies and strategies to help young people follow healthy, active and rewarding life paths."

The survey boasts a broad content. Questions are on a wide variety of outcomes such as health, language, cognitive, social, emotional, and behavioural. Determinants are also surveyed, including characteristics of the child's family, child care, school and neighbourhood. Questions are designed to uncover the results of interactions such as family structure and socio-economic status. Environmental factors are also surveyed.

Sources: NLSCY: http://www.hrdc-drhc.gc.ca/arb/nlscy-elnej/home.shtml; Statistics Canada: http://www.statcan.ca

Table 3: Summary of province-wide examinations

Examinations are tests used to certify the degree to which a student has mastered the syllabus for a course. They usually occur at the end of courses at the highest academic level. Performance on an examination makes up a portion of the final mark for the course. This list also includes proficiency tests given at other levels which students must pass in order to graduate (e.g., Ontario Secondary School Literacy Test). [1]

	Examination & level	Subjects, sources	Percentage of final mark	Marking
British Columbia	Provincial examination program All Grade 12 students enrolled in course	Various core subjects listed at: http://www.bced.gov.bc.ca/exams/handbook/chapter1/whatareexams.htm	40% of final mark	Marked centrally by teachers brought to a common location
Alberta	Diploma exams All Grade 12 students enrolled in course	Various core subjects listed at http://www.learning.gov.ab.ca/k_12/testing/info_students/info_students.asp	Exam mark is worth 50% of the total. A final "blended" mark of at least 50% needed to pass the course.	Marked centrally
Saskatchewan	Diploma exams All Grade 12 students enrolled in course	English language arts, mathematics, and science (chemistry, physics and biology). http://www.sasked.gov.sk.ca/student_records/faq.html	Min. 25% but up to 50% at teacher discretion	Marked centrally
Manitoba	Standards tests—mandatory at Senior 4 (Grade 12) level	Language arts (English, French, immersion) mathematics Complete list at: http://www.edu.gov.mb.ca/ks4/assess/	30%	Marked locally

[1] Traub, Ross. *Standardized Testing in Canada; A Survey of Standardized Achievement Testing by Ministries of Education and School Boards.* Toronto: Canadian Education Association, 1994 provides the general definition of provincial assessments.

* For updates to tables, please consult www.maritamoll.ca

	Examination & level	Subjects, sources	Percentage of final mark	Marking
Ontario	Ontario Secondary School Literacy Test (OSSLT) All students in Grade 10	Designed to determine whether or not students have acquired the reading and writing skills that they are expected to have learned by the end of Grade 9, as outlined in The Ontario Curriculum. http://www.eqao.com/eqao/home_page/07e/7_2_1e.html#1.3	Successful completion of the OSSLT is one of the requirements for an Ontario Secondary School Diploma. Students who are not successful may write the OSSLT an unlimited number of times and will have at least three opportunities to do so prior to the end of Grade 12.	Marked centrally
Quebec	Uniform Ministry Exams All students Secondary IV & V	Must pass the two levels of languages (language of instruction and second language—Fr./Engl) a history, math and science course (with passes in enough other courses with exams at the local level) to graduate	50% of final mark, unless school mark is out of line with exam mark, in which case the exam mark has a higher value	Central marking for multiple choice items. The rest marked locally.
New Brunswick	Middle Level English Language Proficiency Assessment—all students in Grade 8. Reassessment if necessary in Grades 10,11 or 12 English Provincial Exam—Grade 11	English literacy—reading comprehension and written expression	Must pass middle level proficiency exam or earn at least 50% in the Grade 11 English Provincial Exam to graduate	Centrally marked

	Examination & level	Subjects, sources	Percentage of final mark	Marking
Nova Scotia	Nova Scotia Examinations (NSE) All Grade 12 students enrolled in course	Chemistry 12, Cimie 12, English 12, English/communications 12, Physics 12, Mathematics (under development for 2004) http://plans.ednet.ns.ca/about.shtml	30%	Marked locally
Newfound-land	Public examinations All students enrolled in course	Various core subjects	50%	Marked centrally
Prince Edward Island	No provincial exams	Discontinued in 1969		
Northwest Territories	Alberta diploma exams	Same as Alberta	Same as Alberta	
Yukon	B.C. provincial exams Language Proficiency Index Grades 11 & 12	Same as B.C. To provide information about an individual's competency in English.	Same as B.C.	
Nunavut	Alberta diploma exams	Same as Alberta	Same as Alberta	

Table 4: Summary of province-wide assessment programs

Assessments are tests usually administered for program assessment rather than certifying an individual student's achievement. They can be administered at any time during the school year, and they are sometimes only given to a sample of students qualified by grade level and prior instruction to take them. Currently, many provinces administer the tests to all students in a grade level. They may even form part of the final mark (e.g., Ontario Provincial Achievement Tests). However, they differ from provincial examinations in that student promotion does not depend on passing the provincial assessment tests.[1]

	Program and frequency	Grade level/students tested	Subjects tested	Marking	Purpose of test
B.C.	Foundation Skills Assessment (FSA) Annual	All students in Grades 4,7,10	Reading writing numeracy	Marked centrally by teachers in a common location	Info for accountability contracts and school growth plans
	Provincial Learning Assessments Occasional (on a rotating basis with FSA)	Sample of students in Grades 4,7,10	Subject areas not covered by the FSA		
Alta	Provincial Achievement Testing Program	All students Grade 3	Language arts (reading, writing); math (operations and number sense + multiple choice)	Local and central	At the discretion of the teacher, may form part of classroom mark.
	Annual	All students Grades 6 & 9	Same as Grade 3 plus social studies and science	Local and central	Same as Gr.3

[1] Traub, Ross. *Standardized Testing in Canada; A Survey of Standardized Achievement Testing by Ministries of Education and School Boards*. Toronto: Canadian Education Association, 1994 provides the general definition of provincial assessments.
* For updates to tables, please consult www.maritamoll.ca

	Program and frequency	Grade level/ students tested	Subjects tested	Marking	Purpose of test
Sask	Provincial Learning Assessment Program Every 2 years in rotation	Random Sample only Grades 5, 8, 11	Math (95/97), language arts (94/96/98), technological literacy (99)	Central	Results not for individual grading and not to be publicized in a way that enable comparisons between schools, classrooms or divisions
	Curriculum evaluation program	Random sample; Various grades	Varies	Central	Used only to evaluate curriculum
Man	Grade 3 assessment	All Grade 3 students	Reading, numeracy	Local	No centrally produced test; assessment based on classroom work; for reporting to parents.
	Standards tests Annual, but optional—at the discretion of teachers and school divisions	All students Grade 6	English language arts/ Français langue première/ Français langue seconde-Immersion/ English LA-Immersion	Local	Individual and system testing; may count for up to 20% of final mark
		All students Senior 1 (Grade 9)		Local	
	Same as Gr. 6		mathematics/ matématiques		Individual and system testing; may count for up to 25%

Program and frequency	Grade level/ students tested	Subjects tested	Marking	Purpose of test
Ont Provincial Achievement Tests Annual	All students Grade 3	reading; writing; math	Central	20% of final grade
	All students Grade 6	same as Grade 3		20% of final grade
	All students Grade 9	math only		20% of final grade
Que Compulsory exams Annual	All students in Grade 6 (elem) and Secondary III (Grade 9)	French, English (language of instruction)	Local	These are for evaluation of the system. They are not to be used as internal board evaluation tools.
Complementary exams Annual	All students in Grade 3 & 6; optional at secondary levels	English language arts (3 & 6); maths (6); French language of instruction secondary); math (secondary)	Local	
NB Provincial assessments Annual	All students: Grade 3	reading, writing mathematics	Central	
	All students: Grade 5	reading, writing, math, science		
Middle level science proficiency exam	All students: Grade 8	math	Central	

	Program and frequency	Grade level/ students tested	Subjects tested	Marking	Purpose of test
NS	Program of Learning Assessment for Nova Scotia	All students Grade 5 All students Grade 6 All students Grade 8 All students Grade 9	mathematics language arts mathematics language arts	Local Local Local Local	Mostly program assessment except for Gr. 6 language arts which is reported for individual students
Nfld	Criterion-referenced tests (CRT)	All students: Grades 3, 6 & 9	reading, writing, mathematics, science, core French		To determine how well students are meeting the prescribed outcomes.
PEI	No provincial assessment program				
NWT	No mandated assessment programs. Decision can be made by individual boards. Beginning June 2003, five of eight boards will administer Alberta Achievement Tests (All students: for students in Grades 3, 6 and 9. Marked locally)				
Yukon	Yukon Achievement Tests	All students— Grade 3, 6, 9	math language arts		
Nunavut	No mandated assessment programs				

What's the cost of all this testing?

There is scant information available on the financial costs of standardized testing. Especially for the international tests and surveys, the costs are spread over the various partners involved in the exercise and are not easily accessible. The cost in teacher and student time and resources, often called "in-kind contributions," is frequently not calculated. Nevertheless, the information below, collected from news releases and newspaper articles, shows that the costs are considerable. Unfortunately, the benefits, for students and the system, are not at all clear.

National assessments

Federal: Support for SAIP: $1.5 million direct contribution from HRDC (Human Resources Development Canada)

Provincial (shared): Support for SAIP: $1.5 million "in the form of human and material resources"[1]

National clearing house for assessment data: $100 million in 2003-04 for the establishment of the Canadian Learning Institute.[2]

Provincial assessments

British Columbia: $3.3 million (not including high-school exams)[3]

Alberta: Provincial Achievement Testing (Grades 3, 6, 9) and Grade 12 Diploma Exams $12 million per year[4] (as compared to $4 million per year on curriculum[5])

Ontario: Grade 3 and 6 (reading, writing and math) — $6 million each/yr. Grade 9 (math assessment) — $6 million/yr. Grade 10 (literacy test) — $15 million/yr. Cost or of running Education Quality Assessment Office (EQAO) which also administers TIMSS and SAIP — approx. $20 million/yr.[6] Estimates of total cost vary from $50 million to $59 million each year.[7]

Provincial plans (currently on hold) call for more testing to be phased in to the point where there are exams in two core subjects per year from Grade 3 to Grade 11. In June 2001, the Ontario Ministry of Education estimated that a new expanded testing program would cost $16 million annually, in addition to the $33 million already spent testing Grades 3,6,9 and 10.[8] Ontario directors have asked for a three-year moratorium on the expansion of the current testing regime.[9]

Notes

[1] http://www.cmec.ca/saip/indexe.stm

[2] Canada. Government of Canada. Department of Finance. Budget 2003. P. 134. Available online: http://www.fin.gc.ca/budget03/pdf/bp2003e.pdf. It is still too early to tell how much of this amount will be allocated for testing/data gathering at the elementary/secondary level.

[3] Fine, Sean. "Putting education to the test." *Globe and Mail*, September 3, 2002.

[4] Sokoloff, Heather. "The standards of Alberta." *National Post*, Nov. 18, 2002 p.A6.

[5] Hampton, Wayne. "Challenging the testing regime in Alberta." Included later in this collection.

[6] Lipman, Peter. "The Ontario literacy test and the neo-conservative agenda." Included in this collection.

[7] Sokoloff, Heather. "Rough road for testing in Ontario." *National Post*, Nov. 18, 2002 p.A6 mentions $50 million which probably does not include the cost of running EQAO. Peter Lipman in "The Ontario literacy test and the neo-conservative agenda" sets the amount at $59 million by including the cost of EQAO.

[8] Stewart, Margaret. "Perils of testing." Included in this collection.

[9] Lindgren, April. "2nd chance for literacy failures." *Ottawa Citizen* Friday, Feb. 21, 2003. A1-2

Bias in standardized testing and the misuse of test scores:
Exposing the Achilles heel of educational reform

by Diane E. Meaghan and François R. Casas

T he debate over standardized testing needs to be renewed with vigour in light of the recent expansion in the use of such testing across Canada. Especially disturbing is the push to test more frequently, in earlier grades and with greater significance attached to the outcomes,[1] as well as the use of tests in the evaluation of teachers' performance.

Although politicians routinely suggest that standardized testing will result in greater school and teacher accountability, there is mounting evidence that test scores are used mainly for sorting and ranking children, with serious adverse impact on some—particularly low-income and minority children.[2] This becomes particularly problematic when test results are used for student placement and promotion as well as, increasingly, to determine eligibility for graduation. Teaching to the test and subjecting students to "drill-and-practice" sessions are but two of the negative consequences of high-stakes testing.[3]

Standardized testing is an integral component of the accountability-driven, outcomes-based educational paradigm in which gatekeeping based on test results serves to perpetuate and reproduce social inequities. This is most clearly exemplified in jurisdictions where school funding is linked to test scores, with the result that weak schools in low socioeconomic areas are starved for cash and become at risk of further deterioration. Nevertheless, proponents of a market-based approach to education promote testing as the key to expanding educational choice for parents, with a voucher program representing the ultimate expression of such freedom of choice. Similarly, there are serious problems associated with requiring teachers to pass competency tests at regular intervals to retain their licence and the dismissal of teachers and principals based on the test scores of their students.

Upon the release of the results of standardized achievement tests, politicians at all levels customarily make comparisons among schools, school boards, provinces and countries. Parents worry about the chances of their children being admitted into universities, and members of school boards and education ministry bureaucrats praise or lament test results, while the media clamour to publish school rankings based on those results. The public has been brainwashed into believing that testing is a means to ensure educational standards and an objective basis on which to distribute educational resources—despite the lack of compelling evidence that these alleged benefits outweigh the considerable demonstrated disadvantages.[4]

Standardized tests are unlikely to have the desired effects on teaching and learning, and therefore on the quality of education, for a multitude of reasons which include—but are not limited to—the following:

1. These tests divert valuable instructional time from beneficial activities to preparation for testing. Such preparation usually begins weeks before the test date, with a substantial amount of classroom time dedicated to drills, practices, and test-related exercises. Time that would otherwise be devoted to art, music, physical education, and other essential components of a well-rounded education is sacrificed; reading books, writing compositions, and acquiring mathematics problem-solving skills are replaced by attention to word usage and recognition of spelling, punctuation, and arithmetic operations errors.[5]

2. Designed to evaluate responses that are task-oriented rather than skill-focused, standardized tests tend to narrow the curriculum. In particular, the content of tests is often taught at the expense of material that is not tested.[6] Instead of approaching topics from a variety of perspectives, students are trained to interpret passages in isolation and to engage in restrictive writing formats.[7] Higher-order cognitive skills and problem-solving abilities are sacrificed in efforts to raise test scores.

3. Specifically, cognitive processes of analysis, comparison, inference and evaluation are replaced by isolated skills that do not have transferability. The tyranny of the single right answer does not engage students in tasks which require sustained reasoning or an explanation concerning their thinking processes.[8] Teaching techniques that are effective in raising test scores conflict with the kind of instruction that develops critical thinking, reasoning, problem-solving, and creativity.[9]

4. The material tested is often of limited relevance. There is frequently a lack of congruence between the curriculum on the one hand and test questions on the other, with many test items not being taught or focusing on a relatively small portion of the total curriculum.

5. Standardized tests are not suitable for all students: the pressure they exert on children is of a different nature than that encountered daily in the classroom. Test anxiety correlates with damage to self-concept which, in turn, lessens the student's motivation to learn.[10]

6. The format of standardized tests and the testing procedures are antithetical to the ways students collaboratively interact in the classroom setting, responding to the familiarity of the teacher and glancing at other students as they seek information through voice intonation and body language.[11]

Although politicians routinely suggest that standardized testing will result in greater school and teacher accountability, there is mounting evidence that test scores are used mainly for sorting and ranking children, with serious adverse impact on some—particularly low-income and minority children.

7. Research[12] has raised serious doubts as to the technical basis of tests, including their limited reliability, lack of validity and unfairness with respect to the impact that race, gender and family socio-economic status have on test results.[13] Reading tests measure reading skills rather than the ability to read and comprehend, while at the same time, the pleasure of reading dissipates as the emphasis on appreciation of literature gives way to concerns about the mechanics of reading.[14] Mathematics fares no better, with standardized tests failing to distinguish between students who understand

underlying concepts and those who are only able to perform mathematics procedures.[15]

8. Although standardized tests are often referred to as achievement tests, many, in fact, assess abilities that are not influenced by teacher intervention. Test results attributed to teachers' expertise are contingent upon what has been described as *cultural capital*, which includes students' socioeconomic status and exposure to out-of-school experiences.

9. The growing importance attached to test scores in assessing teachers, schools and boards has led to inappropriate and unethical testing practices.[16] Several studies have found that performance in reading and math tests was significantly lower when conducted by independent assessors compared to tests run by school officials.[17]

While these and other shortcomings of standardized testing have been widely debated, we believe that two of the more basic deficiencies of such testing need to be especially emphasized in the renewed debate which we are advocating: the inherent bias in most tests and the misuse of test scores.

A. Bias in standardized tests

Underlying standardized testing is the assumption that students have equal opportunities to develop skills and knowledge and that they will be assessed in an equitable and fair manner. However, a well-founded concern about bias in testing has been documented in a large number of studies. For example, children from disadvantaged backgrounds, special needs students, and children for whom linguistic factors are an issue are likely to fare poorly on standardized tests.[18] This raises important questions concerning the predictive and content validity of such tests, as well as social issues regarding barriers to high-quality education for some students.

Disadvantaged students are more likely to have meaningful instruction in science, arts, and thinking skills replaced by worksheets that drill students in trivial exercises.[19] With test preparation predominating within low-income schools more than within schools in affluent areas, an increasing number of poorer students are able to pass the reading section of standardized tests but are often not able to understand the meaning of or to connect reading assignments with other aspects of the curriculum.[20] Standardized achievement tests may be harmful for the development of young children since this methodology of assessment fails to take into account that children's cognitive abilities develop unevenly in the early years.[21]

In what has been described as "death at an early age," a significant number of children are misclassified as a result of the pervasive use of standardized intelligence and achievement tests in special education and placement.[22] In the United States, this has led to several high-profile court cases alleging cultural bias in intelligence testing, leading to discriminatory placement of students with special needs. Placement in special education programs has thus become stratified along gender, racial and class lines.[23] Galagan[24] argues that learning disabled and low-achieving students cannot accurately be distinguished using standardized tests and that testing has become an expedient way to exclude students from regular education, thus perpetuating a dual education system.

In a study examining the impact of cultural and linguistic differences, the scores of native children in North America were significantly lower than those of non-native children. Similar results were reported in a California study of four million public school children tested in Grades 2 through 11. In what has been described as a two-tiered educational system, students who were fluent in English scored significantly higher in language and mathematics tests than immigrant children whose English comprehension was limited, prompting a judge to issue a restraining order prohibiting the release of the test scores of some 800,000 students.[25]

Underlying standardized testing is the assumption that students have equal opportunities to develop skills and knowledge and that they will be assessed in an equitable and fair manner. However, a well-founded concern about bias in testing has been documented in a large number of studies.

In Canada, an analysis of the scores in a vocabulary test showed that students whose first language was English performed much better than other children.[26] Similarly, the scores on a Canadian Grade 6 standardized social studies test were significantly lower when French immersion students wrote in French rather than English.[27] Desjarlais[28] found that French language schools in Ontario were disadvantaged because of a lack of standardized tests materials for core curriculum subjects.

The bias inherent in standardized tests involves a broad spectrum of bases, including gender and ethnicity.[29] Phyllis Rosser,[30] Director of the Equality in Testing Project, has spent many years investigating the influential Scholastic Aptitude Test (SAT). As far back as 1979, she found that the questions themselves were culturally loaded, enabling students whose cultural experiences parallel those of the test makers—typically white, middle-class males living in metropolitan areas—to perform better than students from different cultural backgrounds. Rosser demonstrated that the SAT systematically underpredicts the performance of females in post-secondary education. Even though girls achieve higher high school marks in all subjects except for mathematics, they receive lower scores on the SAT—thus barring them from the more prestigious universities and programs, with predictable effects on their career prospects and lifetime earnings. This happens despite the absence of evidence that standardized test scores are a better predictor of first year university performance than high school marks.[31] Minority women are doubly penalized, scoring lower than men in their racial groups who, in turn, score lower than white males.

The high correlation between standardized test scores and the socioeconomic status of the family, combined with the increased reliance on tests for university admissions, scholarship awards and employment, explain why education has entrenched a gender and ethnic/racial caste system and has failed to significantly reduce the inequality in the distribution of income. While women have achieved great strides in the labour force, closing the income gender gap has proven much more difficult.

Why are standardized tests biased? The answer lies in part in the questions themselves, which often incorporate gender differences. For example, there are few reading comprehension passages on the SAT about famous women, and it is not uncommon to find negative images of women and their scientific and mathematical abilities. As well, SAT-type tests are biased in favour of males because they tend to suit boys' personalities: males consider tests a game and are more confident in their ability to guess. Females tend to be more cautious and leave more questions unanswered; they perform better on essay tests compared to multiple choice tests, and they score significantly better on untimed assessments when they can work their way through complex solutions.[32] When girls earn higher marks in high school English and mathematics[33] but achieve lower scores in standardized tests, their self-image is adversely affected. In addition to tests confining women and minorities to less prestigious jobs, lower incomes and fewer leadership positions, this loss of self-esteem imparts an additional cost which may be more difficult to quantify but is real nonetheless.

The Canadian academic community has been slow in picking up the challenge raised by these issues and in addressing these challenges. The public is left to believe that the expanded use of testing at all school levels will enhance accountability for teachers and school boards while simultaneously improving the quality of education. Ministry officials, assorted consultants and media experts pontificate about how valuable large-scale tests have become, while a deafening silence surrounds the harmful effects and biases inherent in those tests.

South of the border, tests are well on their way to becoming an end in themselves[34] as well as the main objective of schooling.[35] An entire industry of test preparation materials and courses has emerged to help students and teachers. How much better spent these resources would be if allocated to conduct more research on the predictive validity of tests,[36] on better understanding of problem-solving styles for different genders, and on developing evaluation methods that are more equitable to different genders and racial/ethnic groups.

> The public is left to believe that the expanded use of testing will enhance accountability while simultaneously improving quality. Ministry officials, assorted consultants and media experts pontificate about how valuable large-scale tests have become, while a deafening silence surrounds the harmful effects and biases inherent in those tests.

B. The misuse and abuse of test scores

Aside from the pedagogical issues raised by widespread standardized testing, abuse of test results is neither uncommon nor isolated.[37] Ministry, board, and school officials across Canada may claim that they can avoid the worst problems that have characterized the American experience in this field, but they are unlikely to succeed in preventing the misuse of test scores because they cannot address the root causes of such misuse: namely, a media-driven sensitivity to student performance, itself the consequence of the economists' success in spreading the paradigm that links education and material success.

The most common form of abuse occurs because users of standardized test results and the media ignore the purpose of such tests. Tests were never designed as an instrument for a precise analysis of the merits of a school program: a test given once a year (or in some instances every few years) is hardly an accurate way to evaluate learning. The prevailing use of standardized tests creates a false impression that test performance can be used to rank students, schools, and boards even though sampled learning may correlate poorly with the curriculum.[38] In the United States, standardized tests are routinely used to sort and place students in programs such as remediation, special education, and readiness. However, there is considerable evidence that many students, particularly those from lower-income groups, minorities and females, experience harmful effects and reduced learning opportunities as a result of such uses of test scores.

Students channelled into remediation programs because of poor test performance receive an inordinate amount of drill-for-test instruction and are seldom given the opportunity to read books, write essays, and discuss what they know, leading to a self-fulfilling prophecy of lower achievement and self-esteem accompanied by higher dropout rates.[39] Low test scores too often lead to lower achievement in subsequent schooling and to substantially increase the risk that students will leave school.[40]

The most notorious example of misuse of test results is the SAT. The Educational Testing Service which produces this test insists that it is designed to predict a student's success at the post-secondary level, even though the SAT was never intended to measure what is taught in a particular school or school board. Furthermore, only a fraction of the student population in any one school takes the test in any given year. Yet, each year, school administrators, school board officials, and state and federal legislators brag about or agonize over every minute rise or decline in test scores in their jurisdiction. Students, teachers, schools, school boards, and entire states are judged and ranked on the basis of scores that were never designed or intended for such a purpose. No mention is heard of the fact that a year-to-year increase in a school's average SAT score is achieved by an entirely different group of students, instructed by a number of new teachers, perhaps with a somewhat modified curriculum. The scientific precision associated with, say, the measurement of different brands of baby diapers is imputed to tests such as the SAT. Test scores for different schools or boards published in all the major newspapers are purported to carry a real meaning, though no serious debate can be found of what that might be.[41]

Why is the public and the academic community not rebelling against such flagrant abuses? We can identify several factors that have contributed to the rising popularity of standardized testing:

1. There is a widespread belief that provincial and national tests are prepared by experts. The same parents who might not hesitate complaining loudly to a school principal if they thought that one of their children's teachers was administering tests that were largely unrelated to what was being taught in the classroom, feel helpless when it comes to tests which are prepared outside the school and which are, in most cases, not available for inspection. When errors are discovered in tests, they are not publicized and, in the case of commercially prepared tests, publishers aggressively defend the quality of their tests, citing the degrees earned by their consultants as proof of such quality.

   > Tests were never designed as an instrument for a precise analysis of the merits of a school program: a test given once a year (or in some instances every few years) is hardly an accurate way to evaluate learning.

2. Tests are much cheaper to prepare and to administer when compared with more meaningful methods of student assessment. Not only are comprehensive student portfolios difficult and expensive to prepare, but they do not allow for a quick ranking of students and schools in a society where such rankings have become prevalent in many areas, whether for baseball teams, job seekers, or university applicants.

3. Governments at all levels are under intense pressure to reduce their spending and their debt, with a concomitant emphasis on demonstrating value for money. This has made it imperative to be able to show that schools are delivering quality education. In the absence of the conventional performance indicators available in the business world (profit, P/E ratios, productivity, etc.), test scores provide the illusion of such proof.

4. Starting in the late 1950s, economists have stressed the idea of education as investment in human capital. Increasingly sophisticated measures of the returns to this type of investment have be-

come available and publicized. A bachelor's or a master's degree in every discipline is worth x dollars in additional lifetime earnings.[42] Whereas the majority of youngsters did not complete high school before World War II, the second half of the 20th century has witnessed an explosion in the demand for higher education. With so much pressure on parents to ensure their children's future in an increasingly technological world, presenting parents with an easy-to-understand assessment of the state of the school system and the quality of education has become irresistible.

5. The media have played a significant role in deepening the hysteria around test results. It has become increasingly common for newspapers and magazines to prominently display the results of the latest round of provincial, national or international tests, with little commentary on the numerous difficulties encountered in interpreting those results. Publishing school-by-school lists of test scores is standard practice, much like publishing hockey standings.

6. There is an entrenched business interest in convincing the public that standardized tests are meaningful. The sale of a whole range of screening, intelligence, readiness, and other tests generates in excess of $100 million in revenues in the U.S. The testing mania has also led to the publication of a dizzying array of manuals to prepare students writing these tests, as well as for the teachers preparing the students for the tests.[43] Some of the titles would be humourous if it were not for the serious nature of this issue: you can purchase manuals with such titles as *How to Beat the SAT* and *SAT for Dummies*, with strategies for test taking that include techniques for guessing and other assorted tricks to improve scores. Reading some of these manuals leaves no illusion about how major standardized tests such as the SAT contribute to raising the quality of education. The goal has shifted from learning in order to perform well on a test to "beating" the test.

7. Abuse of test results can also be linked to an increasingly pervasive market ideology. It has become relatively common to hear corporate CEOs and senior government officials referring to students as "clients" or "customers" and to stress the need to borrow from business models in order to improve the quality of educational "outputs." Business representatives are often invited to help shape the curriculum, and business-school partnerships are eagerly encouraged.

Can the misuse of test results be eliminated, or at least minimized? There is little basis for expressing optimism unless all stakeholders acknowledge that misuse is a response to societal problems and to dilemmas and conflicts faced by schools, parents and governments.

Final thoughts: What do test scores reveal?

One of the tragedies in the current rush to expand the use of standardized testing is that little attention is being paid to the research conducted in the past four decades on what factors explain student performance in these tests. The earliest—and still influential—study in this area is the *Coleman Report*[44] which remains unique by virtue of its scope, using data on 645,000 students. Coleman and his associates looked at achievement measures consisting of 10 test scores and 93 possible explanatory variables. The most surprising and controversial result was that non-school variables—chiefly the socioeconomic status (SES) of families in the school district— were the most significant predictors of student performance. Among the school variables, only the verbal ability of teachers appeared to be (weakly) associated with achievement. Some subsequent studies arrived at radically different findings,[45] while others confirmed Coleman's results.[46] Benson[47] subsequently offered four hypotheses to explain the link between SES and student achievement:

- Parents in higher SES areas may spend more time and be more supportive of school achievement.
- School personnel may reinforce the high aspirations of high SES parents.
- Neighbours and members of peer groups may also reinforce parental attitudes.
- The value system of children from high SES areas and their community may stress education as relevant and important, while children from low SES may be exposed to the opposite set of values, caused by high unemployment rates.

Studies on the influence of school inputs (the only variables amenable to changes through educational policies) have been notable both for what they reveal about the relative unimportance of these inputs and for the variations among the conclusions. Richards and Ratsoy[48] have noted that different studies show class size to be positively related, negatively related and unrelated to student achievement. Similarly, the relationship between teacher experience and student achievement differs widely from study to study. Bowles[49] provided a partial explanation for this puzzle by showing that individual resources that have a positive influence in one setting may have little or even a negative impact in a different setting. For example, while the level of parental education was important in schools in the northern U.S., teachers' verbal ability and reading material available in the home were important in southern schools.

Further clouding these issues is the argument that a strong correlation between student achievement and a school or non-school variable does not constitute evidence of causality. Garms, Guthrie & Pierce[50] found that schools with a strong record of student achievement attract highly experienced teachers under policies that give teachers with the most seniority the right of first refusal when vacancies occur. High student achievement may therefore paradoxically "cause" a school to have a more experienced staff! Similarly, it is common for families with a high socioeconomic status to relocate near a school with a strong reputation, driving property values up and chasing poorer families away. In this sense, differences in student achievement may "explain" differences in SES, rather than the opposite.[51]

With so little known about what explains student achievement in standardized tests, it is astounding that government agencies such as the Orwellian-named Education Quality and Accountability Office—set up to create and administer a whole battery of tests across Ontario—would presume that whatever results are observed will reveal some particular strengths or flaws of the school curriculum or school practices. Canadians need and deserve a renewed and well-informed debate over the use and misuse of standardized testing to screen and sort students, teachers and schools, to diagnose student abilities, and to measure achievement or aptitude. It is essential that questions be raised concerning the purpose of administering these tests and whether they adequately measure student learning and school performance. Moving students away from essay assessment and problem solving to multiple choice tests excludes them from educational opportunities and raises serious issues of equity. Before subjecting Canadian schools to such forms of evaluation, careful consideration must be given to the pedagogical and financial costs associated with standardized tests.

Diane Meaghan is a professor of Sociology in the Department of General Education, and faculty representative on the Board of Governors at Seneca College of Applied Arts and Technology. François Casas is the undergraduate chair of the Department of Economics at the University of Toronto.

Endnotes

[1] Evidence of the recent proliferation of standardized tests in Canada can be found in Traub, R. (1994). *Standardized Testing in Canada: A Survey of Standardized Achievement Testing by Ministries of Education and School Boards.* Toronto: Canadian Education Association and in Fagan, L. & Spurrell, D. (1995). *Evaluating Achievement of Senior High School Students in Canada: A Study of Policies and Practices of Ministries and School Boards in Canada.* Toronto: Canadian Education Association.

[2] See Froese-Germain, B. (2001). "Standardized Testing + High Stakes Decisions = Educational Inequity," *Interchange*, 32(2), 111-30.

[3] The term high-stakes testing refers to situations in which test scores alone are used to make decisions regarding tracking, placement, promotion and graduation.

[4] Popham, W. (1999). "Where Large Scale Educational Assessment is Heading and Why It Shouldn't," *Educational Measurement: Issues and Practices*, 13-17; Madaus, G. (1991). *The Effects of Important Tests on Students: Implications for a National Examination or System of Examinations.* Paper presented at the American Educational Reform Association Conference, Washington, DC.

[5] Smith, M.L. (1990). "Put to the Test: The Effects of External Testing," *Educational Researcher*, 20, 8-11.

[6] Haladyna, T., Nolen, S. & Haas, N. (1991). "Raising Standardized Achievement Test Scores and the Origins of Test Score Pollution," *Educational Researcher*, 20(5), 2-7.

[7] New York State United Teachers Task Force (1991). *Multiple Choices: Reforming Student Testing in New York State.* Reports-Evaluation 142.

[8] Haney, W. & Madaus, G. (1989). "Searching for Alternatives to Standardized Tests: Whys, Whats and Withers," *Phi Delta Kappan*, 2(3), 683-7.

[9] Neill, M. & Medina, N. (1989). "Standardized Testing: Harmful to Educational Health," *Phi Delta Kappan*, 6(3), 688-97.

[10] Paris, S., Lawton, T. Turner, J. & Roth, J. (1991). "A Developmental Perspective on Standardized Achievement Testing," *Educational Researcher*, 20, 12-20.

[11] Marlaire, C. & Maynard, D. (1995). "Standardized Testing as an Interactional Phenomenon," *Sociology of Education*, 63, 83-101.

[12] Baker, E., O'Neill, H. & Linn, R. (1993). "Policy and Validity Prospects for Performance-Based Assessment," *American Psychologist*, 48(12), 21-2; Wainer, H. (1993). "Measurement Problems," *Journal of Educational Measurement*, 30(1), 1-21; Burns, M. (1998). *Interpreting the Reliability and Validity of the Michigan Educational Assessment Program*. Standing Committee for the Michigan Association of School Psychologists.

[13] For example, the validity of the Scholastic Aptitude Test (SAT) has been challenged because the test is, in the words of Owen & Doerr (1999), "extremely coachable." These authors point out that a coached student can increase her/his score on average by 110 points. [Owen, D. & Doerr, M. (1999). *None of the Above: The Truth Behind the SATs*. New York: Rowan and Littlefield.]

[14] Guthrie, J. (1998). *Indicators of Reading Education*. New Brunswick, NJ: Center for Policy Research in Education, Rutgers University.

[15] National Council of Teachers of Mathematics (1989), *Curriculum and Evaluation Standards for School Mathematics*. Reston, VA.

[16] Moore, W. (1994). "The Devaluation of Standardized Testing: One District's Response to a Mandated Assessment," *Applied Measurement in Education*, 7(4), 343-67.

[17] Shephard, L. (1991). "Negative Policies for Dealing with Diversity: When Does Assessment and Diagnosis Turn into Sorting and Segregation?," in Hiebert, E. (ed.), *Literacy for a Diverse Society: Perspectives, Practices and Policies*. New York, Teachers College Press.

[18] Hymes, D. (1991). *The Changing Face of Testing and Assessment: Problems and Solutions*. Arlington, VA: American Association of School Administrators; Rodriguez, R. (1996). "Test-Driven Admissions," *Black Issues in Higher Education*, 13(14), 7-9.

[19] Herman, J. & Golan, S. (1992). "The Effects of Standardized Testing on Teaching and Schools," *Educational Measurement: Issues and Practices*, 2(4), 20-5.

[20] Orfield, G. & Wald, J. (2000). "Testing, Testing: The High-Stakes Testing Mania Hurts Poor and Minority Students the Most," *The Nation*, June 5, 38-40.

[21] Sinbkule, J. (1996). *A Study of Standardized Tests and Alternative for Elementary Schools*. M.A. Thesis, Salem-Teikyo University.

[22] Oakes, J. (1990). *Multiplying Inequalities: The Effects of Race, Social Class and Tracking on Opportunities to Learn Mathematics and Science.* Santa Monica, CA: RAND Corporation; Lee, F. (1992). "Alternative Assessment," *Childhood Education,* 69(2), 72-3; James, J. & Tanner, K. (1993). "Standardized Testing of Young Children," *Journal of Research and Development in Education,* 26(3), 143-52.

[23] Marlaire, C. & Maynard, D. (1995). "Standardized Testing as an Interactional Phenomenon," *Sociology of Education,* 63, 83-101.

[24] Galagan, J. (1995). "Psychoeducational Testing: Turn Out the Light, the Party's Over," *Exceptional Children,* 52(3), 288-99.

[25] Guthrie, J. (1998). *Indicators of Reading Education.* New Brunswick, NJ: Center for Policy Research in Education, Rutgers University.

[26] McVey, M. (1991). *A Profile of the Ottawa Board of Education Heritage Language Students.* Research paper 90-05, Ottawa Board of Education.

[27] Samuel, M. (1990). *Language of Testing Effects for Academic Achievement of French Immersion Students.* M.Ed. Thesis, University of Alberta.

[28] Desjarlais, L. (1978). *L'Évaluation du Rendement Scolaire pour Cycles Primaire et Moyen.* Toronto: Ontario Ministry of Education.

[29] Wilson, J. & Matinussen, R. (1999). "Factors Affecting the Assessment of Student Achievement," *Alberta Journal of Educational Research,* 45(3), 267-77.

[30] Rosser, P. (1989). *The SAT Gender Gap: Identifying the Causes.* Washington, DC: Center for Women Policy Studies.

[31] Haney, W. & Madaus, G. (1989). "Searching for Alternatives to Standardized Tests: Whys, Whats and Withers," *Phi Delta Kappan,* 2(3), 683-7.

[32] Owen, D. & Doerr, M. (1999). *None of the Above: The Truth Behind the SATs.* New York: Rowan and Littlefield.

[33] For evidence that this pattern prevails in Canada as well see Casas, F. & Meaghan, D. (1996). "A Study of Repeated Courses Among Secondary Students in Ontario," *The Journal of Educational Research,* 90(2), 116-27.

[34] Brown, S. et al. (1991). *Gender Bias in Testing: Current Debates, Future Priorities.* New York: Ford Foundation Office of Communications.

[35] Madaus, G. (1992). "An Independent Auditing Mechanism for Testing," *Educational Measurement: Issues and Practice,* 11(1), 26-31.

[36] In the *1974 Test Standards* favoured by the American Psychological Association, the concept of test validity was expanded to include the social consequences resulting from the use of tests [Linn, R. (1993). "Educational Assessment: Expanded Expectations and challenges," *Educational Evaluation and Policy Analysis,* 15(1), 1-16]

[37] Cuban, L. (1991). *The Misuse of Tests in Education*. Washington, DC: Office of Technology Assessment.

[38] Downing, S. & Haladyna, T. (1996). "Model for Evaluating High-Stakes Testing Programs: Why the Fox Should not Guard the Chicken Coop," *Educational Measurement: Issues and Practices*, 15, 5-12.

[39] Liberman, A. (1991). "Accountability as a Reform Strategy," *Phi Delta Kappan*, 1(3), 219-25.

[40] Koretz, D. et al. (1991). *The Effects of High-Stakes Testing on Achievement: Preliminary Findings About Generalization Across Tests*. Paper presented at the annual meeting of the American Educational Research Association, Chicago, 1991; Spatig, L. (1996). *Developmentalism Meets Standardized Testing: Low Income Children Lose*. Paper presented at the annual meeting of the American Educational Studies Association, Montreal, 1996.

[41]. For example, the *1999 Report on Science Assessment* published by the Canadian Council of Ministers of Education

[42] Stager, D. (1994). *Returns to Investment in Ontario University Education, 1960-90, and Implications for Tuition Fee Policy*. Toronto: Council of Ontario Universities.

[43] Owen, D. & Doerr, M. (1999). *None of the Above: The Truth Behind the SATs*. New York: Rowan and Littlefield.

[44] Coleman, J. et al. (1966). *Equality of Educational Opportunity*. Washington, DC: Government Printing Office.

[45] Smith, M.S. (1968). "Equality of Education Opportunity: The Basic Findings Reconsidered," in Mosteller, F. & Moynihan, D. (eds.). *On Equality of Educational Opportunity*. New York: Vintage Books.

[46] Hanushek, E. (1972). *Education and Race*. Lexington, KY: Lexington Press.

[47] Benson, C. (1982). "Household Production of Human Capital: Time Uses of Parents and Children as Inputs," in McMahon, W. & Geske, T. (eds.) *Financing Education: Overcoming Inefficiency and Inequity*. Urbana, Ill.: University of Illinois Press.

[48] Richards, D. & Ratsoy, E. (1987). *Introduction to the Economics of Canadian Education*. Calgary: Detselig Enterprises.

[49] Bowles, S. (1970). "Towards an Educational Production Function," in Hansen, W. (ed.) *Education, Income and Human Capital*. New York: Columbia University Press.

[50] Garms, J., Guthrie, J. & Pierce, L. (1978). *School Finance: The Economics and Politics of Public Education*. New Jersey: Prentice-Hall.

[51] The catchment area around Earl Haig Secondary School in North Toronto has become known for the "monster homes" built in adjacent streets for wealthy families anxious to secure spaces for their children in that highly successful school.

How does Canada's education system stack up against other countries?

The news is better than you think.

by John Hoffman

W hen I was in high school I was told that I went to the best school in the world. The logic went like this: Silverthorn was the best school in Etobicoke. Etobicoke had the best schools in Metro Toronto. Metro Toronto had the best in Ontario. Ontario had the best education system in Canada. Canada's education system was the best in the world.

We won't bother to deconstruct that theory. The point is, nowadays we hear little self-satisfied talk about Canada's perceived pre-eminence in education. Throughout the 1980s and '90s, we became accustomed to negative news about our schools. Many of the education reforms introduced in the past decade were prefaced by dire pronouncements that schools were not performing, that our kids didn't measure up. We've heard so much about reportedly mediocre international test scores, kids who can't read and college graduates who can't write a sentence, that recent good news has come and gone without even penetrating our consciousness. Well, listen up for a rebroadcast of the highlights.

Tests of strength?

If international tests are one's standard, Canadian students are doing very well in reading, math and science. Last December, results from the Program for International Student Assessment (PISA), a testing arm of the Organization for Economic Co-operation and Development (OECD), suggested Canadian students were near the top of the international heap. (There is general agreement that PISA is the best-designed international assessment thus far.) Out of more than a quarter of a million 15-year-olds (30,000 from Canada) from 32 countries who wrote the tests, our kids came second to Finland in reading, tied Australia for fifth in math and were also fifth in science—behind Japan, Korea, New Zealand and Finland. (PISA tests 15-year-olds because that's the last year almost all kids are still in school in all countries, which makes the sample more representative of the entire youth population, as opposed to just the brighter and more affluent kids who finish high school.)

A year previously, the media reported that Canadians also scored well in round two of the Third International Mathematics and Science Study (TIMSS), which tested grade-eight students in 39 countries. We tied for sixth in science and seventh in math, an improvement of three places in the standings from the TIMSS 1995, when we narrowly escaped relegation to the "B" pool. With a little more improvement, observers felt we might soon be challenging for a playoff spot, and even find ourselves in the coveted final four. (Notice how tempting it is to slip into sports analogies when talking about international test results.)

In truth, there weren't really any "standings" although a ranked list appeared in the TIMSS '99 Canada Report. What "seventh" in math seems to have meant was that six countries had results that were significantly higher than Canada's. Canada was actually in a clump of 12 countries whose results were considered to be more or less equivalent in terms of statistical significance.

Spin cycle

Although these assessments were designed as a way for countries to compare notes about what teachers were teaching and students were learning, they have been co-opted by the media, politicians and business leaders, who present them as a sort of academic Olympics. International math and science results have become the indicators of our future global competitiveness.

For its part, the Ontario government did some creative presentation of data from the TIMSS '95 to justify its education reforms. Putting Students First, a Ministry of Education pamphlet sent to every house-hold in the province in 1997, showed a graph implying that Ontario grade-eight students came last in the math test (five Canadian provinces participated as quasi-countries). The graph presented the results for the top seven countries followed by those of several Canadian provinces, with Ontario at the bottom—suggesting, by omission, that Canada was at the bottom. The pamphlet didn't mention that 41 countries participated in the grade-eight portion of the study, nor that Canada's standing was actually in the upper middle of the pack, along with countries like The Netherlands, Australia, Ireland, Belgium and France.

There are other reasons to interpret these results cautiously. First, since there is no planet-wide standardized curriculum, different countries teach concepts at different times. So the content of the test is a compromise—a compromise that means some students are grilled on material they haven't been taught. Check this out: The "test curriculum match" (TCM) for Ontario grade-eight students in the TIMSS '95 was 74 in math and 53 in science. That means 26% of the math items and 47% of the science items were not taught in the Ontario curriculum at the time. In contrast, the TCMs for BC were 97 and 98 respectively. Small wonder BC students did the best in Canada.

These assessments have been co-opted by the media, politicians and business leaders, who present them as a sort of academic Olympics. International math and science results have become the indicators of our future global competitiveness.

But this begs the question: Was BC teaching the right stuff and Ontario the wrong? Possibly, although there was much debate about what should have been tested. Phillip Nagy, professor emeritus of education at the Ontario Institute for Studies in Education at the University of Toronto, estimates about half the Ontario grade-eight math and science curriculum at the time was not covered by TIMSS. "We had a much richer curriculum than TIMSS tests," he comments. This would've been true for BC as well, even though its TCM was better. (In fact, TIMSS tests a fairly narrow range of curriculum, although Nagy feels that this is reasonable for a large-scale international assessment.)

Another problem with international tests based on curriculum content is that they compare students in systems that operate quite differently. Canada and the US, for instance, are two of the few countries in the world with comprehensive high schools, where kids of all abilities attend the same school (albeit in different streams). And they tend to take a wide variety of subjects, even at the upper levels of secondary school, while students in western Europe are specializing in as few as three subjects.

On two of the TIMSS '95 tests, which were for math and physics specialists, Canadian and American 18-year-olds were up against students from other countries who were getting up to twice as many hours of math and physics instruction. (The '95 tests are a useful reference since there's been time to analyze the results.) "We have one of the highest levels in the world of high-school students who could drop math but still take it," says Nagy. "The question is, do we want to have 10% of the students taking math, and get better international results, or 20% taking math, and get decent results?"

The tower of PISA

The PISA tests were based less on content and more on literacy, which includes math and science "literacy" as well as reading literacy. In lay terms that means applied knowledge or, as it says in *Measuring Up*, the Canadian PISA report, "the knowledge and skills that are essential for full participation in society."

"PISA was not an assessment of what youth learned during their previous year at school, or even during their secondary school years," says Doug Willms, professor of education at the University of New Brunswick. "It's more an indication of the learning and skill development that has occurred since birth. International assessments are getting better and better. They are addressing a much broader range of questions." This, of course, makes Canada look even better. Our best results came on the best tests. In PISA 2000, the emphasis was on reading. This is significant since reading is arguably a much more universal skill now than expertise in upper-secondary-level math and science, which relatively few people will use in their paid employment. Everyone will have to understand and interpret what they read, and use that data to generate and evaluate ideas.

PISA results provided an overall reading score and subscores in three specific areas: retrieving (locating information in the text), interpreting (constructing meaning and drawing inferences from written material) and reflecting (relating the text to the student's knowledge, ideas and judgments). In the latter category, which, you could say, would require the highest-level thinking, Canada was number one—We're number one, hey. We're number one!—ahead of the UK, Ireland, Finland and Japan.

Beyond scores

If test scores don't turn your crank, here are some other telling facts. According to OECD data, Canada has proportionately more university and college graduates than any other country. We also have one of the highest rates of high school graduation in the 25-to-34 age category: 87%, which puts us on a par with the US, Sweden, Denmark, Germany and Finland.

Here's another good one: adult literacy. According to results from the OECD International Adult Literacy Survey, 57.8% of Canadians aged 16 to 65 are at least at level three (equivalent to high school completion) in prose literacy—namely reading, understanding and finding information in text. That puts us fourth out of 20 countries. We were eighth in document literacy (filling out forms and following instructions). Overall, that's not bad, considering countries like Canada, the US, Australia and the UK have much higher levels of immigration than the Scandinavian and northern European countries, who have the highest adult literacy rates in the world. (Sweden is tops with 72.1 at level three or higher in prose literacy.)

There's one other indication that our education system is holding its own. Asian countries, which routinely kick butt in math and science, are sending people over here to see what it is we and the US are doing because they think we do some things better than they do. Nagy comments, "A few of the eastern Asian countries are concerned they are not teaching creative problem-solving as well as American and Canadian schools."

This doesn't mean things are hunky-dory in every Canadian school, though. "The PISA data show that there are large discrepancies between girls and boys in reading [girls did substantially better in most countries] and large differences between Canadian provinces," says Willms. "Alberta, Quebec and British Columbia were consistently near the top while the Atlantic provinces were closer to the international middle. There were also substantial gaps between social class groups."

In fact, while no one factor explained all the differences between high and low scores in the PISA study, socio-economic status (SES) proved to be the single biggest contributor. In all countries, well-off students did better than their less affluent peers—the difference in international rank was essentially the performance of lower SES students, since students with high SES essentially had similar results in all countries. "Canada's good results show that we do a comparatively good job of educating our less-advantaged youth," says Willms. Interestingly, Saskatchewan has the least stratified scores of any Canadian province

What does all this boil down to? Possibly the greatest lesson from the heap of education data is not that our system is broken and in need of fixing, but that it is a good system that must be protected. It does make sense to try to improve schools. It makes sense to work to improve teaching and curriculum. And, yes, it makes sense to do some testing. But policy-makers should bear in mind the hallmark of Canadian education and our international success is equity. We do a good job of educating students from all walks of life. So any improvements to schools and changes in education policy should be assessed by how well they live up to that core value. It's the reason we have a public education system in the first place—playoff spot or not. ❧

John Hoffman is a regular contributor and columnist for Today's Parent Magazine. This article was originally published in Today's Parent, September 2002 and is reprinted with permission.

Leaning between conspiracy and hegemony

OECD, UNESCO, and the tower of PISA

by Larry Kuehn

It is tempting to believe in conspiracies, to think that events have unfolded because powerful forces have secretly and behind-the-scenes carried out an action that had significant social and political impact. Enough stories have been proven later—the Iran-Contra scandal, CIA engagement in overturning elected governments—that one must at least keep an open mind about the possibilities. But international standardized tests—isn't that going a bit far? Could the PISA exam (Program for International Student Assessment) be a result of a conspiracy?

The PISA exam is the beginning of the testing program of the Organization for Economic Cooperation and Development (OECD). The OECD is a club for the 30 major industrial economies, originally made up of the countries of Western Europe, North America, and Japan. In recent years, some of the emerging industrial countries, such as Korea and post-NAFTA Mexico, have been added.

More than a decade ago, the OECD began a project called the OECD Education Indicators. The central purpose of the Education Indicators was to provide cross-national comparisons about education systems. The OECD has published since 1992 an annual report of indicators called *Education at a Glance*. One of the objectives from the beginning was to develop "performance indicators" as a key part of the system. This phrase is put in quotation marks here because it stands for an entire ideology and technology of control systems being imposed on public services in general and education in particular.

Performance indicators
as a technology of control

The major global corporations that have both production and sales in multiple countries have developed control mechanisms that are based in information technology. Inventories can be maintained on a "just-in-time" basis, keeping down the costs of production. Information about sales can be aggregated quickly, providing indications of the relative success of different parts of the system, and giving feedback that things are going well or need to change. Both of these depend on technology-intensive communication networks providing information on a distributed basis, both to the corporate centre and to the various operations that may be located in a number of countries. This information is supposed to be used to alter aspects of production or sales that don't conform to the need to produce profits.

The OECD Education Indicators project is conceptually based on this model. In its initial stages it identified three aspects of an education production model applied to education—inputs, process and outputs. You can already see from the get-go how the source of the model influences how one thinks about the process and objectives of education.

The ideology of the globalized production model places a priority on "outputs." Profits are the valued outcomes of a capitalist economic system and an entire industry, and technology—accounting and auditing—is in place to identify what those profits are and to give confidence to the shareholders that their return on investment is being honestly reported. However, we have seen with the scandals around Enron, Worldcom, and many other major companies that even with something as concrete as dollars and profits, it is possible for accountants and auditors to fiddle with the results and hide the realities.

The auditing conception of accounting to shareholders has been widely adopted as a method of measuring accountability for government services. The claim is made—rightly—that citizens have a right to know if the government is doing what they want it to do and to use that information to make changes, if desired. The method that has been generally adopted is to try to create an equivalent to the accounting to shareholders. The central mechanism for this is the creation of "performance indicators" that can be measured, narrowing the objectives that can be set to those measurable in some concrete way. As an example, the Deputy Minister of Education in British Columbia has said, "If it can't be measured, it can't be managed." Where this leads is exemplified by the B.C. Ministry of Education performance indicator for curriculum: no curriculum document will be more than five years old. The quality or the relevance of the curriculum are difficult to measure in some standard way, but the number of years since publication is easy to determine. Quality and relevance can never be fixed elements. They change as the social context changes and as one set of ideas gains acceptability over another set. The best that can be done to determine them is to have an ongoing dialogue among citizens, teachers and students—the essence of what would be done in a democratic education system.

In contrast to a democratic dialogue approach where a school community defines goals, the performance indicator system is defined externally to the participants in the education system. Both the framework and the content are determined by bureaucrats or "experts." Under pressure from auditors-general, most governments at both the provincial and federal level in Canada have adopted a model of performance standards and performance indicators for public services. These are promoted as systems of "accountability," and are intended to give assurances to the public that public resources are being used effectively on public programs. These systems are supposed to give direction to the day-to-day work that public employees carry out or that is contracted by government.

Sounds sensible, doesn't it? But take another look. Do either the public or the employees actually doing the work have a role in defining what the performance outcomes should be or what kind of performance indicators should be used to evaluate the services? The claim for public involvement is usually based on politicians being elected to represent the public in the process. Seldom, though, do politicians have more than a cursory role in the process—beyond mandating it through legislation. They are on the sidelines nearly as much as those delivering or receiving a service. It is generally a technocratic process whose shape is driven by the need to produce numbers that are supposed to mean something about the services being provided.

In the education system, standardized tests provide a way to produce the numbers. Some tests, like the PISA exam or the SAIP (the Canadian School Achievement Indicators Program), are aimed at comparing education systems on an international basis (PISA) and national basis (SAIP). Other exams, such as the Foundation Skills Assessment (FSA) in B.C., combine comparing system results between schools and school districts with reports to parents on the performance of individual students. Despite the limits of what these tests tell us, private groups such as the market-promoting Fraser Institute and its clones take these figures and produce league tables, rankings of schools according to the tests, much like a sports league. They reduce education to a race for competitive results rather than the growth and development of each and every young person, regardless of their abilities and circumstances.

While standardized exams seem to produce an "objective" measure, it is important to remember that these are socially constructed, based on a set of assumptions that are generally implicit and seldom debated or widely understood. Even the accounting model on which they are patterned is based on a set of socially-constructed "standards" called GAAP (generally accepted accounting practices). These are developed by "experts," much as the PISA exam was developed by an international group with experience in this kind of audit testing. Reports of the early discussions among the PISA developers shed interesting light on the underlying assumptions. They talked about the difficulty of finding elements of the practice of literacy that have consistency across the many cultures and languages of the countries involved in the testing program. All forms of literature—poetry, fiction, as well as journalism and other forms of non-fiction—are embedded in a culture and language, so one cannot assume that simply translating will really produce comparable testing experiences. The one form of writing that they did think carried across cultures was computer manuals—presumably incomprehensible in any language.

Developing an international test involves complex negotiations, based on assumptions rooted in a social context, culture and language of the test developers. It is also embedded in a particular way of knowing, one that values the appearance of "objectivity" with a heavy emphasis on numbers. None of this complexity is obvious when the results are reported as a single number that fits nicely into a chart or league table. Seldom are the assumptions and structure of the testing model exposed to public view.

So where is the conspiracy?

You are right. What has been described so far is really a case of hegemony, not a conspiracy. Hegemony because performance indicators and finding numbers to define how the standards are met is pervasive. We see it in all areas of government, promoted by auditor-general offices and ideologically by those who want to limit government and make whatever remains of government look as much like the market system as possible. It is a way of understanding that is hegemonic because it is so dominant that it is invisible, and seems to many like "common sense."

How did this system come to dominate education? To a large degree, because it is an adaptation to the education context of a widely used control system. But widely used systems don't come out of nowhere. They serve particular interests and are built on specific decisions by real people who have access to the resources to carry them out. That is where the conspiracy comes in.

This story about the OECD and UNESCO is drawn from a presentation by Dr. Albert Tuijnman at an Edudata seminar in Vancouver in March of 2001.[1] Dr. Tuijnman worked for the OECD centre on education and was an author of the first three issues of the OECD's *Education at a Glance* indicator reports.

> While standardized exams seem to produce an "objective" measure, it is important to remember that these are socially constructed, based on a set of assumptions that are generally implicit and seldom debated or widely understood.

The key to finding the conspiracy (not Dr. Tuijnman's term) is to know that two groups were competitors for carrying out comparative international education studies: the OECD and UNESCO (United Nations Education, Scientific and Cultural Organization). This competition developed in the early 1980s, when Ronald Reagan was U.S. President and Margaret Thatcher the British Prime Minister.

The context was a report from an early international testing program, the Second International Maths and Science Study (SIMSS). It showed unfavourable results for U.S. students compared to those from a number of other countries. These results were used to declare a crisis (always a precursor to change) through the publication of the report called *A Nation at Risk*, claiming that the U.S. had adopted "unilateral disarmament" in education. Failure to lead the world in science and math results was considered to be a disaster in the U.S., similar to the shock of being beaten by the Russians in sending the first human into space in an earlier decade. *A Nation at Risk* kicked off a new direction in international testing studies. Until this point, the international studies had not been based on a "horse race" approach. Rather, they provided data that academics used to explain differences by comparing tested achievement to curriculum, school resources, teaching approaches, and home and social factors, reflecting the reality of the complex that is education.

The U.S. and British governments wanted studies that focused on accountability and performance, measuring "value for money," as accountants understand those terms. They were not interested in the "input" and "process" elements, but in the outputs produced, as determined by testing. It is a compliance audit approach drawn from business.[2] It is sometimes called a "loose/tight" form of management, where outputs (standards independent of time or context) are set centrally and are measured by tests (the tight part), while those working in the system in theory determine how to reach the externally set goals. Detailed knowledge of the social context and the pedagogical and other educational practices are not of significance from this perspective. We'll tell you what to do and you figure out how to do it, is the message—whoever the students are and whatever the resources we give you to carry out the job. And we will test and publish the results to let everyone know who has the fastest horses.

The Reagan and Thatcher governments wanted UNESCO to carry out these output performance indicator types of studies, but UNESCO refused. UNESCO is governed by a general assembly in which each of the more that 150 countries that belong have one vote, regardless of how much they contribute in financing. The cold war was still on, and the U.S. and U.K. saw UNESCO as dominated by leftists and developing countries, so they withdrew in 1986, taking their money with them.

They turned to the OECD as the other international agency that might be used to carry out the mandate for the kind of statistics that the

Reagan and Thatcher governments wanted. However, when they went to the OECD, it did not immediately adopt their position, either. Neither Germany nor France—both still members of UNESCO—wanted to see the OECD carry out what they saw as suspect studies. The U.S. and U.K. then threatened to pull out of the OECD education committee as well—a threat that led the other countries to capitulate and agree to develop international indicators of education systems.

The OECD *Education at a Glance* indicators were first published in 1992, based on the limited data that were available at the time. Much of the information was not really in comparable form. The only outcome data was from the second international math test that was already 10 years old. This was included because of the political imperative to have output data, and its dated nature was used to argue for creating a system to collect outcome data on an ongoing basis.

Although other groups within the OECD education structure were aimed at understanding broader system outcomes, the group designated as Network A was concerned with outputs defined as student performance on tests. The work of this group has been financed primarily by the U.S., and it is this group that developed the PISA exams. These exams are to be given on a three-year cycle to provide ongoing outcome data to feed the OECD indicators, allowing for the ongoing ranking of countries in the horse race winners-and-losers approach.

As Dr. Albert Tuijnman says of the PISA exam:

> . . . *when the OECD designs such a project, it's not driven by scholarly interests, not driven by an interest in academic analysis or hypothesis or data analysis; that means also of course that the data collection itself is not an elaborate data collection that IEA used to do in terms of curriculum analysis and so on; it's a different type of approach. . . The main interest is simply to know where the systems achieve rather than explaining why they achieve like they do.*[3]

The conflict between UNESCO and the OECD reappears in 1997, with UNESCO proposing to set up a World Education Indicators project. The OECD indicators project, of course, provided comparative information among participating OECD countries, which constitute only 30 of the more than 150 countries that belong to UNESCO. A UNESCO project could also have provided an opportunity for a different approach to indicators, one based on getting data to understand relationships within education, not just outcomes.

However, the OECD won out again. Funding from the World Bank that had been intended for financing the UNESCO World Education Indicators project got diverted to the OECD. The U.S. approach to marketing its OECD indicators approach to countries beyond the OECD was to make it seem like the only game in town and the logical way to understand education systems. As an example, the U.S. took the members of the newly established Education Forum of APEC (Asia Pacific Economic Cooperation) to Washington, D.C. in 1997 to be briefed on the OECD Education Indicators. The APEC Education Forum is made up of senior officials in ministries of education, as are the policy bodies within the OECD that define the direction of the outcome measures through the PISA exam.

As Harvey Weiner of the Canadian Teachers' Federation told a conference co-sponsored by UNESCO and Education International, "Globalization has narrowed the scope of education, and hence the individual's objectives to economic targets: best marks, best jobs, best salaries."[4] The OECD, its Centre for Education, Research and Innovation, and the OECD indicators project have all played key roles in this narrowing of education to focus on economic targets.

Dr. Tuijnman's evaluation of the impact of the OECD indicator frameworks is that they have "produced over the last 10 years a very strong tendency to demean." The impact of this has been for "education systems to become more homogeneous, to become more similar." He also points out that "there are very few critical voices outside."

"A very strong tendency to demean" seems like a good assessment of the impact of most of the program of bringing compliance audit techniques from business into the work of education—whether by the OECD, the Council of Ministers of Education Canada, or the Bush administration with its "No Child Left Behind" testing program.

What if UNESCO had been responsible for an international evaluation program?

Could testing and educational statistics have been different if UNESCO had won out over the OECD, both in the '80s and the '90s, when the U.S. and the U.K. and then the World Bank (also controlled by the U.S.) opted for the OECD over UNESCO?

Perhaps not. As described at the beginning of this article, there is a hegemonic conception of performance measures and outputs that dominates discourse on how government is evaluated. It is an element of globalization, of building institutions that promote a particular form of development that is subservient to corporate global interests and brings the technology of control of business into education. It is not a system of democratic dialogue, but one of measurable objectives set by senior officials and evaluated by tools of quantification. And because of the dominant economic position of the U.S., any international system might end up following the ideology and dictates of the U.S.

A description from the UNESCO web page of a publication issued February 17, 2003, shows just how much UNESCO has been brought into the fold of the OECD's human capital approach to understanding education. The World Education Indicators have even been combined to be a UNESCO/OECD program:

> *Financing Education Investments and Returns is the third in a series of publications that seeks to analyze the education indicators developed through the UNESCO/OECD World Education Indicators (WEI) program. The report examines both the investments and returns to education and human capital. It begins by looking at the results of a specially commissioned study of the impact of human capital on economic growth in WEI countries that shows new findings in comparison with OECD countries. It also sets out the context for trends in educational attainment as well as current levels and future prospects of educational participation and expenditure in WEI countries.[5]*

On the other hand, things might have been different. One sees an immediate difference in looking at the names of the two organizations. While the OECD's name is limited to "economic," UNESCO includes education, science and culture, clearly a much broader scope than that of the OECD.

The possibilities of what could have been is reflected in the breadth of the goals that were defined for education in UNESCO's Delors Report on education.[6] It identified four goals: learning to live together, learning to be, learning to do, and learning to know. The OECD, its Indicators Project and the PISA exams are really only interested in the "learning to do" element, the development of human capital for the economic system. A valid assessment system would not just focus on one element, but would be concerned with all four aspects of learning, some of which do not lend themselves at all to testing as a means of assessment.

In fact, there still may be opportunities. According to Albert Tuijnman, the "OECD is no longer the only game in town." He is referring to the new UNESCO Institute of Statistics that opened in Montreal in 2001. It has a particular focus on monitoring progress on achieving the *Education for All* objectives, with significant financing by the Canadian federal government. The *Education for All* campaign is an international effort to ensure that by 2015 all children around the globe have access to at least primary education—an objective that could be achieved much sooner, of course, if only a share of the money spent on bombs were devoted to education.

Indeed, if we accept the claim of the World Social Forum that other worlds are possible, so must other forms of educating and assessing also be possible. The challenge is for us to imagine these, and to rebuild our institutions to make them real. 🌑

Larry Kuehn is Director of Research and Technology for the British Columbia Teachers' Federation.

Notes

[1] Tuijnman, A. (2001). Transcription of a presentation to an Edudata Canada Seminar on May 2, 2001 at the University of British Columbia.

[2] Elliott, J. (2002). "The Impact of Intensive 'Value for Money' Performance Auditing in Educational Systems."

[3] Tuijnman, 2001. p.12.

[4] Weiner, Harvey. EI Newsletter, December 2002.

[5] UNESCO web page. http://portal.unesco.org/, downloaded March 23, 2003.

[6] Delors, Jacques (Chairman), (1996), Learning the Treasure Within: Report to UNESCO of the International Commission on Education for the Twenty-first Century, [France: UNESCO Publishing], p.97.

An overlooked success in an under-appreciated province

By Heather-jane Robertson

A few weeks ago, an earnest-sounding journalist based in Halifax called me with a new twist on the "what do tests tell us?" question. Any educator who deals with the media knows the frustration of trying to answer questions that seem perfectly reasonable, from the layperson's perspective, but which deserve almost impossibly complex responses. The wisest answers to these questions usually begin with the phrase, "Well, it all depends…" Unfortunately, nuanced comments tend to irk journalists who know that their editors/producers are looking for pithy, unequivocal statements that can be ridiculed by the next interviewee. It's called making the news.

Certainly, politicians realize that "it all depends" isn't a vote-getting soundbite. Action, not consideration, is the new measure of leadership. And, as it turned out, it was a politician's "ready—fire—aim" reaction to public criticism that prompted the phone call from Halifax. Canada's results on the OECD's Program for International Student Assessment (1999), known as PISA, had just been released.[1] While Canadian 15-year-olds achieved their best-ever rankings in reading, mathematics and science, the province of Nova Scotia, along with the other Atlantic provinces, had fallen well short of the performance of central and western provinces.[2] Under fire from the opposition and the media, Education Minister Jane Purves announced a quick fix. Her ministry would see that each Grade 4 student would receive a writing handbook. "Grammar is like the rules of the road for effective communication," Ms. Purves explained in a press release, which went on to defend accurate spelling and correct usage as essential "employability skills."[3] When an impish member of the press gallery asked the Minister to define a gerund, she admitted to being uncertain, but ventured that she thought that it had something to do with "i-n-g endings."

I assured the reporter that, in my opinion, there was no known link between the ability to sort gerunds from participles and scoring well on "reading retrieving" and "reading reflecting," nor, for that matter, on students' anticipated success in the labour market, which is the intended focus of the PISA assessment. But I also told him that the report did contain a great deal of information that deserved public attention and debate. Several important findings are buried in the detailed, competent, and clearly written 93-page report on PISA produced by Statistics Canada, some of which are interesting because they are counter-intuitive. The most useful findings were derived by integrating achievement scores with contextual information collected through YITS: the Youth in Transition Survey. YITS questionnaires were administered to the Canadian students who wrote PISA, and to their teachers and principals; parents participated in half-hour telephone interviews. According to StatCan's report,

- Canadian schools have been more successful than most of their international counterparts in mitigating the effects on achievement of students' socioeconomic characteristics. (p.19)

- Moderate use of public and school libraries contributes to high scores, but very frequent use is associated with a drop in reading scores. (p. 21)

- Time spent on homework has a trivial effect on scores in reading, math and science in all but a very few jurisdictions. (p.28)

- Students' sense of "belonging to school" has no significant effect on scores. (p.29)

- Part-time jobs, held by an estimated 40% of high school students, have a negative effect on scores in all provinces. Contrary to several previous studies, labour force participation of even a few hours a week appears to hamper student achievement.(p.28)

- Students who live in single-parent households perform significantly less well than those in dual-parent households. (p.31)

- Parental involvement, as measured by the frequency and nature of their communications with their children, has a surprisingly weak effect on achievement. (p.34)

- Parental participation in homework has a negative effect on scores (p.28)
- French language minorities in provinces outside Quebec score poorly in reading compared with their anglophone counterparts. In most instances, these intra-provincial gaps are substantially larger than inter-provincial variations in reading scores. Results for anglophones in Quebec are equivalent to those of the francophone majority. (p 25)
- Principals in the four Atlantic provinces perceive teacher shortages as causing acute adverse academic effects that are just as severe as those described by principals in the Russian Federation and Mexico. (p.41)
- The achievement effects of "instructional resource adequacy" are trivial in Canada and in most other PISA countries, although principals in five provinces believe that material inadequacies are affecting student achievement. (p.42)

All interesting stuff, and predictably overlooked by the media's preoccupation with rankings. Even a great showing by Canadian students (ranked second overall in reading, next to Finland; fifth in math and science in a field of 32) produced tepid, even critical headlines in the national media. "Canadian teens rate passing grade" begrudged *The Ottawa Citizen*;[4] "Our schools: The best of a bad bunch," according to the *National Post*.[5] Provincial media reported provincial results and skipped the fine print.

But it isn't just the media that are missing the real story. According to this report, although its average scores are slightly below the Canadian norm, the province of Saskatchewan is achieving better equity outcomes than any other province, and better than any of the other 31 countries in the OECD study. Saskatchewan, large in area and in its commitment to education, although small in population and resources, posted astonishing gains in reducing the gap between its poorest and best students, which (as everyone knows) nearly always reflects socioeconomic status (SES).

No small feat in a province where child poverty approaches 20%, where 29% of all children below the age of 5 are poor, and where more than a third of students are Aboriginal, a group for whom the urban poverty rate exceeds 30%.[6] It seems unlikely that spending alone deserves the credit for Saskatchewan's success: In U.S. dollars, Saskatchewan's per-pupil expenditure (1997-98) was just $4,125, when the Canadian average was $4,808.[7] Yet something is happening in Saskatchewan's schools and communities that is transcending SES factors to a degree that most educators would believe is impossible.

Consider these results. Canada's PISA report includes an "inequality index" that measures the distance between the average scores of students ranked below the 10th percentile and those above the 90th. A score of 1.0 indicates no gap; Germany posts the greatest reading gap of 1.85, while the United States scores 1.75. Finland's results are best at 1.52; Canada's are 1.59; Saskatchewan's are 1.57. (p.55).

Even a great showing by Canadian students produced tepid, even critical headlines in the national media. "Canadian teens rate passing grade" begrudged *The Ottawa Citizen*; "Our schools: The best of a bad bunch," according to the *National Post*.

A related measure tells the same story another way. When comparing the average scores of students from the highest and lowest SES groups, relatively homogeneous Japan posts the lowest scores (between .08 and .12) in all three domains tested. (A score of 1 would indicate perfect alignment between SES and scores.) Effect sizes between .34 and .38 are reported for the U.S., putting that country in the company of nations where achievement appears to be most affected by SES, including Mexico and Belgium. Canada's "equality results" are quite encouraging at about .26, but Saskatchewan posts just half the Canadian average at .13 to .16. (p. 70).

Saskatchewan stands out in two more indices of educational equity. The first calculates the absolute difference in average scores in all three domains achieved by students within the lowest and highest SES quartiles. In mathematics, Germany showed the greatest gap at 106; the U.S. scored 95; Canada's average was 65; Saskatchwan's a mere 34. Results for reading and science were almost identical, with Saskatchewan coming second only to Japan in equality of results. (p.71,72) The final equity index measures the effect on achievement of the average SES of the schools students attend. Average school SES has the greatest effect in Belgium (.58) and Mexico (.56), with the U.S. scoring .43 and Canada .27. Saskatchewan recorded an astonishing .12, showing a weaker relationship between school SES and student achievement than any other province or country measured. (p. 79)

In a finding that ought to be making headlines everywhere, this report concludes that in Saskatchewan socioeconomic status exerts no statistically significant effect on student achievement among 15-year olds. (p.78) No doubt the validity of such a remarkable conclusion will generate a great deal of skepticism, and indeed it should. Whether the next round of PISA/ YITS will confirm or confound these findings—or whether there are problems with the data and the analyses—I'm going out on a limb. Something is going on in Saskatchewan that the rest of us should be paying attention to. Even if it requires ending a sentence with a preposition. ◗◖

Heather-jane Robertson is a writer living in Ottawa. She is the vice-president of the Canadian Centre for Policy Alternatives.

This article was originally published in Phi Delta Kappan, May 2002.

Notes

[1] Patrick Bussiere, Fernando Cartwright et al, "Measuring up: The Performance of Canada's Youth in Reading, Mathematics and Science." OECD PISA Study – First Results for Canadians aged 15. Human Resources Development Canada, Council of Ministers of Education, Canada and Statistics Canada. December, 2001. Available at www.statcan.ca

[2] All Canadian provinces were over-sampled to allow interprovincial as well as international comparissons to be made. (Bussiere, Cartwright et al, p. 18)

[3] "More Attention to Grammar in Nova Scotia". Government of Nova Scotia. Press Release. Jan. 14, 2002.

[4] Richard Starnes, "Canadian teens rate passing grade." The Ottawa Citizen, Dec. 5, 2001, p.A8.

[5] Clifford Orwin, "Our Schools: The best of a bad bunch." National Post, Dec. 6, 2001 p. A20.

[6] Kevin K. Lee, "Urban Poverty in Canada." Canadian Council on Social Development. April, 2000. http://www.ccsd.ca/pubs/2000/up/b1-9.html

[7] Ontario Secondary School Teachers Federation, "Ontario ranks 55th in Per Pupil Expenditures." 1999. http://www.osstf.on.ca/edfi/55th.html

No Child Left Behind (NCLB)
A plan for the destruction of public education: Just say "NO!"

by Gerald W. Bracey

T he NCLB is a trap. It is the grand scheme of the school privatizers. NCLB sets up public schools for the final knock down.
Paranoia? Hardly. Consider that the Bush administration is
de-regulating every pollution producing industry in sight while cutting
Superfund cleanup money. It has rolled back regulations on power plants
and snowmobiles and wants to take protection away from 20,000,000
acres of wetlands (20% of the total). President Bush's response to global
warming: "Deal with it!" by which he means, adjust to it while we make
the world safe for SUVs. The President wants to outsource hundreds of
thousands of government jobs to private corporations.[1] He wants to get
the government out of government.

Would an administration with such an anti-regulatory, pro-private
sector policy perspective turn around and impose harsh, straitjacket requirements on schools, demands that would bankrupt any business? Of
course not. Unless it had an ulterior purpose.

Recall that the president's original 2001 proposal provided vouchers
to let children attend private schools at taxpayer expense. Congress, chas-
tised by the massive defeats vouchers suffered in referenda in California
and Michigan in the 2000 election (voucher proponents outspent opponents 2-1, but the measures went down in flames, 70-30, in both states),
stripped the voucher provisions from the bill. They didn't strip them
from Karl Rove's mind. After the 2002 elections, the Wall Street Journal declared "GOP's Election Gains Give School Vouchers a Second

Wind."[2] They'll be back. In fact, they already are. President Bush has put $75 million for vouchers for the District of Columbia in his 2004 budget proposal and some congressmen want to extend their use to other cities as well.[3]

Mission impossible

There are any number of impossible-to-meet provisions in the NCLB, but let's take just two of the most prominent: those for testing and for teacher qualifications. The federal government cannot force NCLB on states, but any state that wants NCLB money must agree to test all children in Grades three through eight every year in reading and math and, two years later, science as well. The tests must be based on "challenging" standards and schools must show "Adequate Yearly Progress" (AYP) until, after 12 years, all of the schools' students attain the "proficient" level. The school must demonstrate AYP overall and separately for all major ethnic and socio-economic groups, special education students and English Language Learners. And pigs will fly.

The massive testing requirements alone will force many states to spend massive amounts of money to develop, administer, analyze and report the test results and other data needed for mandatory "report cards" schools must develop and send to parents. Many states will have to abandon their own programs laboured over for the last decade—or two. Their costs may well exceed what NCLB provides. An analysis by Rutland, Vermont School Superintendent, William Mathis, found that the state will receive $52 million dollars from NCLB, but that it will cost the Green Mountain State $158 million to implement the law's provisions.[4]

The word "proficient" is a trap, too. According to the law, each state decides how to define it, but the word already has great currency in education circles as part of the lingo surrounding the National Assessment of Educational Progress (NAEP). It is one of the NAEP achievement levels, the others being "below basic," "basic" and "advanced." Not many children attain the proficient level on NAEP tests

Although in common parlance, the NAEP achievement levels have been rejected by everyone who has ever studied them: UCLA's Center for Research on Evaluation, Student Standards and Testing (CRESST)[5], the General Accounting Office[6] and the National Academy of Sciences[7], as well as by individual psychometricians such as Lyle Jones of the University of North Carolina.[8] The studies agree that the methods used are flawed and, more importantly, the results don't accord with any other data.

For instance, Jones pointed out that American fourth-graders were well above average on the mathematics tests of the Third International Mathematics and Science Study (TIMSS), yet only 18% reached the proficient level and a meager 2% scored at the advanced level in the 1996 NAEP mathematics. Similar low percentages are seen in the 1996 NAEP Science assessment and TIMSS Science where American fourth-graders were third in the world among 26 nations. Finally, on the 2000 NAEP reading assessment, only 32% of fourth-graders attained proficient or better, but that American 9-year-olds were second in the world among 27 countries in the international reading study, *How in the World Do Students Read*[9,10]? It makes no sense that American kids do so poorly on domestic measures such as NAEP but stack up well against the rest of the industrialized world.

When NAEP was first introduced, the enabling law forbade it to report at the state level. Congress revised the law in 1988 to make state reporting possible and currently about 40 states volunteer (and pay) to receive state-level information. Under NCLB, state-level NAEP goes from voluntary to mandatory. All states must participate in the biennial NAEP reading and math assessments to "confirm" their own results. Studies have already shown that a much smaller proportion of students reaches proficient on NAEP than on the various state tests. Because the NAEP levels are exceedingly high, Robert Linn, co-director of CRESST observed that even getting all children to even the "basic" level on NAEP would constitute a mighty challenge.[11]

The NCLB bill contains incentives for states to start at a low level (to have any prayer of achieving AYP). This is why, on a preliminary analysis of "failing schools" in various states, Michigan, with high standards had 1513 failing schools, and Arkansas, with low standards, had none. Yet on the fourth grade NAEP reading assessment in 2000, Michigan had 28% of its students at or above proficient while Arkansas had only 23. Differences like this will turn into discrepancies between what the state assessments say and what NAEP says about how many students in a state are or are not proficient. Critics and profit seekers will take the discrepancy between the state results and the NAEP results as evidence that the schools are still failing and that the states and districts are lying to their citizens about school quality.

Districts and schools that fail to make AYP are subject to increasingly severe—and unworkable—sanctions. Their staffs can be fired, their kids sent to another district, the district abolished.

Using the original formulation, the White House's own calculations revealed that had NCLB been in place for a few years, about 90% of the schools in North Carolina and Texas would have been labeled "failing schools." North Carolina and Texas? These are states that have been singled out in recent years for their progress on a variety of tests. If they can't meet the standards, what hope is there for the rest? None—that's the purpose of the law. The National Conference of State Legislatures estimated that 90% of all schools would fail while simulations by the Council of Chief State School Officers put the failure rate at only 88%.[12] As a consequence, some wags are beginning to refer to the law as LNSS: Let No School Succeed.

Greasing the skids for vouchers

In a move clearly aimed at greasing the skids for vouchers, the U. S. Department of Education put out regulations that make no sense at all. As a first step to quashing failing schools, children in those schools must be offered the option of going to a more successful one, successful defined solely in terms of test scores. It does not matter if the "successful" schools are already stuffed to the gills. They must hire more teachers (where they will find them is something of a mystery), bring in trailers or build more classrooms (where they will get the money is something of a mystery). They must, in the words of Under Secretary Eugene Hickok, build capacity. Only if the arriving students would so crowd the schools as to violate fire or other safety and health codes, can they be denied access. Thus, in theory, we could face a situation in which virtually all students attend schools currently enrolling only 10% of students. In some places, one must truly wonder where kids will go. Los Angeles has enough classroom space for 145,000 high schoolers. The district currently has 165,000 with a projected 200,000 by 2005.[13]

The NCLB bill contains incentives for states to start at a low level. This is why, on a preliminary analysis of "failing schools" in various states, Michigan, with high standards had 1,513 failing schools, and Arkansas, with low standards, had none.

There are more than a few technical problems with the concept of AYP. Researchers have found that test scores at the school level are quite volatile from year to year.[14] According to RAND researcher David Grissmer, the tests would not identify the good and the bad schools, but only the lucky and unlucky ones.[15] Not only are the test scores volatile, most of the volatility is associated with factors that have nothing to do with what goes on in the classroom.

No one has given any consideration to student mobility. Nationally, 20% of American students change schools each year. In urban areas the figure is more like 50% and in some instances, the students in a building at the end of the year are not those who started there in the fall. How, then, can the school be considered failing or succeeding?

Similarly, nothing in the law takes into account the phenomenon of summer loss. This is critical. Disadvantaged students show substantial summer loss while middle class and affluent students hold their own in mathematics and actually gain over the summer months in reading. One study found that poor and middle class students gained the same amount during the school year, but, because of summer losses, the poor students fell farther and farther behind their middle class peers as they moved from first to fifth grade.[16] Thus schools that actually make adequate yearly progress during the school year will get labeled as failures because of what happens during the summer months.

Moreover, no one has given any attention to what happens when large numbers of children leave "failing" schools for more successful ones (the U. S. Department of Education has given large grants for publicity campaigns to insure that parents are aware of this option). Suppose the arriving students raise the average class size from 22 to 29 students. This alone could easily transform a successful school into a failing one.

And what kinds of test scores will the arriving students bring? The legislation demands that schools give priority to the neediest students— those with the lowest test scores. The arrival of large numbers of low-scoring students might well convert a successful school into a failing one. At the same time, since the departing students take their low scores with them, the sending school's test scores will automatically rise. But if the sending school gets out of the failing category, it doesn't get the kids back. It only gets to stop paying for their transportation, thereby turning NCLB into an unfunded mandate on parents.

The above problems present sufficient difficulties for schools, but their lives become more arduous because they must disaggregate the data below the school level. We have mentioned already that school-level test scores show volatility from year to year. Imagine what kind of instability we'll see when we have to report by smaller units: blacks, whites, Hispanics, Asians, Native Americans, special education students, kids on free-and-reduced price lunches, and English Language Learners. And if one group doesn't show AYP, the school takes the hit.

When the pre-ordained high failure rate occurs, vouchers and privatization will be touted as the only possible cures. Subsequent to the voucher defeats in Michigan and California, advocates have stopped touting vouchers as a cure-all for the whole nation on market grounds and have started pushing them for poor people on civil rights grounds. They contend that middle class people aren't interested in vouchers because they think their public schools are good (they're right).

But with the high failure rates guaranteed by NCLB, even those good schools will fail—51% of the schools North Carolina recognized for "exemplary growth" failed under NCLB.[17] Conservative school critic, Denis Doyle wrote that the NCLB means that the nation is about to be "inundated in a sea of bad news" and that the schools are going to get "pole-axed."[18]

> In some instances, the students in a building at the end of the year are not those who started there in the fall. How, then, can the school be considered failing or succeeding?

The privatizers will shout "The school system has proven it is an ossified government monopoly that can't reform itself (Chester Finn shouted precisely this in 1998 in the Wall Street Journal[19]). You've had your chance. We warned you. We gave you *Nation At Risk* over twenty years ago. Nothing has changed. It's time to apply American business expertise to education." Right, as in Enron, Tyco, Global Crossing, Imclone, WorldCom, and the 993 companies that have "adjusted" their accounting reports in the last five years, and the myriad dot.coms that failed because their officers didn't have a clue about how to run a business (How come no one ever criticizes business schools?).

Here comes the private sector

Chris Whittle and his Edison Schools Inc. will likely be waiting. Edison stock has been as high as $39 a share, but in February, 2003 it was hovering around $1.35; in ten years, the company has failed to show a profit for even one quarter. Recall that Whittle announced his plan for a national system of private schools in 1991 when President George Herbert Walker Bush was riding high after the Gulf War. So certain was a Bush re-election that the most likely Democratic candidates declined to run and left the certain defeat to the Governor of Arkansas.

Whittle's original grandiose plan prophesied 200 private schools by 1996 and 1000 by 2000 (he currently manages, not owns, about 130 public schools). He said it would require about $1 billion to create a prototype of his scheme and another $2 to ramp it up to a national scale. Where on earth would he get that kind of money? Whittle said it would come from bankers and investors. Three billion from investors who had already lost about $400 million on his earlier adventure, Channel One?

Whittle actually needed President Bush and Secretary Alexander to push their school voucher plan through Congress. Then children could use those vouchers to attend Edison schools.

When the unthinkable happened and President Bush lost, Whittle had to fall back on managing a few public schools. Whittle no doubt already has an advertising campaign ready for when the failing grades start arriving. He will then portray the Edison "model" as the only means of consistently achieving AYP, even though evaluations have found Edison achievement results mixed at best and a dozen schools that Edison lists as showing "positive" trends have terminated their contracts.

Former secretary of education William J. Bennett will also be waiting. Bennett now heads K12, Inc. After decades of warning people that computers offer no educational advantages, Bennett converted and is now CEO of this company that produces on-line curriculum materials. The "supplementary services" provisions of NCLB offer Whittle, Bennett and other private companies opportunities after the public schools "fail."

The testing requirements alone are enough to consign the schools to failure. The requirements for "highly qualified" teachers simply hit the schools while they're down. All current teachers in schools receiving NCLB funds must be "highly qualified" by 2005-2006, as must anyone who was hired after the 2002-2003 school year began. By "highly qualified," NCLB means those who hold at least a bachelor's degree, have full state certification (or have passed the state's licensing exam), and who have not had any certification requirements waived on "an emergency, provisional, or temporary basis."

There are nationwide shortages of people with such qualifications in mathematics, science and special education—and in the cities. Chicago says 25% of the teachers in low-performing schools don't meet the requirements[20], while Baltimore put the figure at 31%.[21] A 2003 survey commissioned by *Education Week* shows that 22% of all high school students take a course from a teacher without even a minor in the subject. For high-poverty high schools, the figure is 32% and for high-poverty middle schools it is 44%.[22] These precise figures are recent but the teacher qualification problem has been known for some time. We can only assume that the framers of the legislation knew in advance that states could not meet the requirements. They just didn't care.

Even classroom paraprofessionals must have completed two years of college and have an associate's degree or have passed a state test on content and teaching skills. New hires must meet this requirement as of January 8, 2003; existing paraprofessionals have four years to ratchet up their credentials.

Paraprofessionals are low-salaried staff who often come from lower-income neighborhoods. Many urban education experts contend that they are the best possible candidates to become accredited teachers—they are familiar with the situation and know what they're getting into and have shown that they can deal with it. But there is no federal money to assist them to their degrees and if they should attain one, they will no doubt find more attractive salaries outside of the school. And better working conditions – NCLB greatly restricts what services they can provide to children. They can't teach, for instance unless, "directly supervised" by a teacher.

A 2003 survey commissioned by *Education Week* shows that 22% of all high school students take a course from a teacher without even a minor in the subject. For high-poverty high schools, the figure is 32% and for high-poverty middle schools it is 44%.

Harry Reid, the Democratic whip in the Senate is said to have gathered some education lobbyists together and asked, "How on earth could you have let this happen?" ("on earth" was not actually the phrase he used). How, indeed? Well, money can be attractive and addictive. How else to explain why so many Senators and Representatives endorsed President Bush's proposal? Senators Kennedy and Miller now say President Bush didn't deliver the promised dollars—their versions contained $10 billion more than the $1.4 billion of new money actually appropriated.[23] Some states are already thinking that their costs—in dollars, not even counting hassle—might well be more than they get from NCLB. David Shreve of the National Conference of State Legislatures estimates that the cost of program to states could run as high as $35 billion.[24]

Thomas Gaffey, a state legislator in Connecticut says, "I'm sitting here shaking my head. I knew this was loaded with problems, but what the heck was going through their minds?"[25] What indeed? States should look at the lucre-drug that Bush and the NCLB are offering them and just say "No!" ◗◖

Gerald W. Bracey is an independent researcher and writer living in Alexandria, VA. His most recent books are The War Against America's Public Schools *(Allyn & Bacon, 2002),* What You Should Know About the War Against America's Public Schools *(Allyn & Bacon, 2003), and* Put to the Test: An Educator's and Consumer's Guide to Standardized Testing *(Revised edition, Phi Delta Kappa International, 2002). He holds part-time positions with George Mason University in Fairfax, Virginia and the High/Scope Educational Research Foundation in Ypsilanti, Michigan.*

This article is reprinted with the author's permission from No Child Left. Volume I, Number 2, February, 2003. http://www.nochildleft.com/2003/feb03no.html

Notes

[1] Lee, Christopher. "35 Senators Oppose Outsourcing Plan." *Washington Post*, February 5, 2003, p. A21.

[2] Tomsho, Robert. "GOP's Election Gains Give Vouchers a Second Wind." *Wall Street Journal*, November 11, 2002, p. 1.

[3] Strauss, Valerie. "President to Push Vouchers for D. C." *Washington Post*, February 8, 2003.

[4] Johnson, Sally West. "Mathis Rips Feds Over School Act." *Rutland Herald (Vermont)*, February 5, 2003. The analysis can be obtained by emailing William Mathis at wmathis@sover.net.

[5] Linn, Robert L. *Standards-Based Accountability: Ten Suggestions.* Policy Paper, Center for Research in Evaluation, Standards and Student Testing, 1998.

[6] General Accounting Office. *Educational Achievement Standards: NAGB's Approach Yields Misleading Interpretations.* Washington, DC: Author, June 1993, Report GAO/PEMD-93-12.

[7] National Academy of Sciences. *Grading the Nation's Report Card: Evaluating NAEP and Transforming the Assessment of Educational Progress.* Washington, DC: National Academy Press, 1999.

[8] Jones, Lyle V. *National Tests of Educational Reform: Are They Compatible?* Princeton, NJ: Policy Information Center, Educational Testing Service, 1997. Accessible at www.ets.org/search97cgi/s97_cgi.

9 U. S. Department of Education. *The Nation's Report Card: Fourth Grade Reading 2000*. Washington, DC: Author, Report No. NCES 2001-499, p. 15.

10 Elley, Warwick P. *How in the World Do Students Read?* The Hague, Holland: International Association for the Evaluation of Educational Achievement, 1992. Available in this country through the International Reading Association, Newark, Delaware.

11 Linn, Robert L., Eva L. Baker, and Damian W. Betebenner. "Accountability systems: Implications of the No Child Left Behind Act of 2001." *Educational Researcher*, August/September 2002, pp. 3-16.

12 Information can be found at the organization's websites, www.ncsl.org, and www.ccsso.org.

13 Ross, Randy. "School Choice Where None Exists." *Education Week*, December 4, 2002, p. 37.

14 Kane, Thomas J. and Douglas O Staiger. "Volatility in School Test Scores: Implications for Test-Based Accountability Systems." In Diane Ravitch (Ed.). *Brookings Papers on Education 2002*. Washington, DC: Brookings Institution, 2002.

15 Olson, Lynn. "Study Questions Reliability of Single Year Test-Score Gains." *Education Week*, May 23, 2001 p. 9. Author's note: it might seem that David Grissmer made his remark a year before the Kane and Staiger research appeared. Dave made his comment when the Kane and Staiger paper first appeared in 2001, but it was not published formally until 2002.

16 Alexander, Karl L., Doris R. Entwistle, and Linda S. Olson. "Schools, Achievement and Inequality: A Seasonal Perspective." *Educational Evaluation and Policy Analysis*, Summer, 2001, pp. 171-191.

17 Simmons, Tim. "U.S. Standards Perplex N.C. Schools." *Raleigh News & Observer*, June 2, 2002, p. A1

18 Doyle, Denis P. "AYP Revealed, Now What?" *The Doyle Report*, June 4, 2002. "AYP Once More Once," *The Doyle Report*, June 13, 2002. www.thedoylereport.com

19 Finn, Chester E., Jr. "Why America Has the World's Dimmest Bright Kids." *Wall Street Journal*, February 25, 1998, p. A22.

20 Gewertz, Catherine. "City Districts Seek Teachers With Licenses." *Education Week*, September 11, 2002, p. 1.

21 Walsh, Kate. *Teacher Certification Reconsidered: Stumbling for Quality*. Baltimore, MD: The Abell Foundation, 2001.

22 Education Week. *Quality Counts 2003: If I Can't Learn from You—Ensuring a Highly Qualified Teacher in Every Classroom*. Bethesda, MD: Author, January 9, 2003.

23 Robelen, Erik W. "Democratic, GOP Education Plans Differ by Billions." *Education Week*, March 27, 2003, p. 1.

24 Frahm, Robert A. "Lawmakers Hear Criticism of Education Reform Law." *Hartford Courant*, February 8, 2003, p. 1.

25 Ibid.

Measuring up to the league in England and Wales

by Marita Moll

Children in England take more standardized tests than anywhere in Europe—up to 105 national tests in the first 11 years. (Schmidt, 2002)[1]

In England and Wales, they are called "league tables," but Canadians will recognize the pattern from the Fraser Institute school ranking project.[2] Rankings based on tests that evaluate teachers and schools are published in newspapers and on the Internet. Of course, such simplistic measures ignore contextual issues and often stigmatize schools that may be exemplary despite the fact that, for a variety of reasons, they did not make the Top 10 list. "It's a quasi-market system that creates an internal market within the public sector," said Tony Brockman, president of the National Union of Teachers (NUT), the largest teacher union in the British Isles. "Globalization has highlighted education as one of the last great frontiers for privatization," he warned during his visit to Canada in 2001.

Recently, British authorities have been experimenting with a "value-added" league table that measures change in student performance on standardized tests applied at ages 7 and 11. Results of the pilot project show differences between schools to be much smaller than on the original ranking based on straight test results. Sadly, even marginal differences are accentuated in any ranking system. Brockman observes that, "in reality, these ranking systems often amount to nothing more than tables of social deprivation."

Name and shame

Operating hand-in-hand with the league tables is a draconian school inspection regime carried out by freelance inspectors employed by private companies. These inspectors observe classes, grade teachers, examine school policies, gather views from parents, evaluate test results, and produce a public report on each school. "It's a classic 'name and shame' exercise," said Brockman. Schools determined to be failing have two years to show improvement before a "fresh start" program kicks in. At this point, new administrators are usually appointed and all current teachers may be declared redundant. "This way of trying to help schools has been a complete failure. The inspectors simply issue the report and leave without offering any recommendations for improvement." The cracks in the inspection process, which is managed by the Office of Standards in Education (OFSTED), are beginning to show.

"In reality, these ranking systems often amount to nothing more than tables of social deprivation."

The head of the program was recently fired. There is an attempt to make the process more comparative as opposed to absolutist, and to take into account funding and teacher shortages, as well as social deprivation in some areas, as contributing to school difficulties.

Drawing on the work of John McBeath, a pioneer in the field of school self-evaluation at the University of Strathclyde, NUT has proposed a tool-kit for school self-evaluation that addresses the qualitative as well as the quantitative aspects of schooling. These school self-evaluations are grounded in the different perspectives of children, parents, school governors, teachers, and senior management, who come together as stakeholder groups to determine the conditions for effectiveness in their particular context and to develop a plan for improvement.[3] In this model, the government inspectors would simply evaluate the school's own processes and intervene only when they were deficient.

Brockman notes that the government has recently found a new role for OFSTED—the evaluation of local school authorities (LEAs)—the British equivalent to our school boards/districts/commissions. Failing LEAs are usually privatized and their services are put out to tender. Firms running prisons and immigration detention centres figure prominently among the applicants for these contracts.

In Ontario, the Conservative government recently fired school boards in Toronto, Ottawa and Hamilton for challenging the government's funding allocations by refusing to balance their budgets. These boards were put "under supervision." One wonders if this privatization model could be the next remedy for non-compliant school boards in Ontario. ◑◐

Marita Moll is a freelance writer and educational researcher based in Ottawa. She is a research associate with the Canadian Centre for Policy Alternatives.

Notes

[1] Schmidt, Sarah. "The A-level debacle." *National Post*, November 20, 2002.

[2] For more information on league tables, see: http://www.ioe.ac.uk/media/r000221.htm.

[3] For information and references, see *The School Self-Evaluation Tool Box by* Kathryn Riley and John McBeath, 2000. http://www1.worldbank.org/education/est/resources/domains/Quality%20assurance.htm.

League tables cause student burn out

Some experts believe that exam mania could scar the emotional health of a generation of children because of its relentless appetite for high grades at almost any cost. A paper for the Institute of Public Policy Research published in the summer argued that high-achieving students could become success "junkies" and lose sight of themselves, only feeling accepted if they got straight As, while those who didn't make the exam grade could feel like failures.

The paper, *Learning to Trust and Trusting to Learn* by Elizabeth Hartley-Brewer, cited the apparent rise in eating disorders, burn-out, male disaffection and behaviour problems, even in the more academic schools, as signs that all is not well.

It argued that schools which focus too heavily on getting children through exams and pushing themselves up local league tables by hook or by crook risk damaging children's—and teachers'—emotional health and skewing broader educational objectives in the process. The latest official study acknowledges that one in 10 children aged five to 15 will experience a clinically defined mental health problem.

"I think there is a horrendous amount of pressure being put on young children, which is changing the nature of childhood," says Elizabeth Hartley-Brewer. "There is an unhealthy and neurotic perfectionism developing among children which involves a strong desire to avoid mistakes."

This can lead to children under-achieving to avoid the risk of failure and, she says, schools have to provide an environment in which children feel valued beyond delivering "success" to parents, the school or the government.

"When there is so much pressure and focus on doing well, children can feel they are only being valued for being successful, so they can become depressed if they are not.

"They are working for and trying to meet someone else's expectations. They end up with very little pleasure from their own work and they can end up losing the plot—burnt out or opting out."

Excerpted from: Wendy Berliner. "Success, the new drug" U.K Guardian, Thursday November 22, 2001

Japan and Finland

Two test cases

by John Hoffman

J apan came first in math and Finland came first in reading in the Program for International Student Assessment (PISA), a testing arm of the Organization for Economic Co-operation and Development (OECD). What can we learn from them?

Japan

Education is hierarchical and intensely competitive in Japan. High schools are ranked by how many students they send to the top universities (which are also ranked), and all high schools and universities have entrance exams that are weighted in difficulty according to the school's ranking. Some universities have so-called "escalator schools" so there's a high school, elementary school and even a preschool that feed into the university. Entrance (even to preschool) is by testing.

According to OECD figures, Japanese students do the least amount of homework but spend the most time attending subject-related courses (as opposed to piano lessons, etc.) outside of school hours. This probably reflects the number of children who attend juku or "cram schools"— private after-hours schools designed to supplement regular instruction and boost chances of passing entrance exams. A total of 10% of Japanese students attend private schools (in Canada it's about 6%).

Although this system seems elitist to us, it's actually thought to have been an important factor in introducing more equity to Japanese society after World War II, by providing a mechanism for social mobility through merit as opposed to social status.

The typical Japanese elementary class size is up to 40, substantially larger than in Canada. But observers say Japanese classes tend to be quieter and more orderly than ours. They also don't include students with learning disabilities or special needs (these kids go to separate schools). Japanese teaching in math and science emphasizes basic knowledge and operations more than we do, although recent reforms point to a shift towards creative problem-solving in the curriculum.

Finland

Kids don't have to start school until age seven in Finland, though many attend daycare and preschool. Finland doesn't seem to emphasize early childhood education as much as other European Union countries. How, then, do these kids top the world in reading scores? Borje Vahamaki, a professor of Finnish studies at the University of Toronto, offers two observations: "One is that Finnish is very logical and easy to learn for native speakers [for foreigners it's actually one of the most difficult languages]. It's extremely phonetic. It writes the way it sounds and it sounds the way it writes," Vahamaki explains. "The entire vocabulary comes from Finnish roots. There are no words with Latin, Germanic or French roots, as there are in English." For example, the Finnish equivalents for big words like individuality are words any five-year-old would know, Vahamaki says. Most Finns also get a lot of practice in linguistic detail since they learn two other languages (including English) in the course of their schooling.

Another big factor is the social and political history of Finland in the last 200 years. "For many years, Finland was ruled by the Swedes and then it was part of Russia, so the Finnish people and their language were marginalized," Vahamaki explains. "In the latter half of the 19th century there was a national movement to raise the level of education of all Finnish people, which at that time was behind the rest of the Western world. For a Finn, one of the most patriotic things one can do is to become well educated." ❧

John Hoffman is a regular contributor and columnist for Today's Parent Magazine. This article was originally published in Today's Parent, September 2002 and is reprinted with permission.

Is there any merit in merit pay?

by Marita Moll

Imported from the U.S., where it continues to fail as a useful system for teacher remuneration, performance-related pay (PRP) is a tool that flows logically from the current mania for measurement activities.

"It's ironic that the system of connecting teacher pay to test results was one of the issues that led to the founding of the NUT 100 years ago," says Tony Brockman, president of the National Union of Teachers, the largest teacher union in the British Isles.

Research and practice have continuously found PRP systems to be counterproductive and even destructive. "One of the real impacts of a system that bases teacher pay increases to student performance is that teachers of disadvantaged students are rarely eligible for such increases," he noted. To reduce such obvious inequities, the processes tend to become increasingly complex creating mountains of paperwork. The system introduced in England and Wales includes teacher characteristics as well as student test results among the criteria. It can take three days to fill in the application form.

As a result of intensive lobbying and a court challenge, the NUT achieved important improvements to the original proposal including additional funding, a set of appeal mechanisms and a review of the entire process in 2002. In the meantime, NUT is developing an alternative that would connect teacher pay increases to the identification of professional development needs and the accreditation of enhanced qualifications.

Testing undermines education in Korea

by Adam Woelders and Emily Moes

F our months ago, we got married, took a short honeymoon, came home, packed and headed to South Korea within two weeks. We shared the dream of traveling and teaching. We were hired through the Korean government and assigned to the Board of Education in the southern island province of Jeju-do. We work as English instructors in several different schools as well as conduct teaching methodology and conversation workshops for local teachers.

We both looked upon the new Liberal government as a breath of fresh air for the education system in British Columbia. From our perspective as new teachers, there appeared to be a lot of current practices in schools that needed some alteration or change. The use of increased standardized testing, greater accountability through school rankings, and even charter schools did not seem like bad ideas for the welfare of students.

Our perspective on education has radically changed since coming here. Korea has virtually no natural resources, so education pulled this country from the devastation of the Korean War to industrialization and prosperity in the last two decades. In this Confucian-influenced society, a child's education is considered to be the single most important goal of Korean society.

Yet at some point, a problem emerged. Koreans are flocking to Australia, America, Britain, and Canada. The reason? For many, it is to ensure that their children avoid the Korean public education system, unaffectionately known by some students as "exam hell." We have seen and experienced here that increased testing does not make teachers more accountable or give students more choices. It has the opposite effect.

The entire education system, year after year of schooling, is geared entirely to the tests. Principals and administrators are concerned only with how their schools fare competitively against others. The test results are only used to publicly determine which are the best students and then to categorize them.

The students achieving the best scores are sent to specialized charter schools for an education in technology, science, or other pursuits. The poorer test achievers are sent to industrial schools. The career and lifestyle choices for both high achievers and low achievers are limited early in their life. During a recent conversation workshop, one teacher told us: "I wish I could go back to my first year of middle school and study harder for a test. I scored low on one test and couldn't go to the high school or university I wanted to." School prestige and rankings have become so important here that she was too embarrassed to tell us what schools she ended up attending.

Industrial schools here have become completely ghettoized, whereby students, teachers, and parents alike regard such schools as temporary depots for poor students who have no hope of post-secondary education. Such schools have few materials and equipment; meanwhile more prestigious schools receive private-sector funding and can afford large screen televisions, video projectors and a disproportionate amount of multimedia equipment. Emily teaches English at a science high school that has class sizes of 20 students, and a total student population of 70. The school is three years old and has a multimedia lab that contains many more computers than students. Across town, I teach at an industrial high school that trains students for careers in the hospitality industry. Classes in a dilapidated building have at least 45 students and multi-media equipment is scarce. Some of these students study English diligently in the hopes of going to another country to attend university. "I cannot have a good job or education here because I go to this school. Studying English can help me," said one student. The injustice is compounded by the reality that these students are taught a watered-down curriculum but required to write the same government tests.

Koreans are flocking to Australia, America, Britain, and Canada. The reason? For many, it is to ensure that their children avoid the Korean public education system, unaffectionately known by some students as "exam hell."

Because of the importance of tests at all levels of the school system, an incredible amount of unnecessary and unproductive pressure falls on the shoulders of students and teachers. Teachers feel such a personal sense of responsibility for their student's scores that they never take a day off, no matter how sick, nor will their principal allow them to. The irony is that even with this sense of responsibility, teachers do not know names of many of or much about their students. Teachers cannot help but be more concerned with their reputation among administrators than they are with their students. When asked what should change in Korea, one teacher said, "teacher's need more time to talk with students."

Emily's co-teacher, a Korean with more than 20 years experience, was amazed at how much Emily learned about her students in one class simply because she taught a lesson where students took a break from examinable material and were encouraged to "share their dreams." One problem is that teachers are routinely tested, observed, and graded by local administrators and school-board inspectors. Their performance affects many aspects of their careers including salary, promotions, and where they are placed to work. It is not uncommon for teachers to rehearse the same lesson several times in anticipation of an inspection. One elementary school teacher told us that, "many teachers are so worried about their scores that they forget about their students. It's very stressful," she said.

Students themselves lead mundane lives once they reach high school, relegated to a routine of little sleep and constant studying. Little time is available for extra-curricular activities. In this highly competitive system, there is no special education, and few placements are available for students with learning disabilities or handicaps.

Given these shortcomings in the public system, many parents resent the government spending tax dollars on education. Instead many parents are now opting to spend small fortunes sending their children to tutors and private institutes once their regular school day is over. It is not uncommon to find students who study or attend classes from early morning to midnight.

Creativity, innovation, critical thinking, and problem solving are reluctantly marginalized by teacher-directed lessons focused on textbook-based memorization and factual knowledge—testable stuff. The result is thousands of students who never challenge the status quo, nor imagine creative solutions to existing social and economic problems. We wandered into a pizza restaurant one night in Seoul and met a man who had worked for Samsung, Korea's largest tech company, for seven years.

He explained that since King Sejong invented Hangul (the Korean writing system) in the 1500s, nothing produced in Korea has been innovative. Most Korean products are copied from foreign manufacturers, many Hyundai cars for example, need Japanese engines. "This," the former Samsung employee said, "I blame on the education system here."

The economic impact is further exacerbated by attitudes toward an individual's academic record. Last week the Korea Herald reported that among the students surveyed at Korea National University, one of Korea's three most elite colleges, over half of them said they wished they were born in another country. The students cited the education system as among the top three problems in Korea. A recent article in the Asian edition of *TIME* magazine reported that most Korean companies hire exclusively from the prestigious high schools and universities, with little regard for a person's qualifications or skills. No wonder Korea's economy is falling behind its Asian competitors.

Our supervisor here in Jeju, Lee Young-sook, has experienced many frustrating years as a teacher and administrator relentlessly fighting for change. But she admits, "Nothing can ever change until we change our competitive attitude and thinking that testing is so important." Her daughter is studying English in preparation for possibly studying abroad when she is old enough for high school. In working with her and many other teachers here, we have come to see that many of the proposed ideas for change in our own system do not work in practice because they do not serve students nor give them increased choice, sense of value, or lifestyle. We have also come to appreciate our system of education and the teachers working within it for their commitment to the welfare of students above all other concerns.

Overall, our brief experience has made us much more aware of what teachers in B.C. have fought for on behalf of students in the past, and it has made us determined to return to B.C. with the desire to protect what we now have. Our hope is that our current government will honour their commitment to public education and seek to do what is right for students, not what looks good to the taxpayers or the private sector. As we have seen in Korea, such a strategy has had a dramatically negative effect on this society and economy. 🦋

Adam Woelders and Emily Moes are B.C. teachers working in Korea.
This article was published in Teacher Newsmagazine *(British Columbia Teachers' Federation) Volume 14, Number 4, Jan./Feb. 2002.*
Reprinted with permission

Testing companies fail the grade

In September 1999, [CTB/McGraw-Hill] admitted that it had incorrectly scored the reading and math tests of more than 8,600 [New York] city students. Thousands of third and sixth graders were erroneously sent to summer school because of the mistake, a miscalculation of the percentile score that showed how the students compared with a national sample. The error made it look as if test scores had dropped precipitously from the year before, which influenced the decision of Rudy Crew, then the chancellor, to remove a number of superintendents.

In June 2001, the [New York City] Board of Education accused CTB/McGraw-Hill of miscalculating yet another set of scores, this time on a sixth-grade reading test. Board officials were convinced that the scores were too high, but the testing company insisted there was no error. The dispute was never resolved.

Earlier this year, the Board of Education complained that the testing company had not accurately scored the seventh-grade reading test. Harold O. Levy, then the chancellor, refused to release the seventh-grade scores, which some officials said showed a sharp decline. The scores still have not been released, but CTB/McGraw-Hill has insisted that they are accurate.

Harcourt Educational Measurement [which has been contracted to provide reading tests for third, fifth, sixth and seventh graders beginning this school year] has been accused of miscalculating test scores in Georgia, Delaware and California. . . .

Excerpted from "After Disputes on Scoring, School System Switches Provider of Reading Tests" Abby Goodnough. New York Times, September 28, 2002.

Putting ETS to the test

by Patricia McAdie and Erika Shaker

"No scores of any kind of test of subject matter knowledge are
related to teacher effectiveness. There is no reason to expect that
future use of teacher competency tests will have any impact
whatsoever on the quality of teaching in the public school."
— Don Medley, senior research scientist at ETS.[1]

T he Educational Testing Service (ETS) is a private, so-called non-profit, American corporation. As a non-profit corporation, they are exempt from corporate and property taxes. ETS has recently been given the contract by the Ontario Government to develop the entrance to the profession test for prospective teachers.

ETS was created in 1947 by the American Council on Education, the Carnegie Corporation, the College Board and the Carnegie Foundation for the Advancement of Teaching. For fiscal year ending June 1998, they had real estate valued at $133.4 million (US) and held $34.8 million in cash and $132 million in stock. They have more than 2100 employees. In 1998, their president earned $467,481 plus $49,664 in deferred compensation. They administer the SAT, GRE, LSAT, MCAT (Medical College Aptitude Test), TOEFL (Test of English as a Foreign Language), and PRAXIS (Professional Assessments for Beginning Teachers), as well as a number of others. The SAT is given to over 5 million students every year. ETS has been called the "creator of gatekeeper exams that have sorted America's educated society for more than five decades."[2]

The current president of ETS, Kurt Landgraf, is a former CEO of DuPont Pharmaceuticals.

Three for-profit subsidiaries have been created by ETS: the Chauncey Group International, in 1996, to handle much of the employment testing business, ETS K-12 Works, in 2000, and ETS Technologies, also in 2000, focussing on online learning and assessment applications. They also own stock in Sylvan Learning Systems.

Following are some of the problems that have been encountered over the years with ETS, their tests, and their approach to the people taking the tests. This is by no means an exhaustive list, nor does it address many of the inherent problems with multiple choice, standardized tests in general.

2001—Almost 400 colleges and universities in the U.S. have stopped using the SAT in their admissions requirements after many studies have concluded that standardized tests do not add significant information to predict how students will do. In fact, the SAT explains only about 16% of the variation in freshman grades. The tests also have been shown to be biased against minorities and women.

1999—ETS agreed to cancel unusually low computer-based Graduate Record Exam (GRE) scores for one student, paying for her time and registration fees. The student was surprised by her low score on the computer-based GRE so took the pencil-and-paper version. She scored significantly higher on the second test, jumping from the 3rd to the 84th percentile of test-takers. ETS had claimed that the two tests were equivalent. The student was assisted by free legal assistance in challenging the low score from the computer-based test. ETS settled the case out of court. The GRE and other tests are no longer available in pencil-and-paper format.

1998—ETS moved to computer administration of the Graduate Management Admissions Test (GMAT). Because there were too few testing sites, long waiting lists developed, as long as four months in parts of Europe and Asia. Some test takers encountered computer programming flaws while taking the test; the entire national computerized GMAT system crashed while 1300 students were taking the test.

1995—Before phasing out the National Teachers Exam (NTE), announced at least 3 years earlier, thousands of New York City public school teachers received termination or demotion notices. Most of these teachers were from minority groups and many with 10 or more years of experience. They had failed the NTE. Independent studies have found that the NTE cannot predict teacher competence.

1995—ETS could not find 60 SAT answer sheets submitted by a high school in New York City. Although they offered a free make-up exam, the timing was very inappropriate. After much pressure, an alternative time was agreed to. Soon after the retest, ETS found more than 2/3 of the missing answer sheets, even though all had been in the same package. ETS unilaterally informed the students that the scores from the retest would not be reported.

1995—In 1991, a student took the SAT while suffering the effects of mononucleosis. He took the exam again six months later and scored significantly better. ETS would not release his second scores, claiming that he had cheated. After years of fighting in the courts, including appeals by ETS after losing in lower courts, the student finally won his case, but not until after he had failed to get in to the college of his choice and failed to get a swimming scholarship.

1993—A research study jointly published by the College Board and ETS concludes that males do better on multiple-choice questions than females. The gender gap narrows or disappears for essays, word problems or other construct-response questions. ETS's tests are virtually all multiple choice format.

1992—ETS announced that they would replace the National Teachers Exam (NTE) with a new test. The NTE was widely criticized as having almost 40% of the questions with either no one correct answer or more than one correct answer. Prospective teachers who failed the test subsequently passed licensing require-

©2002

"Make tests! That's where the money is."

ments. How many prospective teachers never pursued a teaching option after taking this faulty test?

1989—7 students out of 79 taking Advanced Placement Exams in California admitted to cheating. ETS invalidated the scores of all 79 students and mandated re-tests. This is the same scenario as documented in the 1988 Hollywood movie "Stand and Deliver."

1989—A Federal District Court Judge issued a ruling that struck down New York's system of awarding college scholarships on the basis of the SAT scores.

1989—A book published on teacher competency tests, including ETS's National Teacher's Exam (NTE), concluded that at least 38,000 Black, Latino, and American Indian and other minority teacher candidates were barred from teaching by teacher competency tests.

1982—Four boys are accused of cheating on the SAT. After a year of trying to get ETS to withdraw their accusation, the boys filed suit against ETS. In a book exposing many problems with the SAT, it is stated that ETS said privately that they "didn't really think the boys had been cheating on these tests, and that the charges would have been dropped if the boys had abandoned their protest."[3] ◖◗

Notes

[1] Quoted in "Standardized Tests and Teacher Competence," by Bob Schaeffer, *School Voices*, Fall 1996, reprinted on FairTest www.fairtest.org/empl/ttcomp.htm

[2] David Hoff, "Testing ETS," *Education Week*, December 1, 1999.

[3] David Owen with Marilyn Doerr, *None of the Above, Revised and Updated. The Truth Behind the SATs*, 1999, p.155.

Sources

Fairtest Examiner, various issues (www.fairtest.org)

"SAT + ETS = $$$," Rethinking Schools, Spring 2000 (www.rethinkingschools.org)

Education Week, various issues (www.edweek.org)

"Making Another Big Score," Time, June 12, 2001

ETS websites (www.ets.org, www.etsk-12works.com, www.etstechnologies.com)

RESEARCH REPORT

Educational evaluation in school systems of the Western Hemisphere
A comparative study

This is an edited version of a study coordinated by Lidia M. Rodriguez (2002) on behalf of the of the Civil Society Network for Public Education in the Americas (Red SEPA). As part of this study, reports were submitted by network members in Argentina, Chile, Costa Rica, El Salvador, Honduras, Panama, Quebec and Mexico. (See appendices for information on Red SEPA, list of organizations participating in the study and evaluation report guidelines.)

A. A comparison of educational evaluation policies

Since the 1990s, public education systems in all of the reporting countries have witnessed a tendency to adopt new models of educational evaluation influenced by neoliberal concepts of production, human capital and supply and demand.

Argentina

In Argentina, this model became state policy with the adoption of the Federal Education Act of 1993, which created a National Department of Evaluation. The scheme involves the application of standardized testing—generally multiple choice exams—to a sampling of schools throughout the country. This model has two negative effects: it reduces student evaluation to mere measurement, and it turns the learning process into an output. The results obtained via these exams are used for the compilation of school rankings according to student output.

Within this framework, the most important activity of the Department of Evaluation from its inception has been the implementation of what are called "Student Evaluation Operations." Under this program, "proficiency exams" are administered to students in a number of elementary schools chosen out of a national sample, and also to all students in their last year of high school. The Minister of Education in the government of President de la Rua (ousted in the Argentine rebellion of December 2001) upgraded this department to an Institute of Evaluation.

Chile

In Chile, the national system of student evaluation started in 1982, during the military dictatorship, with the Scholastic Performance Evaluation (PER). This test was applied from 1982 to 1984 to the 4th and 8th year students, in all the national schools with the exception of those located in rural areas. The tests measured performance in Spanish and mathematics. The results, which provided a comparative measure between schools with similar characteristics, were sent directly to the schools to be distributed to the teaching staff and to students' parents.

In 1988, the Ministry of Education launched the National System of Educational Quality Measurement (SIMCE) which had many similarities to the PER with respect to the courses evaluated, the schools where it was applied, and its national and standardized character. In addition, it incorporated admissions tests at the national level, and it was also applied to the natural and social sciences in a sample of schools and courses up until 2001.

In March 1990, the dictatorship approved the Constitutional Act on Learning (LOCE), which mandates the Ministry of Education not only to systematically apply a national evaluation program, but also to publish each school's results in the press. Beginning in 1995, the SIMCE has been applied by means of a standardized test that measures the performance in basic education at the 4th and 8th grade. The SIMCE is now applied to rural schools with more than five students in grades 2, 4 and 8, and the results are published in a newspaper with national distribution. The system has been universalized and the ranking is widely publicized.

The current government and all the preceding democratic governments have shown little interest in changing the LOCE, although the current government has taken partial measures to mitigate the damaging effects of these tests on the quality and equity of the education system. Specifically, it has attempted to develop tests that measure not only simple knowledge, incorporating some open-ended questions, leaving out of the ranking the results of tests administered to children with special needs, and obtaining additional data to conduct cross-tabulations that might explain the results (social and economic background of the student, degree of education of the parents, etc.). Chile has incorporated the TIMSS (Third International Maths and Science Study) and the adult competence tests of the OECD, making great effort to promote the results. In addition, a variety of international tests are being independently used in some of the private schools of the elite, where the SIMCE results would not present significant inter-school variance and therefore wouldn't be useful to highlight competitive academic advantages.

El Salvador

In El Salvador, an evaluation system—the Aptitude Test for High School Students (PAES)—has been used since 1995 to measure the output of students in the last year of high school. The test measures knowledge and aptitudes in math and science. El Salvador does not participate in international testing.

Honduras

The Honduran Minister of Education is promoting an ongoing evaluation system that, because it is being imposed without significant consultation, is facing resistance. The argument against this system is that the incidence of the following conditions makes it impossible to carry out the new evaluation requirements in an effective way:
- The existing high student-teacher ratio.
- The lack of infrastructure, equipment and resource materials.
- The deteriorating condition of school buildings.
- Student malnutrition.
- Academic overload.

The proposals of the IMF and the World Bank regarding public education imply that education quality is not compatible with expanded access. Therefore, they require that governments ignore demands for full access to all citizens and that education systems focus on the value-added development of basic human resources, but with lower levels of skills and training. Similarly, they call for teachers' wage demands to be disregarded.

Mexico

In Mexico, a final multiple-choice exam for primary and secondary school students was first administered in schools in various regions of the country starting in the mid-1990s. The data gleaned from these exams only became public at the end of the decade. The same approach has been more recently applied to both senior high school *(preparatorios)* and post-secondary education.

The privately owned National Centre for Post-Secondary Education Evaluation (CENEVAL) was created in 1994, but it only administered admission and completion exams in the institutions that chose to hire its services. By the late 1990s, the services of CENEVAL extended to all of the country, but the Centre still tested only a relatively small number of students (less than one million students yearly, while the overall national registration figure is close to 30 million).

In the year 2000, however, as part of its educational proposals, the newly elected administration of President Vicente Fox proposed the creation of a National Institute for Educational Evaluation. This institute, which has not yet been established, would be in charge of evaluating student and teacher performance at all levels, from pre-school to university. There is no general regulation overseeing evaluation, except for institutional evaluation or evaluations under official agreements. There are also a few evaluation service companies from abroad (U.S.A) selling their services in Mexico, such as College Board, which evaluates candidates for admission to various public universities.

Panama

In Panama, a national evaluation system was established with the passage of Bill 47, which became law in 1946. Even though it covers all academic and administrative levels of the system, it is only applied to students, not to teachers or other sectors of the education system. It is considered obsolete by the teachers' union FREP because of the broad generalisations used in the selection of evaluation criteria. In addition, the results do not provide corrective or motivational action, unless the school principal takes the initiative to do so.

Currently, a new proposal for student evaluation has generated a significant amount of discussion and opposition from various sectors.

Quebec

In Quebec, a long-time policy of final evaluation upon completion of the secondary education level involves exams in French language (composition), English language, mathematics, and science. The exams correspond to 50% of the final mark for the last grade. As part of the neoliberal policies of "responding to consumer demand," school rankings are now being published based on the results from these tests. The objective is to facilitate the selection of schools by parents based on the published performance ratings. This is part of the Public Education Act's thrust of mandating schools to be directly accountable to their communities with respect to the quality of their service. The changes to the Public Education Act introduced in 1997 have given new responsibilities to individual schools, creating in each institution a board made up of teachers, parents, and community members.

Québec's Minister of Education has introduced measures and is putting pressure on schools to base their direct accountability to the community on results that can be compared between schools. The goal is to make it easier for parents to choose a school for their children, as contemplated by the law. In September, 2000, the Minister imposed on each school the obligation to create a three-year "success plan", with a yearly evaluation, based on school completion rates and reductions in course and grade repetitions.

The Minister made public declarations in March 2001 regarding the tying of funding to school results and the evaluation of teaching staff. But faced with opposition from the teachers union, these new measures have not been put forward to date, and schools continue with the implementation of their basic "success plans".

The changes in the Schools Act and subsequent policies have contributed to a fostering of competition between schools. A CD-ROM containing data to compile a ranking of schools has been distributed. The media and a conservative 'think-tank' published the results, comparing public and private schools without giving any consideration to the selective admissions procedures that many private institutions have in place. Not surprisingly, the private and public schools that choose their students based on admission tests were at the top of the ranking.

Québec's Education Minister recently reiterated his intention to impose a province-wide French language exam at the end of primary school. In 2002, the Minister proposed that standardized exams be administered to students in various primary school grades.

In recent years, Quebec has participated in international examinations in science and mathematics. The results for 9 and 13 year old students have been included in the *Education Indicators*, a yearly publication that contains various education data, such as statistics on graduation rates, grade repetition, per student spending, proportion of the GDP spent on education, comparisons with other provinces and the U.S., etc.

Education in Canada as a whole, traditionally the domain of each province, is experiencing centralizing tendencies under the pressure of the globalization process. The Canadian government states that it wants to guarantee "the quality of its human resources". There are pressures to introduce a common curriculum in all the provinces, which already exists for the sciences and social studies. The Western provinces have developed some common curricula, as have the Eastern ones. But the government of Quebec has criticized these initiatives, which it considers interference in an area that is exclusively of provincial authority.

B. Overall impact of neoliberal policies on education and perspectives of teachers' unions

The organisations participating in this study maintain that, in their countries, neoliberal policies have not produced improvements in education and have exacerbated pre-existing problems in public school systems.

Argentina

In Argentina, the implementation of neoliberal policies has resulted in the complete fragmentation of the system and has failed to improve the quality of learning or professionalism in the teaching career. In all respects, the neoliberal concept of evaluation has not permeated the education practices of the majority of teachers. But the evaluation program has a significant impact on the definition of the real curriculum that is taught in schools. Evaluations carried out through the program operate as a mechanism of bona fide central control that contravenes the commitment to institutional autonomy. This system of measurement promotes teaching only what is to going be evaluated, which is decided by the national state. The evaluation program has also played the role of political propaganda, at least until 1999. Each year, we witnessed an event of great magnitude in which the results of the evaluations were made public and schools with the highest rankings were awarded prizes.

At its Education Congress, CTERA stated that it is necessary to recuperate the tradition of evaluation and its pedagogical fundamentals as a means to obtain information that contributes to the construction of social relations based on solidarity and democratic relations instead of competition.

In this respect, CTERA proposed the creation of a Federal System of Evaluation with the participation of national and provincial governments, teachers' unions, and other civil society organizations. It also proposed the creation of evaluation systems at various levels: national, provincial, local, and institutional.

The Congress also stated that it was essential to include education workers and the whole of society in the definition of what and how to evaluate. It also argued that the object of evaluations is the education system as a whole, making sure it guarantees its own unity, universal access to knowledge, and the development of state policies that improve the system. For an evaluation of this type to be possible, it would be necessary to create a new way of organizing the school system and the work of teachers, the creation of institutional time blocks that lend themselves to evaluation, and appropriate training to make it work.

Chile

With regards to improving the quality of education, the effectiveness of the SIMCE and PER depends on how quality is measured. But even from the narrow and simplistic conceptualization of measurement by means of standardized tests, these systems' effectiveness cannot be counted as positive. The results from year to year have not improved in a statistically significant way, and comparability of results is technically limited. There has been a larger advance in the second year of application, but this is largely accounted for by the practice effect.

In relation to the control of education, these tests have had a profound effect, specifically as follows:

1) One of the central preoccupations of the teaching establishments and the teachers is for the students to get good results, and as a result the curriculum (in all its dimensions) is adapted to that goal. The content and objectives measured by the tests become the focus, and are often pursued by means of mock testing.

2) The so-called decentralization of the curriculum loses its meaning, because the main areas of focus become those that are measured by the test. As a matter of fact, any time freed up at the edu-

cational establishment tends to be used for courses or activities oriented towards improving student results in the tests.

3) According to official discourse, the incorporation of international tests is intended to homogenize the curriculum at the international level, which has not occurred in practice. However, this orientation has clearly negative effects on the cultural development of the curriculum and the student.

In terms of teaching performance, these tests are a fundamental transgression of the boundaries of professional autonomy, as teachers feel pressured by the results.

The effects of the SIMCE on educational policy relate particularly to the singling out of schools. The information obtained from administering the SIMCE has allowed the Ministry of Education to select the schools with lowest results, to which it administers specific programs (such as the P-900 and 'Schools For Everyone'). A negative effect of this singling out is that, in the educational establishments that "benefit" from these programs, all of the actors in the teaching community feel stigmatized. In addition, these establishments are entered in the competitions for other general programs, where the best ranking schools stand a better chance.

The SIMCE has become central to the application of politics of the market to education, because the published rankings are used as a competitive advantage to attract more students to the high ranking schools. This issue matters because the state subsidies are allocated to the schools on the basis of student enrollment figures.

Amongst its most perverse effects, the SIMCE has brought about the segmentation of education, inequity, valorization of private education, and as a consequence, the de-valorization of public education, as part of the hegemonic discourse that has been assimilated in one way or another by the teaching sector itself. It is well known that the cultural and social situation of the students is a significant factor in determining the results of standardized tests on learning. As the public municipal system is the main provider of education for popular sectors of society, it shows the lowest results year after year. The most neoliberal sectors of society use these results to support their permanent discourse on the need to privatize education in order to improve its quality.

The results also contribute to the stigmatization of popular sectors of society and the segmentation of education. The popular sectors are increasingly concentrated in the municipal education system, and the middle class in the private subsidized system. SIMCE is one of the major factors contributing to this segmentation.

The hegemonic discourse of SIMCE's standardized evaluation met with some dissident voices within the teaching profession and in the academic world. However, these voices were not powerful enough. As the struggles and hopes of both sectors were focused on more urgent themes as a result of the deterioration of the military dictatorship, new authorities took up the hegemonic discourse in a transfer that in one way or another happened without much resistance. In addition, the discursive forces of the neoliberal right were highly influential.

It was towards the second half of the 1990s when the perverse effects of the system became more obvious, and the dissident voices were progressively articulated and introduced in some circles within the Ministry of Education. While some improvements have resulted from this response, it has yet to achieve enough power to realize substantive modifications to the system.

Costa Rica

In Costa Rica, the union (SEC) has proposed an evaluation system with a corrective, rather than repressive character and which provides a comprehensive evaluation that facilitates addressing deficiencies as well as improving the quality of education. Taking these things into consideration could resolve the problems associated with the unilateral imposition of standardized examinations.

El Salvador

In El Salvador, the government has been implementing education reform for the last seven years. While this reform has not produced many real changes in the national education system and has not improved its quality, it has given the government more control over teaching practices and has resulted in five years of frozen wages. As part of this reform, funding of schools has been gradually passed down to the general population as the state contributes less and less to the public school system. ANDES 21 describes this as a sort of veiled privatization of public education.

Honduras

According to the report from Honduras, the neoliberal evaluation methods proposed in that country are overly weighted with economic objectives of privatization. Education is considered one of the largest remaining potential markets, whose volume and control would generate enormous profits.

The teacher organizations and the previous Honduran government, however, reached consensus on one of the priority goals, to increase the reach of the education system by means of an increase in the number of teachers, education centres, and the education budget. The new administration, that took office in early 2002, however seems less willing to continue down this path.

The Honduran education unions believe that the neoliberal development model has been unable to meet its stated goals. It has increased unemployment and reduced the education and health budgets disproportionately to population growth. Neoliberalism has increased the difficulties faced in meeting basic needs in these areas, and has increased the gap between the well-being enjoyed by the countries of the Northern Hemisphere and the poverty of the countries of Central and South America. More wealth has accumulated in fewer hands, and poverty has increased.

Mexico

According to the Mexican report, the accumulation of evaluation data has been unable to contribute to the development of a plan for improving the quality of education. Instead, it has been effective in transforming teaching methods to focus on output in order meet the requirements of standardized evaluation. What is rewarded becomes the priority and what is not rewarded is considered a waste of time. The use of surveys by students to evaluate teachers (especially at the post-secondary level) forces teachers to act in accordance to the questions on the evaluation form. There is also a profound individualization of the struggle to improve wages: it becomes a strictly personal affair with each educator on a different pay scale. (Merit pay at the k-12 level can be up to 20—30% of a teacher's pay. In the post-secondary level it can reach up to 60%.)

Panama

In Panama, the teachers' union –the Panamanian Educators Reform Front (FREP)– sees traditional student evaluation as problematic, in that students receive corrective feedback at the diagnostic, formative and summative level, but other components of the system do not. FREP considers that a full evaluation of the education system has not yet been conducted, and as a result important changes have not taken place to correct the lack of appropriate infrastructure for schools and the lack of essential learning materials. The education authorities lack commitment in dealing with what is required, because the proposed education policies are not followed up. The union believes that student evaluations must also be more holistic in nature, evaluating the learning process and not just outputs.

The report from FREP in Panama also states that neoliberal policies have failed to produce the promised improvement to education. On the contrary, these policies have generated inconsistencies, and they have increased debt. Teachers are in control of education in the classroom, but they face a series of limitations that sometimes obstruct their work. Teachers have expressed their disapproval of the small amount of participation they are allowed. School principals spend more time on administrative issues than on working with teachers and students, and supervisors spend most of their time in their offices. The work of the teachers is complex because they have to attend to the administrative and pedagogical aspects of the classroom on top of the multiple parallel programs that create limitations to their work. Their wages, in spite of being the highest for teachers in Central America, don't reflect the higher cost of living in the country.

Quebec

In Quebec, the CSQ argues that centralized evaluation is a control mechanism that obstructs the movement towards decentralization and supports the commodification of the learning process. It should be noted that the movement toward decentralization in schools is accompanied by a centralizing tendency that promotes the introduction of more controls and measurement of results and output. This tendency supports the mercantile process of competition between schools, by introducing a common measurement that permits the comparison of schools and provides "objective" information to the "education consumers" in the selection of the school that "responds to their preference".

The union proposes that the Minister of Education conduct public consultations before making any decisions relating to this issue.

Faced with the Public Education Act requirement that each school be accountable to its community for the quality of its services, the union took a proactive position. It proposed a model that would include a report on the socio-economic and socio-educational context of schools and on the measures taken by school boards to improve the situation of the students. Schools have welcomed this model.

With regards to the ministerial pressures to base accountability on results that can be compared between schools, the union has strongly criticized the project. The CSQ sees the measure as a relinquishing of the responsibility for education quality by the state, which will carry negative consequences, such as pressure for schools to expel students with difficulties, and the need to devote excessive time to prepare for exams in order to improve their ranking.

The union proposed a different model, suggesting measures to act on the reasons behind student failure without tying these measures to the results of the testing. This model received the support of parents' organizations and many intellectuals who had strongly criticized the mistakes in the data contained in a CD-ROM sent to the schools to prepare their local plan. In the end, a compromise was reached between the Minister and the union, which has resulted in a mixed evaluation system.

The CSQ defined three elements to be considered with regards to the current evaluation movement. In the first place the strong social pressures for quality education and criticism of the current situation must be taken into account. It is important to try to respond to concerns about the quality of public education with proposals and arguments that take into consideration not only working conditions but also education in general: services, content, evaluation, etc.

Second, in the current context, the pressures in favour of school choice by parents are very strong. If we can argue that primary schools must be neighbourhood or community schools, it is more difficult to do so for secondary education. The danger lies not in the possibility of parental choice, but in the strategies adopted by schools in order to better position themselves in this "market", such as developing exclusive educational projects reserved to the best students only.

The third element to consider is that there is a strong movement, which includes many parents, in favour of staff and school evaluation. Many teachers in Quebec favour a certain kind of evaluation because they feel that it contributes to the quality of the profession. From this perspective, it is important to formulate alternative positions, including mechanisms for staff evaluation, in collective negotiations and to oppose the movement for competition between schools. ❧

Lidia M. Rodriguez is a researcher with the Confederation of Education Workers of Argentina (CTERA) and was the coordinator of this study.

This report is one of the research projects carried out by the Civil Society Network for Public Education in the Americas (Red SEPA) as part of its Initiative for Democratic Education in the Americas (IDEA). Research for this report was coordinated by Confederation of Education Workers of the Argentine Republic, with the collaboration of researchers from educators' organizations and NGOs from Canada (Quebec), the United States, Mexico, Chile, El Salvador, Costa Rica, Panama and Argentina. This report was translated from the Spanish by Pablo Mendez. Other documents of the IDEA process can be accessed at the Red SEPA's web page at www.vcn.bc.ca/idea.

Appendix 1: Organizations participating in this research

1. Confederación de Trabajadores de la Educación de la República Argentina – CTERA (Confederation of Education Workers of the Argentine Republic)

2. Colegio de Profesores de Chile – CPC (Chilean Teacher's College)

3. Sindicato de Trabajadores de Educación de Costa Rica – SEC (Union of Costa Rican Education Workers)

4. Asociación Nacional de Docentes de El Salvador – ANDES 21 de Junio (National Teachers Association of El Salvador)

5. Colegio Profesional de Superación Magisterial de Honduras – COLPROSUMAH (Honduran Teachers Professional Development College)

6. Coalición Trinacional para Defender la Educación Pública – Sección Mexicana (The Mexican Section of the Trinational Coalition to Defend Public Education)

7. Frente Reformista de Educadores de Panamá – FREP (Panamanian Educators Reform Front)

8. Centrale des Syndicats du Québec – CSQ

Appendix 2: Guidelines used for evaluation reports from each country

1. The current state of education evaluation policies in your country
a. The creation of national evaluation systems
   i. the year they were established
   ii. the regulations that govern them
   iii. the levels (ie grades) that are involved
   iv. general characteristics
   v. other pertinent information
   vi. the incorporation of international testing into the education system
b. Evaluation of teachers
   i. The state of advance in the testing of teachers
   ii. productivity (merit) pay
   iii. any other pertinent information
2. The effects of neoliberal policies on public education
a. In relation to their stated objectives: improvement of education quality, transformation of the education system, etc.
b. In relation to their non-explicit objectives: monitoring teaching, teachers workloads and salary, education financing etc.
c. Their capacity for intervention in teaching methods and concepts. For example modifications in the ways that teachers carry out testing, rankings of schools by parents or other organizations, etc.
d. Any other related information
3. Alternatives and resistance
a. Alternative evaluation methods that have been proposed by teachers or other organizations.
b. Opinions, articles and speeches critical of neoliberal evaluation methods that have been generated by intellectuals and/or education experts.
c. Perceptions that parents have of neoliberal and other evaluation methods.
4. The position of the teachers unions:
a. Toward neoliberal evaluation methods in general
b. Towards teacher evaluations
c. Toward productivity (merit) pay
5. Any other points related to evaluations that you think it would be important to include.

Appendix 3: Information on Red SEPA

What is the Civil Society Network for Public Education in the Americas (Red SEPA)?

Public education is facing challenges that are an outgrowth of globalization—challenges that manifest themselves in ways that are increasingly common among different countries. In the Americas, the process of creating a Free Trade Area of the Americas (FTAA) includes initiatives directly related to education. Governments of the Western Hemisphere are negotiating the creation of the FTAA through a series of meetings called the Summit of the Americas Process.

As the decision-makers in government and business organize on a hemispheric level, so too must civil society organizations concerned with the future of education in the Americas. The Red SEPA has been organized to bring together civil society groups throughout the Americas that have an interest in protecting and enhancing public education as a basic institution of democratic development and human rights. It works in conjunction with other civil society groups concerned about the impact of the FTAA and other processes on education and social services.

Currently about 100 educator, student, support staff, parent, indigenous, women's and community organizations from 24 American countries participate in the Red SEPA.

What does the Red SEPA do?

The Red SEPA is conducting research, developing communication networks and publications, and holding conferences. These are aimed at building an understanding of the impact of neoliberal policies on education and proposing alternative approaches that are consistent with strong and democratic public education systems.

The network also helps to mobilize support for educators, students and others who face repression in their own countries for activities in support of democratic and public education.

PART 3

Soap, SAIP or standardized test: what is the PCAP?

Calling the tune

A rare challenge to the CMEC's testing regime

by Marita Moll

October 2, 2002—The Council of Ministers of Education,
Canada's (CMEC) national testing project, SAIP,
"may fall victim by 2004 to federal cuts," says the National Post.[1]

SAIP (Student Achievement Indicators Program) is a pan-Canadian testing program that measures the reading, mathematics, and science skills of a random sample of over 35,000 13- and 16-year-olds across Canada.

The SAIP program has depended, since its inception in 1993, on an annual $1.5 million grant from Human Resources Development Canada (HRDC). HRDC, for its part, said no final decision had been made on funding. But a spokesperson pointed out that Canadian students also write an international assessment. "The education ministers know they have two big assessments out there and they have to decide where to go next," said Allen Zeesman, director-general of applied research at HRDC.[2]

The other "big assessment" on the CMEC's horizon is called the Program for International Student Assessment (PISA). PISA is a project of the Organization for Economic Cooperation and Development (OECD) implemented in Canada by HRDC, CMEC, Statistics Canada, and Provincial Ministries and Departments of Education and Labour. Like SAIP, PISA tests reading, mathematics, and science skills. In the last round (2000), approximately 30,000 Canadian 15-year-old students from more than 1,000 schools participated in PISA.

Although there is clearly some overlap, SAIP and PISA are very different tests. SAIP is developed in Canada with the intention of producing indicators that can be compared inter-provincially. PISA is developed by a team of external "experts," and is based on complex negotiations among 32 countries to accommodate for social, cultural and language differences. It is a process that can lead to bizarre results. According to one observer, the only form of writing experts could agree was testable across cultures was the writing of computer manuals. "Presumably incomprehensible in any language," says Canadian educational researcher Larry Kuehn.[3]

November 19, 2002—A national meeting recommends an educational information clearinghouse.

The *Canadian Learning Institute* (CLI) first appeared in a speech delivered by HRDC Minister Jane Stewart on behalf of the Prime Minister to the *National Summit on Innovation and Learning* held in Toronto on November 18 and 19, 2002:

"The education ministers know they have two big assessments out there and they have to decide where to go next."

I am confirming tonight that the federal government is prepared to work with its partners to develop the Canadian Learning Institute. To create a locus for information and research on learning. (sic) *But it will require a collaborative partnership with provinces and the private sector to make it work. Tonight I challenge all of us to get together and make this concept a reality.*[4]

One of the background documents for the Summit indicates the importance of PISA to that federal policy agenda. "For many students, Canadian school systems work well. The 2000 Program for International Student Assessment (PISA) placed Canadian 15-year-old students second in reading, sixth in math, and fifth in science." The document goes on to list four milestones for children and youth in the federal government's "innovation strategy." Making Canada "one of the top three countries in mathematics, science, and reading achievement"[5] tops the list.

If it was a trial balloon, the first flight of the CLI was smooth sailing. With uncharacteristic speed (for policy circles), the Summit's final press release, issued the second (and last) day of the Summit, announced that conference participants had recommended that the establishment of the CLI be one of the next steps in a Canadian innovation and learning agenda.[6]

Other than the Conference Board of Canada, whose CEO was one of the co-chairs of this event, and a long list of federal cabinet ministers, it is unclear exactly who (and more interestingly, who was not) in attendance at this meeting. The press release says there were "over 450 leaders in the private sector, voluntary sector, non-governmental organizations, academia, and other levels of government."

There must have been some representation from provincial departments of education—although perhaps not from the highest levels. Nevertheless, the next development seemed to take provincial education ministers entirely by surprise.

January 28, 2003—the Ottawa Citizen *leaks the news that the federal government is preparing a "back door answer to a national education strategy."*[7]

The federal plan to kick-start the CLI was formally announced as part of the spring 2003 budget package. "This budget sets aside a one-time contribution of $100 million in 2003-04 for the establishment of the *Canadian Learning Institute.*"[8] A key objective of the Institute is to broaden and deepen data and information on education and learning. "The institute will also develop indicators to measure how successful Canada is at getting its people ready for the knowledge economy,"[9] said Shirley Seward, head of the Canadian Labour and Business Centre, part of a team holding consultations with key partners of the proposed initiative.

The provinces were quick to recognize a potential threat to their jurisdictions. "I don't know what this Learning Institute could possibly contribute to our agenda," said Dianne Cunningham, Ontario's Minister of Training, Colleges and Universities and chair of the CMEC, on the day of the budget announcement.[10] The provincial education ministers claimed to be completely in the dark about the proposed Institute. After the announcement, Lyle Oberg, Alberta's Minister of Learning, angrily accused the Prime Minister of intruding into their jurisdiction with a plan to set up another "legacy" project like the Canadian Millenium Foundation.[11]

He may have had reason to be concerned. The veiled threat by Zeesman in November was a federal challenge to the CMEC suggesting that it rationalize the testing programs. Documentation from the Summit indicates that the feds were placing their priorities on the international assessments, not on SAIP. There were plenty of vested interests at stake here as the provinces regrouped to consider their next move.

April 2, 2003—The CMEC attempts to firm up its position as the czar of elementary/secondary testing.

Following a conference in London, Ontario, the CMEC issued a press release announcing the new Pan-Canadian Assessment Program (PCAP). "The ministers confirm their leadership in assessment and are developing a major streamlined and forward-looking assessment program aimed at improving learning."[12] But it was evident in the details that the federal threat to withdraw funding was heard loud and clear. The PCAP will replace SAIP, says the CMEC. While assessing the same subject matter, "the beauty of PCAP is that it enables us to assess the performance of our education systems here in Canada but also dovetails with the important international assessments we are doing through the OECD. By integrating existing testing programs, PCAP greatly eases the testing burden on schools."

According to an internal CMEC memo, this integration would be achieved by testing 13- and 15-year-olds rather than 13- and 16-year-olds. This aligns PCAP with PISA, which tests 15-year-olds. The internal memo explains that the PISA round could contain a supplemental "Canadian option." PCAP could be administered in non-PISA years, following the PISA model of major and minor domains (subject areas), and could focus on domains not assessed by PISA. This would enable comparisons between PISA and PCAP data. The memo also notes that, at some point, the "Canadian options" added to PISA could also be available to provincial jurisdictions so that they could "link PCAP to their own jurisdictional assessment" and by extension to PISA. It sounds like a data gatherer's dream come true.

In an attempt to turn the tables on the federal CLI initiative, the press release also notes that provincial ministers are seeking a meeting with Jane Stewart "to discuss the . . . Canadian Learning Institute and potential duplication with CMEC's activities."

Time for some critical thinking

This is an interesting power struggle, as far as it goes. The CMEC, so far, has operated its testing programs on a very "closed shop" basis. The entire testing program has yet to come under intense scrutiny from the wider education community. A rare challenge was mounted by Heather-jane Robertson, during her tenure as Director of Professional Development at the Canadian Teachers' Federation (CTF). Ms. Robertson's extensive investigation into the SAIP process and the flaws exposed by this investigation were presented to CTF's CMEC Advisory Committee in the fall of 1999. But the material was clearly "too hot to handle." The CTF moved quickly to silence the challenge. Some of the material was later presented by Ms. Robertson and educational evaluation expert David Ireland at meetings of the Canadian and American educational research communities. It is published for the first time in *Passing the Test: The False Promises of Standardized Testing*.[13]

The document goes on to list four milestones for children and youth in the federal government's "innovation strategy." Making Canada "one of the top three countries in mathematics, science, and reading achievement" tops the list.

Now the CMEC has proposed a major restructuring of the national testing agenda in response to the federal demand that the organization "get its testing act together." However, the challenge to the national testing agenda does not go far enough. If the SAIP process was flawed, will the PCAP process be any better? Will some of the flaws exposed in the research presented by Robertson and Ireland finally be addressed? How valid is the PISA process, given its "lowest common denominator" approach. Beyond "bragging rights" for national governments at international meetings, do these tests serve a useful purpose for Canadian students and Canadian education?

And, most importantly of all, why should we spend our precious tax dollars on unnecessary international or national tests while we have to sell hot-dogs and hold garage sales to fund essential resources like textbooks and paper? Tests, national and international, do not improve learning but they do create increasingly stressful conditions for students and teachers, in addition to stigmatizing some schools that don't make it to the top of the school ranking lists.

"All that data from tests which you subject to every statistical manipulation known to humans is probably not worth the paper it's written on," suggests David Ireland, Canadian educational researcher and testing expert.[14] So let's test our air and water and leave education to the educators. We already know the ingredients for successful learning: dedicated teachers, healthy students, caring communities, and adequate resources. ❧

Marita Moll is a freelance writer and educational researcher based in Ottawa. She is a research associate with the Canadian Centre for Policy Alternatives.

BREAKING NEWS: According to various news reports in December 2003, the CLI appears to have undergone a name change even before its official launch. Watch out for a new policy think-tank called the Canadian Council on Learning which will most likely be headquartered at the University of British Columbia. The proposed council, though federally funded, will operate at arm's length from the federal government. Quebec, objecting to any federal intrusion into matters of provincial jurisdiction, has, so far, declined to participate in this new learning partnership.

Notes

[1] Sokoloff, Heather. "Education ministers fear cutbacks to nationwide student testing." *National Post*, Oct. 02, 2002.

[2] Ibid

[3] Kuehn, Larry. "Leaning between conspiracy and hegemony: OECD, UNESCO, and the tower of PISA". in Moll, Marita (ed). *Passing the Test: The False Promises of Standardized Testing."* Ottawa: Canadian Centre for Policy Alternatives, 2003.

[4] Chrétien, The Rt. Hon. Jean, Prime Minister. Opening speech delivered by the Hon. Jane Stewart, Minister of Human Resources Development, November 18, 2002 to the National Summit on Innovation and Learning. Available at: http://www.innovationstrategy.gc.ca/cmb/innovation.nsf/ MenuE/NationalSummit_speeches

[5] Canada. Government of Canada. *Backgrounder: Children and Youth.* Available at: http://www.innovationstrategy.gc.ca/cmb/innovation.nsf/ Backgrounders/BG10-NS

[6] Canada. Government of Canada. "Participants Commit to Action at the

National Summit on Innovation and Learning." Press release, Toronto, Nov. 19, 2002. Available at: http://www.innovationstrategy.gc.ca/cmb/ innovation.nsf/releases/

[7] May, Katherine. "Feds enter education with learning institute. Think-tank viewed as way to influence provincial jurisdiction." *Ottawa Citizen* Jan. 28, 2003.

[8] Canada. Government of Canada. Department of Finance. Budget 2003. P. 134. Available online: http://www.fin.gc.ca/budget03/pdf/bp2003e.pdf

[9] May, Katherine. *Ottawa Citizen* Jan. 28, 2003.

[10] Sokoloff, Heather. "Provinces decry federal foray into education." *National Post.* Feb. 18, 2003.

[11] ibid

[12] Council of Ministers of Education, Canada. Improved learning focus of new pan-canadian assessment program. Press release April 2, 2003. Available http://www.cmec.ca/releases/2003-04-02.en.asp

[13] Robertson, Heather-jane and David Ireland. "Report on the 1998 SAIP Reading and Writing II Assessment: Implications for Educational Policy and Practice. A Case Study." Executive Summary; and Robertson, Heather-jane and David Ireland. "Form and substance: Critiquing SAIP" in Moll, Marita (ed.) *Passing the Test; The False Promises of Standardized Testing. Ottawa: Canadian Centre for Policy Alternatives, 2003.*

[14] Ireland, David. "The test validity construct." A summary paper delivered at the Annual Meeting of the American Educational Research Association, New Orleans, 2002

Bogus points for the national testing agenda

by Heather-jane Robertson

In their hapless search for the Holy Grail, Monty Python's disturbed band of knights and rogues encounter the Keeper of the Bridge of Death. The Keeper poses three high-stakes questions that must be answered to his satisfaction—or the unfortunate test-takers will be thrown into the Gorge of Eternal Peril. Sir Lancelot knows his name and passes easily, but Sir Galahad suddenly forgets his favorite colour and is summarily hurled into the pit. When crafty King Arthur figures out how the testing system works, he trips up the Keeper with a question of his own. The Keeper suddenly finds himself tossed into his own Gorge. Test-meisters beware: this may be a parable for our times.

While educators in many countries have had long experience with the Keeper and his games, Canada is a relative newcomer to national testing. The Council of Ministers of Education Canada (CMEC) introduced the School Achievement Indicators Program (SAIP) in 1993. Until the 1990s, provincial jurisdiction over education included absolute autonomy in deciding how to evaluate the quality of education offered within each province. "Indicators" that might measure this success were not particularly sophisticated, since data collection had not yet become the chief function of provincial ministries of education.

But the tide of American criticism that began with *A Nation at Risk* soon washed over Canada's borders, and by the early 1990s Canada's business élite had taken up the call for higher standards and more standardized testing as its preferred remedy for flaccid educational productivity. CMEC responded with SAIP. Business was so proud to be associated with this initiative that early rounds of SAIP were funded, in part, by Spar Aerospace and the Investors Group Inc. Such corporate lobbyists as the Conference Board of Canada and the Business Council on National Issues (BCNI) signaled their support for national testing. But, naturally, they were critical of the results and demanded more tests and higher stakes. The BCNI urged the provinces to adopt a single national exit exam that would reflect business priorities, and it even offered to design the test. It seems that the Keeper of the Bridge wears pinstripes and lives on Bay Street.

The most recent SAIP results, released in March 1999, report how a sample of Canadian 13- and 16-year-olds from each province and territory performed on reading and writing tests conducted in 1998.[1] Reporters who glanced through CMEC's press release searching for the tasty bits that could be excerpted and massaged into headlines must have been disappointed. Even by CMEC's somnolent standards, these SAIP results were ho-hum. Sixteen-year-olds performed better on the same test than 13-year-olds. Girls outperformed boys. Average kids produced average results. More bad luck: media pundits who had counted on electronic access to SAIP information had no story at all. CMEC's website was down on its biggest day of the year.

Despite almost interchangeable provincial results, CMEC did its best to turn this non-story into a media-worthy event, issuing embargoed press releases and convening a poorly attended press conference. The media saw no reason to challenge the premise that desirable curriculum reforms could somehow be intuited from second-decimal variations in provincial results. Some ministers were quick to agree. Challenged in his legislature to defend a slight dip in Alberta's results, Education Minister Halver Johnson admitted, "We have some work to do"—despite the fact that Alberta's results surpassed Canadian norms, albeit by insignificant percentages.

Meanwhile, Ontario's education minister, perhaps somewhat buoyed by his recent announcement of an entirely new high school curriculum (to be released and implemented in the same month), used Ontario's SAIP results as a platform to defend his controversial reforms. Despite having been taught the "old" curriculum that the minister has dismissed as vague and unchallenging, Ontario's students had posted results in 20 cases out of 20 that differed insignificantly from national means. Undaunted by this good news, the minister told his constituents that "average is not good enough" and that his reforms would vault Ontario students to the number-one ranking they deserved. Apparently, the minister had not been briefed on the sad reality of the arithmetic mean. Given that Ontario is home to 2.2 million students, their performance will always determine what is "average" for English-speaking Canada—no matter how well or poorly they do.

All this is familiar territory to anyone who follows high-stakes testing. Complex outcomes and poorly isolated variables are served up to those eager to defend pre-existing agendas, from tighter teacher surveillance to buying more technology. As long as the public maintains a naive confidence in the irrefutable objectivity of statistics, a graph here and a chart there can leverage support for provincial reforms that could never survive nuanced deliberation.

Nor are SAIP's effects limited to making short-term political hay. SAIP has driven a remarkable degree of curriculum homogenization within a country that has considered local control of curriculum to be a virtue rather than a liability. The Western and Atlantic provinces have come together to design outcomes-based curricula closely aligned with SAIP. In 1997, CMEC issued what it called a framework for K-12 science education, an initiative that was widely perceived as its first foray into national curricula. It is now undertaking "complementary studies" in language arts, a precursor to devising another national framework.

This drift toward creating a national curriculum marks a significant shift in Canadian education policy, yet it has provoked almost no public debate and little insider consternation, other than in Quebec, the sole province that has declined to embrace CMEC's version of curriculum. Outside Quebec, all seems quiet. Decades of curriculum debate and jurisdictional jealousies have been finessed in the pursuit of the level curriculum field required to play the testing game successfully.

This game follows a set of rules that ensures that some players will have an excellent view of the Gorge of Peril. When a jurisdiction does poorly on SAIP tests, the media will assist in pushing students and teachers over the edge as politicians look on. But politicians counting on leveraging political support for reform from their provincial system's results risk being disappointed when their systems do well. Education ministers may have to face embarrassing questions about why they have been so insistent on education reform and so critical of their system's shortcomings. From a political perspective, it would be much more reassuring if every jurisdiction's inadequacy could be guaranteed.

Enter "expectations." In 1998, CMEC decided that SAIP results would be reported in relationship to "public expectations of student performance." Claiming to be too resource-strapped to use any other method, CMEC developed a shortcut process of chatting up focus groups to generate numbers that are then represented as public opinion. CMEC now reports all SAIP results by comparing them to expectations set in this haphazard way.

The media duly reported that, in the most recent tests, Canadian students had failed to live up to the public's expectations, but no reporter questioned how these expectations were set. The public might have been interested to learn that its views were generated by 85 people invited by their respective ministers of education to guess how well students should perform on tests that these judges weren't even allowed to see. Quick, now, reader-on-the-street: What percentage of 13-year-olds should fall in each of the five performance categories in reading?

True, some of the participants in the focus groups were teachers, but teaching experience alone does not guarantee knowledge of the diversity of students and curricula on which any reasonable national expectations would need to be based. For this and other expectation-setting sessions, other participants are drawn from "the community," but CMEC will not divulge exactly who attends or why specific individuals are chosen. Although the focus groups' expectations are parsed to the percentage point, all other pertinent information is under wraps—an interesting feature of a process allegedly devoted to public accountability. Not only does CMEC keep the names and backgrounds of the attendees to itself, but even the documents participants use during the process are confiscated by CMEC staff after each event. The only records of these sessions are those that have been leaked by angry participants.

> The public might have been interested to learn that its views were generated by 85 people invited by their respective ministers of education to guess how well students should perform on tests that these judges weren't even allowed to see.

These notes from the underground make interesting reading. According to one participant—who was willing to make her notes public, but not her name—the two-day session to set expectations for SAIP reading and writing did not go well. Participants demanded detailed information about their tasks and repeatedly questioned their own fitness to perform them. Some participants walked out of the sessions, infuriated by the whole exercise. Their frustration is understandable. According to CMEC's own documents, participants were told that they were to estimate how students would actually perform; to say what was acceptable; to state what they would consider realistic, not idealistic expectations; and to determine a "realistic should." No wonder they were confused.

Confusion soon turned to consternation. According to participants' reports, it seems that the CMEC staff—employed by the folks with the greatest vested interest in certain kinds of results—encouraged a negotiation process designed to push expectations well beyond actual results. After some small-group discussion and two rounds of balloting, student test results were revealed to participants. It was obvious that everyone was facing an unexpected glitch. In almost every category, both 13- and 16-year-old students had outperformed the group's preliminary expectations! Nearly all participants viewed this as a worrisome turn of events.

Those convinced that schools were failing—whatever the test results said—responded by ratcheting up their expectations to validate their pre-existing assumptions. Others who saw themselves as education-friendly were worried that, if their expectations appeared to be set too low, politicians would use good test results to claim that their cuts to programs and budgets had been harmless. After the student results were reported, the participants balloted one last time. Expectations suddenly jumped by as much as 10% in 13 of the 20 categories and were nudged down marginally in only three. Our new national expectations for how well students should read and write are no longer norm-referenced or criterion-referenced, they are politically referenced.

And so 85 frustrated folks—minus the defectors—massaged the data and their limited knowledge of students, curriculum, testing, and politics into expectations and percentages, complete with medians and inter-quartile ranges. At the SAIP press conference, when I asked whether CMEC considered its expectations to be valid, I was assured that we could all have absolute confidence in these numbers. Later, I told my friend Mark Zwelling, president of the polling firm Vector Research and Development, how CMEC comes up with its numbers. I asked for his professional opinion on whether another 85 people could be expected to generate similar results at another time. When he stopped laughing, Mark had only one comment on CMEC's process: "It's bogus."

A suitably Pythonesque comment on a process and a set of tests that deserve to sink to the very bottom of the Gorge of Eternal Peril.

Heather-jane Robertson is a writer living in Ottawa. She is the vice-president of the Canadian Centre for Policy Alternatives. This article was originally published in Phi Delta Kappan, May 1999.

[1] School Achievement Indicators Program: 1998 Report on Reading and Writing Assessment (Toronto: Council of Ministers of Education Canada, 1999).

Report on the 1998 SAIP Reading and Writing II Assessment

Implications for educational policy and practice

by Heather-jane Robertson and David Ireland

Editor's note: Since this report is too long to be reproduced here, we are including instead the Executive Summary (below) and a paper based on the report "Form and Substance: Critiquing SAIP."

The provinces and the territories, through the Council of Ministers of Education, Canada (CMEC), developed the School Achievement Indicators Program (SAIP) to assess the performance of 13- and 16-year-old students in mathematics, reading and writing, and science. According to CMEC, the information collected through SAIP assessments can be used by each province to set educational priorities and plan program improvements. Results of these assessments are claimed to provide those responsible for education systems "with well-researched, reliable data upon which to base important decisions that will improve student learning."[1]

This case study of CMEC's report on SAIP Reading and Writing (1998) sets out to determine whether in fact this assessment generated the "well-researched, reliable data" that could serve this purpose, that is, to determine whether SAIP achieves its own objectives.

Key findings

The report identifies no new problems, and provides neither explanations nor solutions for them.

The study identifies five problems related to student performance that could respond to policy intervention. However, these particular problems have been well known to policy-makers for some time. The report does not explain why these problems exist; nor how student performance responds to policy or practice.

The report represents problems in misleading ways.

The problems are presented as generalizations that distort the findings of the assessment. The problems identified by the data are not that "boys do worse than girls" or that "francophones outside Quebec do worse than francophones inside Quebec," but that *some* boys and *some* francophones demonstrate these characteristics. Without an explanatory analysis of these refinements of the general problem, it is impossible to conclude what kind of changes would yield improved results.

The report misrepresents what was tested.

The Reading test is not just a test of reading; it tests the ability of students to provide answers to questions in a particular, desired manner that requires imagination, writing ability and motivation, as much as (if not more than) reading ability. The Writing test makes erroneous assumptions about the association among writing elements and ignores the extent to which writing depends on the skills of reading.

The methods used to produce students' scores are not reliable.

In Reading, the criteria pertaining to levels of achievement are not always distinguishable; for example, the descriptors for levels 1 and 2 are almost identical.

In Writing, the dimensions of writing used to establish the scale points are assumed to be correlated, which means that each student is expected to have equal control over each of the elements of writing (content, organization, mechanics, style).

The level of achievement reported for each student is global. This ignores any higher achievement the student may have shown during the assessment.

The determination of student levels of achievement is overly complex.

The student questionnaires provide no useful information.

The presentation of the results of the questionnaires divides the 13-year-old students into those who achieved at level 2 and below, and those who achieved at level 3 and above. Since level 2 is the expected level of achievement for 13-year-olds, the distinction that is made between successful and unsuccessful students is completely distorted.

The proportions of subgroups are improperly calculated when questionnaire data are being analyzed. This negates virtually all the conclusions associated with contextual variables.

Gender differences are not included in the analysis of questionnaire data, even though gender differences in results were alleged to be one of SAIP's most significant findings.

The problems identified by the study have been well known to policy-makers for some time. The report does not explain why these problems exist; nor how student performance responds to policy or practice.

Most of the questions have no potential explanatory value and have no significance for policy decisions, since they do not deal with issues that policy-makers can control.

Many of the questions are ambiguous; it is difficult to know what respondents meant when they selected an option, which makes any inferences drawn from them invalid.

The data presentation is misleading.

The achievement graphs combine "all the students who achieved at a level and above", thus making it appear that almost every student achieved at the lowest possible level. This presentation obscures the real distribution of achievement.

The graphs invite simplistic comparisons that violate a central principle of statistics, namely that insignificant differences should be ignored.

Conclusion

This report concludes that the 1998 SAIP Reading and Writing II Assessment collected no information which could be used appropriately to:

- Set educational priorities
- Plan program improvements
- Support important policy decisions that will improve student learning.

Having failed to meet CMEC's stated objectives for SAIP, this assessment appears to have been a waste of students' time and public resources. When placed alongside the other well-documented deficiencies of SAIP, there is little reason to support the perpetuation of the School Achievement Indicators Program. ❧

November 1999

Heather-jane Robertson is a writer living in Ottawa. She is the vice-president of the Canadian Centre for Policy Alternatives.

David Ireland is a retired test-director, who was in charge of research and evaluation with the former Carleton Board of Education in Ottawa. In retirement, he has written many reports and papers critiquing the tests administered at government levels to Ontario students (EQAO, SAIP, and International Studies) and the use made of them.

[1] See, for example, the Communiqué of the CMEC "Results of Second National Reading and Writing Test Released," March 10, 1999.

Form and substance
Critiquing SAIP

by Heather-jane Robertson and David Ireland

ABSTRACT: *The Council of Ministers of Education, Canada (CMEC) claims that its School Achievement Indicators Program (SAIP) can be used by each province to set educational priorities and plan program improvements because SAIP provides "well-researched, reliable data upon which to base important decisions that will improve student learning".[1]*

SAIP's opponents primarily contest its use and expansion by identifying its role in promoting regressive educational reforms,[2] or by describing how high-stakes testing undermines goals such as increasing opportunity for disadvantaged.[3] However, there has been little commentary on the quality of the tests themselves, their administration or the quality of the published data that are intended to guide policy decisions. This paper examines certain aspects of the 1998 SAIP Reading and Writing II Assessment in some detail, and concludes that critics would be well-advised to add the technical shortcomings of SAIP to their analyses.

The Council of Ministers of Education, Canada (CMEC), administer the School Achievement Indicators Program (SAIP) to assess the performance of 13- and 16-year-old students in mathematics, reading and writing, and science. According to CMEC, SAIP results are intended to provide those responsible for education systems:

- with well-researched, reliable data
- upon which to base important policy decisions
- that will improve student learning[4].

CMEC contends that the information collected through SAIP assessments can be used by each province to set educational priorities and to plan program improvements.

SAIP 1998, Reading and Writing II

In April and May 1998, SAIP Reading and Writing Assessments were administered to a random sample of 46,000 students drawn from all Canadian jurisdictions. The total sample comprised 24,000 13-year-olds and 22,000 16-year-olds, approximately 34,000 of whom wrote in English and 12,000 in French.[5]

Performance criteria were described for 5 levels for both assessments. Thirteen-year-old students were expected to achieve at level 2 and above; 16-year-olds were expected to achieve at level 3 and above. The assessments and scoring criteria were the same for both groups tested. The percentage of students at ages 13 and 16 that were expected to score at, above and below the "acceptable" level of performance was established through an elaborate (and contested) expectation-setting process designed and carried out by CMEC staff.[6]

The key findings for Canada, as described by CMEC in its Report on Reading and Writing II[7] held few surprises:

In Reading:
- 78% of 13-year-olds achieved at the expected level (2) or better.
- 69% of 13-year-olds achieved levels 2-3; 9% were judged to be at levels 4 and 5.
- 72% of 16-year-olds achieved at the expected level (3) or better.
- 24% of 16-year-olds performed at level 4 and 10% at level 5.

In Writing:
- 95% of 13-year-olds achieved at the expected level (2) or better.
- 52% of the 13-year-old students were at level 3, and 16% were at level 4.
- 85% of 16-year-olds achieved at the expected level (3) or better.
- 30% of 16-year-olds were at level 4, and 9% were at level 5.

- 16-year-olds performed better, on average, than 13-year-olds in both subjects.
- Approximately twice as many boys as girls failed to reach the expectation for their age group in both subjects.
- Significantly more girls achieved at higher levels than boys.
- For both subjects and for both age-groups, francophones living outside Quebec achieved significantly less well than Quebec francophones, and less well than the population as a whole, regardless of language.
- Students enrolled in second language programs, or who had previously been enrolled in second language programs, had greater difficulty than students who wrote the test in their first language.

Predictably, these results received only limited media attention. Officials were understandably uncertain about the touted "policy implications" of the findings; one went way out on a limb by commenting that the ministries "may want to take a look and see where there [was] something they could do." Media commentary showed a brief interest in what *The Globe and Mail* called the "unconscionable" gender gap, and then the story disappeared.

SAIP 1998, Reading and Writing II: A critique

Neither ministers nor the media questioned the quality of the data or CMEC's interpretation of its findings. It seems to be generally taken for granted that SAIP assessments are objective and competent, even when they are unflattering. Debate over SAIP, such as it is, tends to focus on political rather than technical issues. However, it is our contention that there were multiple, unacknowledged problems with the design, administration, evaluation and interpretation of SAIP Reading and Writing II that deserve the equal attention of critics.

These problems can be grouped into seven clusters.

1. Deficient problem identification and analysis.

Although the SAIP Report on Reading and Writing II identified a number of widely acknowledged problems, it contributed little to their refinement, and nothing to their resolution.

With respect to gender differences, one Minister (correctly) identified the problem as "world-wide" in scope. But problems that are common and widespread are not necessarily simple. When boys show lower achievement in reading and writing tests than girls, it may be interpreted as "boys have a problem." However, in this round of SAIP, many boys achieved just as well as many girls. At age 13, in Reading, 70% of the boys achieved at level 2 or better (compared with 86% of girls); 60% of 16-year-old boys achieved at level 3 or better (compared with 82% of girls). The SAIP report attributes the differences in achievement between boys and girls, among other factors, to this different rate of sexual maturation or "cultural influences". Maturation may be a problem, but some boys—quite a lot of boys—seem to mature (or do well in reading tests) at the same rate as girls.

Linguistic minorities everywhere face challenges in reading and writing. Predictably, SAIP II reported that, on average, Quebec francophone students outperfomed francophones outside Quebec, but there are francophone students, hors du Quebec, who achieve comparably to Quebec students. Amongst 16-year-old francophones, 59.9% of Manitobans, 65% of Ontarians, and 68.1% of New Brunswickers achieved at level 3 and above in Reading, compared with 79.4% of Quebec students.

Thus the problem is not the performance of "all boys" or "all francophones outside Quebec", but the performance of some within each group. Nothing in SAIP identifies the additional characteristics that distinguish low from high-achievers, and (given neither gender nor language is determined by public policy) what policy levers, if any, might make more students successful within each group. For that matter, nothing in this report sheds any light on how achievement for any student could be improved.

2. Erroneous assumptions about what the assessments measure.

The SAIP Reading test is not simply (or even primarily) a test of reading; it is predominantly a test of students' propensity to answer questions in a pre-determined, particular and desired manner that is not divulged to the test-takers. While responses to the Reading questions do require a certain understanding of the text, to score well requires students to intuit, for example, that a level 5 response requires *analytical*, *insightful*, and *substantiated* judgments—or at least long ones.

The SAIP report demonstrates how these criteria were applied by providing examples of student responses to the following question about an excerpt from an Alice Monroe short story, *The Red Dress:*

> *"Considering Raymond's behaviour and comments on the walk home, what do you conclude about his experience that night compared to the narrator's?" (p.8)*

Nothing in this (dreadfully-worded) question signals the student to generate "analytical, insightful and substantiated" judgments. But perhaps the length of the response matters more than its "insightful" content. Response exemplars for level 3 consist of only one or two lines of text, for example:

> *"That this night wasn't as big a deal to Raymond as it was for the narrator. He wasn't as shy & didn't care as much as she does about everything." (p.8)*

But the exemplars for level 5 consist of 5 or more lines, for example:

> *"He probably spent the whole time with the 'guys' arguing about a hockey game. He doesn't really care about any of the girls. Just dances for the sake of dancing, talking for the sake of talking. We can see this because he didn't even seem to notice that he was now talking to the narrator instead. The narrator learned to listen, be more understanding, not so scared of failure. Raymond is full of himself & doesn't care & probably had just another boring night." (p.9)*

Did the students whose responses were judged to be at level 3 believe they had answered the question adequately? Could the level 3 students have written more lines if they had known they were supposed to? Why did the student who responded at level 5 write so much? Is more always better? It seems that both exemplar respondents were sufficiently accomplished to understand what this part of the story was about—they were both readers.

3. Unreliable methods of evaluation (and/or score production)

The methodology used to produce students' scores is highly questionable, and not consistent with widely-accepted practice:

3.1. *The scale-points used to separate levels of achievement are not always discrete or defensible.* In SAIP's rating system, each student's work is judged to be at one of 5 levels of achievement, according to criteria described in the report and illustrated by exemplars. To be meaningful, these criteria should differentiate clearly among performance levels.

For example, in Reading, (in which 21% of the 13-year-olds failed to reach the level 2 standard), the differences between level 1 and level 2 performance should have been clearly evident, since these divide the "successful" student from the "unsuccessful". This was not the case. The following compares SAIP's criteria for Levels 1 and 2, for Reading. The few differences between the two sets of criteria are highlighted:

Level 1	Level 2
The student reader applies those reading strategies needed to construct and interpret *elementary or* surface meaning from straightforward texts/questions and some *degree of* surface meaning from some more complex texts and/or questions by responding to: • conventional vocabulary and syntax; • concrete details and information and uncomplicated elements of characterization and conventional organization; • directly stated or strongly implied ideas and key points.	The student reader applies those reading strategies needed to construct and interpret surface and/or *directly implied* meaning from straightforward texts (*including* questions) and surface meaning from some more complex texts and/or questions by *attending and responding* to: • conventional vocabulary and syntax; • concrete details and information and uncomplicated elements of characterization and conventional organization; • directly stated or strongly implied ideas and key points.

These criteria, although presumably intended to separate acceptable and unacceptable responses, are virtually identical. Nothing of substance distinguishes level 1 from level 2 performances.

The exemplars for levels 3 and 4 present a similar problem. The criteria for these levels are not identical, but are very similar. At level 3, the criteria include surface interpretation of some *"more sophisticated texts"*, whereas at level 4, the interpretation is of *"sophisticated texts"*; at level 3, the student makes *"informed and clearly supported judgments of a certain degree of complexity"*, while at level 4, the student makes *"thoughtful, complex, and well supported judgments"*.

When so little distinguishes one level from the next, much is left to the subjectivity of markers. Ordinarily, quality controls are built into the marking process in an effort to ensure consistency, but there are indications that there may be significant variability in SAIP's practices in this regard. For example, Crocker[8] found that for some SAIP tests, the odds were only slightly better than random that two markers would put the same paper in the same achievement category (p.20-24).

3.2. SAIP treats the dimensions of writing as if they are always correlated, and expects each student to have equal control (or lack thereof) over each of the elements. Students who were assessed in Writing were to have been judged on the following dimensions:
- understanding and control of the elements of writing
- integration of the elements
- meaning the writing conveys
- writer's voice/tone/stance
- writer's interest in the task
- awareness of the reader
- controlling idea and its development
- control of style, syntax, and the rules of language; frequency of errors

While these dimensions guiding the evaluation of writing are quite common, most evaluation rubrics also indicate how responses should be evaluated when writing quality is uneven. Markers will encounter samples in which, for example, the content (idea, development, and support) is strong, but style and mechanics are weak. Guidelines are usually established to assist markers in deciding how to rate such a piece. But the SAIP report makes no mention of the possibility that mastery may be uneven, and provides no guidance for rating a "mixed" paper.

3.3 Not every dimension of writing receives equal attention: SAIP's exemplars emphasize "mechanics." The two exemplars selected to illustrate performance at levels 1 and 2 contain frequent mechanical errors of all kinds. At levels 3 and above, such errors are much more infrequent, which may (or may not) demonstrate the correlation amongst each of the elements of writing. But mechanics do not always improve at the same rate as other elements of writing.

The SAIP report includes one student response that is an exceptional example of a paper that shows both weak mechanics and powerful writing. It is the second longest piece (about 640 words) amongst the exemplars. These anomalies are ignored in SAIP's commentary, which is limited to a "2" and the remark that "development is sketchy and/or inconsistently maintained. The writing conveys simple and/or uneven meaning"—this about a piece in which the writer describes his mother's abusive relationship, in which her partner broke the baby's arm!

3.4. *Global scoring underestimates many students' capabilities.* Students' results on individual SAIP test items are not reported, only their global performances. In practice, however, students may demonstrate considerable variability during a two-and-one-half hour test, which is itself varied by question type and degree of difficulty. In order to assign a single "global" level to each paper, scorers were to take into account how many multiple-choice questions the students had answered correctly and the "depth, subtlety, and complexity" of students' answers to the open-response questions. Finally, each student's booklet of responses was assessed at the *one level* at which the student demonstrated "consistent" success—the level *he or she never fell below*. Strictly applied, this rule means that one poor answer would invalidate a paper that was otherwise of very high quality.

4. Apparent variations in test difficulty seem to have been ignored.

According to the SAIP 1995 Reading and Writing Assessment Technical Report (the Technical Report for the 1998 assessment is not yet available), the Reading booklets were arranged in the following manner:

- There were four reading passages in each of three booklets, which were randomly distributed.
- The number of questions in each booklet varied: 19 in booklet 1; 25 in booklet 2; 23 in booklet 3.
- Each question in each booklet was assigned a targeted difficulty level, e.g., level 2, level 3.
- Each question was also assigned a range of difficulty around the difficulty level, so that a question aimed at level 2 might also be expected to produce a level 1 or a level 3 response.
- Markers were allowed to assign only the levels associated with each question. For example, a level 2 question could not generate a level 4 or 5 response. However, a response to a question anticipating a level 3 or 4 might be graded as a level 1 or 2 answer. If these levels were not indicated as "acceptable" for a particular question, the response was assigned to the "below level 1" category. There is no "above level 5" category.
- The distribution of targeted levels in the three booklets varied. In booklet 1, six of the 19 questions (32%) were targeted for level 2, while 12 (64%) of the questions included level 2 in their range. In booklet 2, 11 of 25 questions (44%) were targeted for level 2, while

19 (76%) included level 2 within their range. In booklet 3, of 23 questions, 7 (30%) were targeted for level 2, while 12 (52%) included level 2 in their range. Thus it appears that booklet 2 was a substantially easier booklet than the other two. The report does not address this imbalance, or how it influenced results.

- In booklets 1 and 2, level 2 answers were expected in three of four passages, but not in the fourth, as they were in booklet 3. However, booklet 3 was almost bipolar, since its questions were based on two reading passages aimed at levels 2 and 3, while the questions based on the other two passages were aimed at levels 4 and 5. For the three booklets in English (1994), it appears that the percentage scoring at level 2 on the third reading passage for booklets 1 and 2 was relatively high; on booklet 3 it appeared to be lower. The technical report does not explore these problems of validity and reliability.

5. Variables in the testing situation were ignored.

Aspects of the testing situation may well have influenced the results of the assessment. First, all students knew that the tests did not "count", that is, how they performed would have no effect on their school grades. This may well have affected the motivation of students to perform well, and it may have affected motivation differentially. For example, the research on gender differences would suggest that, in the absence of consequences, boys may have been less motivated than girls to perform well.

Each student's booklet of responses was assessed at the *one level* at which the student demonstrated "consistent" success—the level *he or she never fell below.* Strictly applied, this rule means that one poor answer would invalidate a paper that was otherwise of very high quality.

Second, at least for the 16-year-old group, the logistics of the assessment were inconvenient and may have impaired performance. SAIP chose a random sample within a school for good reason: intact classes are not a random grouping of students. However, such sampling cuts across classes and, in semestered schools, includes students who are not taking pertinent courses that semester. In every case, an assessment of two-and-one-half hours disrupts students' regular timetables, which means that students forced to be absent from other classes may have missed an anticipated event or have been assigned extra homework. Students may well have resented their bad luck at being chosen to write a test that "didn't count", which hardly inspires peak performance.

As well, students who were chosen to complete the Writing component, rather than the Reading component, were also expected to read and review a booklet prior to the actual scheduled assessment, a task that usually became homework. In some schools, no doubt teachers made an effort to motivate students and encourage them to prepare. But in others, staff may have been as irritated as the students at this expectation and the interruption in their programs, and they may have conveyed this message to their students. Again, the effect on students may have been differential if research on gender differences, motivation and compliance are considered. Boys may well have been less motivated to perform well than were girls, which may explain their comparatively weaker performance.

6. The background questionnaires solicited meaningless information that is presented in misleading ways.

CMEC has been under some pressure to provide "contextual" data to help policy-makers make sense of SAIP results. Thus all SAIP students were required to complete a questionnaire that asked about the their backgrounds, and about their practices and attitudes towards either reading or writing, depending on which test they were to write. CMEC presented some of this information alongside student achievement data. However, these background questions provide little useful information, and in fact, invite harmful speculation about the relationship between context and school performance. There are at least seven problems associated with these questions and their use:.

- *The data presentation changes the rules about what constitutes success.* The tables presenting the relationship between the questionnaire information and achievement for 13-year-old students groups results according to whether students scored at "level 2 or below" or at "level 3 or above". *Yet level 2 is the expected level of achievement for 13-year-olds*, and thus the relationship between the questionnaire information and achievement is meaningless, at best, and often misleading

- *The information derived from the questionnaires is not analyzed by gender or language, even though achievement differences associated with gender and language are identified as key findings of this assessment.* A gender-based analysis might have revealed something about the distinctive characteristics of low-achieving boys and high-achieving girls that might inform policy—one of the key purposes of SAIP. Nor is the questionnaire information analyzed for francophone students by province, even though the lower performance of francophone students outside Quebec was also a key finding.

- *Many of the questions have little explanatory value.* What relationship to achievement could be derived from answers to:
  - How many television channels do you get in your house?
  - How often do you write letters or use e-mail? (Why only these two writing activities?)
  - To do well in language arts, do you need natural ability or good luck?

  Not surprisingly, none of these variables was found to predict success or failure in Reading and Writing: second language students scored at both levels; a significant number of students who said they liked to read and write "a lot" scored at the lower level; having one computer or more at home did not predict success. Even the questions that specifically asked about reading and writing appear to not correlate significantly with achievement.

  > Students may well have resented their bad luck at being chosen to write a test that "didn't count", which hardly inspires peak performance.

- *A substantial number of questions are ambiguous.* For example, students are to answer "How much time each school day do you usually spend reading for enjoyment and/or general interest?" How did students understand this question? Is "school day" the time they actually spend in school, or school-related activities, or is it a synonym for week-day? Other querulous examples include:
  - In the questions about *liking to read and write a lot*, one response option is "I like to read/write some of the time,

depending on what I'm reading/writing". Did students see this as an "inferior" response compared with "I like to read/write a lot" or was it just a more realistic response? In other words, is there any significant difference between the two answers?

- Amongst the options for the most preferred type of reading are "on computer screens" and "information". It would be useful to see the original question, which may clarify the ambiguity, but computer screens may contain very little information or a great deal of information depending on what has been accessed.

- What do students mean when they agree that "you" need good luck or natural ability to do well in school? Do they mean that they have the required good luck or natural ability, or that others do? The intention of the question is unclear.

- *The questionnaires are intrusive and serve no meaningful role in policy development.* What might Ministers of Education do, even if a correlation between watching Cable TV and writing proficiency were to be established? Policy decisions can only be made about phenomena over which the policy-makers have some control.

TABLE 12: 1994—1998 Comparison of Number of Books Students Report Having in Their Home				
	13-year-olds		16-year-olds	
	1994 (%)	1998 (%)	1994 (%)	1998 (%)
Less than 50 books				
Reading	12	17	15	19
Writing	12	18	15	20
50 to 100 books				
Reading	32	38	33	37
Writing	36	38	35	36
More than 150 books				
Reading	54	44	52	43
Writing	52	43	50	43

Source: Page 107, 1998 Reading and Writing Results, CMEC.

- *The questions lack specificity.* In general, the questions are not specific enough or are incomplete. What students watch on television may be more significant than how many channels are available to them; what students do on a computer is probably more important than whether there is one in the home. Having access to a computer—at school, or at the library, or even at a friend's home—may be more important than owning one. A student may believe and therefore claim "you need to read or write a lot to be successful", but does the same student actually read or write a lot?

- *Results are implausible.* Some results are sufficiently unlikely that the entire body of data becomes questionable. For example, in 1994 and 1998, both 13- and 16-year-olds were asked to estimate how many books they had in their homes.

According to SAIP/CMEC, the number of students with less than 50 books has increased by up to 50%, while those with more than 150 books has decreased by almost 20% in only four years. Such changes in book ownership over such a short period of time are quite astonishing and have certainly not been reported by any other source. Indeed, we are told book reading and sales of books have never been higher. If these data are accurate, this is indeed "news". If they are inaccurate however, should we have confidence in the other questionnaire results?

7. The presentation of the data misrepresents results and invites misinterpretation.

The presentation of the data in CMEC's report merits particular attention. Data presentations, particularly graphic presentations, are intended to facilitate understanding so that the reader can see, at a glance, how data are distributed. The bars or the curves in the visual presentation should make it evident that "more" occurs in one place and "less" in another. This rule also applies to tables of figures, in which one should be able to see immediately how the numbers being reported compare to each other.

But the data presentations in this SAIP report consistently defeat this purpose. Their effect is to obfuscate the data and disguise the import and/or the limitations of the data.

The Achievement Graphs: The graphs of student achievement make it very difficult to see the details of actual results and their significance. Data for student achievement are reported in terms of the percentage of students who achieved at a particular level *and all those students who achieved at higher levels.* As a result, almost 100% of the students appear to be scoring at level 1—the lowest level.

The SAIP report presents Writing results for 13-year-olds as follows: (p.28)

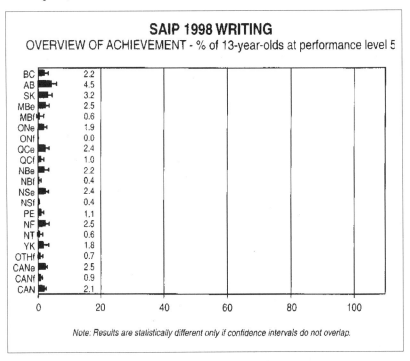

The more conventional presentation of the same data would look like this:

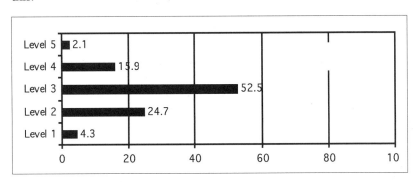

CMEC's visual portrayal of SAIP results is misleading in several ways. It is impossible to get an accurate impression, at a glance, of how well students are doing. In fact, it is made to appear that the greatest number of students did badly— at least, no better than level 1. It is also impossible to see the distribution of student achievement from SAIP's chart, which is, in all cases, a curve around the expected level. A more conventional representation would also show improvement (albeit predictable) between ages 13 and 16. Finally, it is impossible, without undertaking a series of complex calculations, to work out actual student results. A useful graph serves to simplify rather than complexify data.

Other SAIP graphs, especially those that compare provincial and territorial results, make little attempt to distinguish between statistically significant and insignificant data. All differences are presented as equally meaningful. Although there is passing reference to confidence intervals, without magnifying glasses and straight-edges, it is almost impossible to distinguish between significant and insignificant differences.

For example:

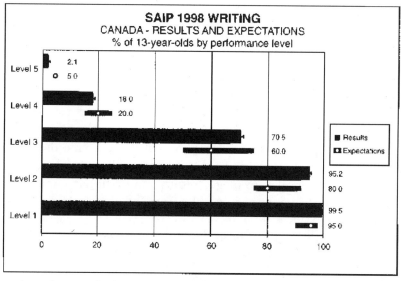

At a glance, which jurisdictions showed significantly better or worse results than their neighbours?

The Questionnaire Data: Three problems contaminate the presentation of questionnaire data. One of the most serious errors in the report is how "successful" and "unsuccessful" students are grouped when survey data are presented. In the SAIP report, the 13-year-old students are grouped according to whether they achieved at "level 2 or below" or at "level 3 or above." Yet this age group was *expected to achieve at level 2!* Because of the decision to group level 2 (13-year-old students) as "unsuccessful", a large percentage of students (36.5% in Reading, and 24.7% in Writing), are included in the "lower" group. As a result, the correlation between either group's performance and the questionnaire ("context") results are meaningless.

This problem is compounded when the students in each of these subgroups are treated as equal and separate populations. These groups are not equal in size, since half of a small group is smaller than half of a large group, even though both represent 50% of their own subset. The SAIP report commits a serious mathematical error when it treats the subgroups as equivalent populations. All results determined in this manner are false.

In the following example (Reading, 13-year-olds), the SAIP report places about 60% of the students in the lower group (because of the way level 2 students were assigned), and 40% in the upper group, yet SAIP's calculations assume these two populations are of equal size in subsequent calculations. Thus, when SAIP reported equal percentage "results" on particular variables, it should actually have reported a 6 to 4 ratio in favour of the lower group, or 50% more. When these two errors (assuming both groups are of equal size, and reversing dependent and independent variables) appear together, the results are entirely misleading.

For example, SAIP's Table 11 (p. 107), presents a chart in which the number of books in the home is compared with performance on the Reading assessment.

13-year-olds Reading: Number of Books in the Home		
	SAIP Presentation	
	Level 2 and below (%)	Level 3 and above (%)
None	2	1
Fewer than 50	21	11
50—150	40	36
150+	38	53
Source: Page 107, Results of Reading and Writing 1998, CMEC.		

From this chart, it appears that a greater percentage of students at level 3 and above have more than 150 books in their home (53%), compared with students at level 2 and below (38%).

But if the relationship between variables had been constructed correctly, the appropriate question would be: "What percentage of students who have x number of books in their homes do well or poorly on this test?" A chart answering this question (with SAIP data) would look like this:

"What percentage of students who have x number of books in their homes do well or poorly on this test?		
	(Reading, 13-year-olds)	
	Level 2 and below (%)	Level 3 and above (%)
No books in home	71.0	29.0
Fewer than 50	73.0	27.0
50—150	61.5	39.5
150+	50.0	50.0

Thus the correct response to the question, "what proportion of students having more than 150 books at home score at each of the two achievement levels?" is an equal proportion, or 50%. The SAIP report, however, claims "a larger proportion of students who report having a very large number of books in their homes score in level 3 and above."

(p. 197). This is demonstrably false. The same flawed approach to drawing inferences is repeated throughout this section of the report. These
distortions are compounded for data on 13-year-olds, since level 2 students, who should have been included in SAIP's "successful" category,
are instead grouped with the "unsuccessful" level 1's.

A second example of bad data analysis is found in the presentation of
the results for the question: "Which of the following do you have in
your home? No computer; one computer; more than one computer?"
These results, as displayed in the report, are presented in the shaded
columns of the table below; the recalculated results for the whole sample of students are reported in the other columns. (The recalculation
treats each population as a proportion of the total.)

Number of computers at home compared with Reading achievement

From Table 14, page 108.
SAIP presentation of data compared with the corrected sample.

	(%) 13-year-olds (SAIP Report)		Corrected sample			(%) 16-year-olds (SAIP Report)		Corrected sample	
	2 and +	3 and -	2 and +	3 and -		2 and +	3 and -	2 and +	3 and -
No computers	31	22	18	9		36	23	10	16.5
One computer	54	60	32	25		52	59	15	42
More than one computer	15	18	9	7.5		12	18	3.5	13

According to SAIP's presentation of the data (which treats both "2
and –" and "3 and +" as equivalent populations), it appears that for 13-
year-old students, having a computer provides a slight advantage on the
Reading test: 60% of those scoring at level 3+ have a computer, compared with 54% who score at level 2-. But when the data are recalculated, the reverse is true: a greater percentage of 13-year-old students
with one computer score at level 2- than at level 3+(32% to 25%).

It would also seem that having more than one computer is slightly detrimental to performance (9% at levels 2- compared with 7.5% at levels 3+). In the older age group, only when the sample is corrected can it be seen that 3 to 4 times as many students with more than one computer score at level 3+ compared with those who score at level 2-. (However, it is likely that "having more than one computer" is a proxy for high family income. Note that "use" of the computer is not explored.)

For those students without a computer, the recalculated data show that twice as many 13-year-olds score at levels 2- than at levels 3+ (18% of the sample compared with 9%). In the older age-group, SAIP's presentation of the data suggests that a student without a computer does less well; however, when the data are recalculated, more students without a computer at home score at levels 3 and above than at levels 2 and below (16.5% of the sample compared with 10%).

These examples of SAIP/CMEC's limited mathematical competence raise questions about the prevalence of less-easily-identified errors in data analysis and manipulation.

Conclusion

The current CMEC—sponsored review of SAIP, which is taking place after, rather than before, a five-year federal funding commitment, is unlikely to admit to how little SAIP provides as a return on public investment.

In addition to telling us nothing new,

- The report provides no explanations for its findings that could be translated appropriately into policy recommendations.
- The results of this assessment are highly questionable. The criteria for assigning students' work to particular levels fails to provide clear direction. Problems with the criteria and, subsequently, with the reliability of marking are manifest.
- The data are presented in confusing ways that invite misinterpretation.
- The responses derived from the background questionnaire fail to provide any illuminative information and, in fact, distort correlations between achievement and contextual variables.

Criticizing SAIP's expectation-setting process, CMEC's lack of transparency and repeating the general critique of the negative effects of standardized testing in education reform have not effectively weakened support for SAIP. But these are not the only grounds on which SAIP can be challenged. We believe that critiquing SAIP from the perspective of its technical quality and the validity and reliability of its numbers should be part of any strategy that seeks to challenge its continuation.

Heather-jane Robertson is a writer living in Ottawa. She is the vice-president of the Canadian Centre for Policy Alternatives.

David Ireland is a retired test-director, who was in charge of research and evaluation with the former Carleton Board of Education in Ottawa. In retirement, he has written many reports and papers critiquing the tests administered at government levels to Ontario students (EQAO, SAIP, and International Studies) and the use made of them.

This paper was presented at the Canadian Society for the Study of Education Meeting (CSSE), May 25, 2000, Edmonton, Alberta.

Notes

[1] Council of Ministers of Education, Canada (CMEC) (1999a, March 10) *"Results of Second National Reading and Writing Test Released"* Communique

[2] Robertson, H-j (1998) *No More Teachers, No More Books: The Commercialization of Canada's Schools.* Toronto: ON McClelland & Stewart, Inc.

[3] Froese-Germain, B. (1999, November) *Standardized Testing: Undermining Equity in Education.* Canadian Teachers' Federation.

[4] Council of Ministers of Education, Canada (CMEC) (1999a, March 10) *"Results of Second National Reading and Writing Test Released"* Communique

[5] Council of Ministers of Education, Canada (CMEC) (1999b, March) 1998 *SAIP Reading and Writing II Assessment.*

[6] Robertson, H-j (1999, May) *"Bogus Points"* [In Canada Column] Phi Delta Kappan 80(9) p. 715-716

[7] CMEC (1999b).

[8] Crocker, R (1997) Review of the School Acheivement Indicators Program. Prepared for CMEC.

Testing the limits

by Patricia McAdie

Standardized testing at the elementary level in Ontario began in 1997. This is not the first time that we have had province-wide standardized tests, but it is the first time that these tests have been used for such young students. Grade 3 and 6 students are now tested every year in reading, writing, and mathematics. Plans are under way to bring in more standardized tests in Grades 4 to 11 in other subject areas.[1]

Is this what we want for our students? For our teachers? For public education? Do the results provide any useful information or help improve our education system? The short answer is no. This focus on standardized testing and a rigid curriculum that goes with it has changed the nature of public education in Ontario and elsewhere, but not for the better.

Some find standardized tests as an indicator of the success of our education system appealing. Some parents feel confident that the results of the tests give an accurate picture of the achievement of their child and of the education system as a whole. Regardless of where in the province you may live, each child gets the same test and presumably is scored in the same way. It also appears to take the politics out of education by providing a so-called objective measure of achievement. The disagreements between teachers and the government can be ignored—at least when it comes to how well their child is doing.

We have been told repeatedly by politicians, the media, and those advocating for privatization of education that there is a crisis in education. This crisis, they say, is the result of an approach to education that favoured child-centred policies that did not teach the basics. The claim is that Canada, and particularly Ontario, has not measured up on international tests and students are graduating that cannot read or write adequately.

With all these supposed problems, standardized testing, along with its partner, standardized curriculum, are portrayed as the solution. Bring in the tests, bring in the rigid standardized curriculum, and then we will have an education system that meets the goal of ensuring that our society is ready for the new global economy.

Policymakers like standardized testing. Robert Linn, a specialist in education measurement, outlines this appeal:

- They are relatively inexpensive, compared with reforms such as reducing class size or improving professional development for teachers;
- The testing can be externally mandated without relying on substantive changes in the classroom;
- Testing changes can be rapidly implemented—"within the term of office of elected officials";
- Results are visible, especially when reported to the media.

    Poor results in the beginning are desirable for policymakers who want to show they have had an effect. Based on past experience, policymakers can reasonably expect increases in scores in the first few years of a program…with or without real improvement in the broader achievement constructs that tests and achievements are intended to measure. The resulting overly rosy picture that is painted by short-term gains observed in most new testing programs gives the impression of improvement right on schedule for the next election. [2]

The news releases from the Ontario Ministry of Education are interesting to follow from year to year. Before the new curriculum was in place, the test results were described as reflecting the poor common curriculum of the previous government. Then the results on the tests got better, but there was room for improvement. Each year they are described as getting better as a result of the reforms in curriculum, testing, the new standardized report card, but they are never quite good enough. More testing is brought in and more reforms are instituted.

The figures reported in the news releases are most interesting. In 1997, 50% of students in Grade 3 scored at Level 3 or above in reading.

But these students were using the old curriculum, so the results were not good enough. The next year, the Ministry of Education news release states that 42% score at level three; it states that only 34% scored at this level in 1997. What the release fails to mention, however, is the percentage of students scoring at level 4 in both years—16% in 1997 and 4% in 1998. The total of level 3 and 4, which is the usual measure, is then 50% for 1997 but only 46% for 1998. This is a significant drop in scores when students go from the old curriculum to the new "improved" curriculum. Maybe it takes more time to get used to the new material.

This focus on standardized testing and a rigid curriculum that goes with it has changed the nature of public education in Ontario and elsewhere, but not for the better.

In 1999, the news release says there was a 13% increase in mathematics scores, but only states that the reading results were similar to the previous year. In fact, there was a 1% decline in reading scores. The news release for the 2000 results gives no numbers for any of the results. In 2001, the news release reports figures for Grade 3 mathematics (up from 43% in 1998 to 61%, both numbers the same as reported by EQAO), but no other Grade 3 results are reported. For Grade 3 reading, the actual results show a small increase. In fact, by 2001, Grade 3 students are now performing at the same level as they were with the old curriculum. We have gone full circle. It took four years with the new curriculum to achieve the same level as with the old curriculum. Do these news releases sound like political messages, rather than reporting the results? Depending on the political agenda, the reports vary.[3]

The latest example of reporting the data to fit a political agenda is for the Ontario Grade 10 literacy test. Students first wrote the test in 2000. The results from the first year did not count, and the students knew that. Beginning with the 2001-02 year, students must pass the test in order to graduate from high school. The results from the second year were reported as 75% passing, compared with 68% in the first year. EQAO has always reported results using Method 1, which includes all students in the cohort, whether or not they actually took the test—until now. For the first time, they have switched to Method 2, which includes only those students who actually wrote the test. Under Method 1, 69% passed the test this year, compared with 61% last year. It appears that

75% sounds more acceptable than 69%. It remains to be seen whether Method 2 will be used to report test results from now on.

There are a growing number of books and countless articles and monographs pointing out various problems with standardized testing.[4] Yet we continue, adding more tests, publishing the results in newspapers, checking the rankings, comparing one school, board, province, or country with another. We have more than enough evidence that such tests are inappropriate and even damaging. So why do we continue with them?

Because the people that are making the decisions don't really care about the research. They are concerned with promoting a different agenda, one that values markets, profits, and social stratification. The results are presented to support the arguments.

Do these news releases sound like political messages, rather than reporting the results? Depending on the political agenda, the reports vary.

The annual budget for the Education Quality and Accountability Office (EQAO) in Ontario is about $50 million. They administer the provincial Grade 3, 6, and 9 tests, the Grade 10 literacy tests, the national SAIP, and the international TIMSS tests. This cost does not include other Ministry costs or district school board costs associated with preparation, administration, and follow-up of the tests. It does not include the time spent in class preparing for the tests and administering the tests. It does not include the time spent at the school or the school board on various aspects of the tests. This is a huge investment for something with very questionable return.

And this does not include the costs of the growing test preparation companies. For $10, you can buy *Help Your Child Prepare for Ontario Grade 3 Language Tests*, or *Help Your Child Prepare for Ontario Grade 6 Mathematics Tests*, or *Helping Your Child Prepare for Ontario Grade 3 Mathematics Tests*. You can enrol your child at Sylvan for a few hundred dollars. You can hire a private tutor for hundreds of dollars per year. It is estimated that the tutoring and test preparation industry is worth close to $4 billion![5]

The tests represent a distinct shift in focus from learning to performing, from thinking to performing or responding. Essay questions must be answered with five paragraphs. Short answer questions must be no less than three sentences and no more than five. Multiple choice questions are becoming more abundant. They do not allow for creativity, for differences, for explanations, or for more than one right answer.

> *"If one mousetrap catches one mouse everyday," she reads slowly, "and two mousetraps catch four mice, and three mouse traps catch nine mice, and four traps get sixteen mice, then how many traps will be needed to catch twenty-five mice?" … "How many traps then, Jiri?" asks the teacher.*
>
> *Jiri smiles. His glasses are filthy. His whiskers shine. "One," he says…. "Of course, you would need almost a month."[6]*

How would this response be scored?

Standardized tests do not improve student learning, but they do help to separate the winners from the losers. Bringing these tests into the elementary level ensures that young children are initiated into the competitive world of markets and meritocracy. Lisa Graham Keegan, Arizona Superintendent of Education and an advocate of standardized testing, refers to "gatekeeper skills."[7] In other words, not everyone should be allowed to pass through the gate, to pass, to succeed. You can't have winners if you don't have losers. "Such tests do not measure creativity, judgment, persistence, higher-order thinking, stamina, motivation, imagination, determination, sense of craft or civic mindedness."[8] But that is not the point of the tests. The point seems to be to stratify students.

Is there a legitimate reason for trying to construct better standardized tests? Some, such as James Popham,[9] argue that you can develop fair, appropriate standardized tests that would address accountability. Others, such as Alfie Kohn,[10] argue that no form of standardized testing is appropriate; to address accountability, we should look at more subjective measures—observe you child's behaviour, visit the school, talk with the teachers.

"It's only the <u>illusion</u> of a level playing field."

None of this means we should not or cannot hold high standards for students. "Having high standards is not the same as having common standards for all, especially when they are tied to a lock step of age or grade level."[11] Teachers do expect the best from their students. What Ontario's schools need are the resources to be able to ensure a high quality education system for all students—lower class sizes, particularly in the early grades, more resources, more supports for students and teachers, a full range of programs.

And none of this means we should not or cannot be accountable. Accountability is not the same as testing. Accountability should be a measure of the purpose we hold for school. If we are interested in democratic citizenship, then look at voting rates, particularly among young people, volunteering and participation in the community, crime rates. If we are concerned with social efficiency, of educating our future work force, then look at students' ability to take their place in the workforce (not unemployment levels, which measure market factors, not the ability of the workforce). If we are interested in social mobility, in perpetuating the meritocratic, class-based society, then keep the tests.

Public education is more than just public ownership of the schools. It should include public control for the common good, for a common purpose. Public education should be the responsibility of all of us, not left for a handful of politicians. ❧

Patricia McAdie is a research officer with the Elementary Teachers' Federation of Ontario.

Notes

1 Provincial standardized tests are also given in Grade 9 mathematics and Grade 10 literacy. Students must pass the Grade 10 literacy test in order to graduate from secondary school. PEI is the only province that does not administer provincial exams at some level. Alberta, Manitoba, New Brunswick, Newfoundland, and Ontario all have provincial tests for Grade 3 students. New Brunswick does not report the results for individual students. BC starts testing at Grade 4, and Saskatchewan begins at Grade 5. Saskatchewan's testing is only a sample of students and is only reported at the provincial level.

2 Robert L. Linn, "Assessments and Accountability," *Educational Researcher*, March 2000, Volume 29, Number 2, 4-16.

3 The Ministry of Education news releases can be found on their website at www.edu.gov.on.ca. The EQAO reports can be found at www.eqao.com.

4 See, for example, Alfie Kohn, *The Case Against Standardized Testing*, 2000, W. James Popham, The Truth About Testing, 2001, Bernie Froese-Germain, *Standardized Testing: Undermining Equity in Education*, 1999, FairTest website www.fairtest.org.

5 "*The Education Industry Reports. Pre-K-12*," February 7, 2002, eduventures.com.

6 Richard Scrimger, *Of Mice and Nutcrackers: A Peeler Christmas*, Tundra Books: Toronto, 2001, 75-77.

7 *PBS Online Focus, School Testing*, Feb. 15, 2001—www.pbs.org/newshour/bb/education/jan-june01/testing_2-15.html

8 G. Bracy, "*A Lesson Plan for the Schools With Little Learning Behind It*," Center for Education Research, Analysis, and Innovation, Jan. 28, 2001.

9 For example, see *The Truth About Testing. An Educator's Call to Action*, 2001.

10 For example, see *The Case Against Standardized Testing. Raising the Scores, Ruining the Schools*, 2000.

11 Robert L. Linn, "Assessments and Accountability," *Educational Researcher*, March 2000, Volume 29, Number 2, 4-16.

Ontario Grade 3 student achievement

by Stéphane Tremblay, Nancy Ross
and Jean-Marie Berthelot

An important measure of children's well-being is their academic performance. Previous research has shown that the socio-economic status of students and features of the home environment may have a large impact on academic achievement. Teaching practices, class size, parental involvement with the school and school neighbourhood characteristics may also exert incremental effects on academic performance.[1]

This study identifies factors that influenced Ontario Grade 3 student achievement in reading, writing and mathematics in 1996-97. An "ecological" approach is taken to examine these factors including characteristics of individual students and their families (student level); teachers and classrooms (class level); and schools and school neighbourhoods (school level).[2]

The face of Grade 3 in Ontario

In 1997, few Grade 3 Ontario students had a first language that was not English (5%) and few were enrolled in French immersion programs (4%), yet nearly one-quarter came from homes where a language other than English was spoken. More than half the students (54%) had home computers, but 70% of Grade 3 classes had limited or no access to computers in their school. About 59% had more than 100 books available to them at home. Grade 3 classes were frequently split-grade (47%) and were often taught by teachers with no more than 10 years of teaching experience (63%). Most schools were public schools (69%) and were in urban areas (83%).

Based on this profile, a reference group was created to assess the impact on test scores of changes in student, class and school characteristics. The reference group embodies the most common characteristics of Grade 3 students: that is, it represents an English-speaking girl in a public school, with a reference score of 51out of 100 who is not in a split-grade class and whose school is located in an urban neighbourhood with a median household income of $42,500 (among other characteristics.)[3] The model developed for this study show test scores change when a student's characteristics deviate from that of the reference group. Thus, for example, being a boy would reduce the test score by 3 points to 48, compared with 51 for the reference group, even when all other characteristics remain the same.

Girls with computers and books at home do better

Students' sex, language and socio-economic background were all significantly associated with student achievement on the tests. For example, girls scored 3 points higher than boys. These results generally echo those of other researchers.[4] Grade 3 students whose second language was English recorded performances 3 points lower than those whose mother tongue was English. If English was not the dominant language spoken at home, the students' performance was about 1 point lower than that of students from English-speaking homes. French immersion programs had no effect on test results.

> Students' sex, language and socio-economic background were all significantly associated with student achievement on the tests.

The socio-economic status of students' families were approximated by two proxy measures: the availability of more than 100 books and a computer at home. Students who had both of these resources scored an average of 6 points higher than those who had neither. This implies that socio-economic status plays a significant role in student achievement. Past studies have suggested that parental involvement in children's education is associated with a wide range of positive outcomes for elementary school children, including higher student achievement.[5] Grade 3 students whose parents were not involved with the school scored 1 point less than the rest. Interpreting the meaning of the association between parental involvement and student achievement, however, is not straight forward. It may be that parental involvement is a marker for parental enthusiasm and positive parenting style.[6]

What you should know about this study

Data in this article come from two sources. The1996-97 Education Quality and Accountability Office(EQAO) database for Ontario provides data on province-wide standardized academic achievement tests. The EQAO data used in this study consist of student scores on 14 performance assessments in mathematics, writing and reading; information on four background questionnaires completed by students, parents/guardians, teachers and principals; and a student information form completed by teachers. These questionnaires provide information on student, family, teacher, class and school factors related to student performance. The 1996 Census of Population collects data about the socio-economic status of residents in the school's neighbourhood (e.g. educational attainment) and whether the school is located in an urban or rural environment. In urban areas, school neighbourhoods are defined as the area within walking distance of the school, measuring a 1.6-kilometre radius. In rural areas, "neighbourhood" is defined as the census sub-division in which the school is located.1

Target population and sample size

The target population consisted of all Grade 3 students enrolled in English-speaking schools in Ontario for 1996-97 (typically children about 8 years old). Excluded were those students who were exempted from the test or whose records had missing information. The sample used for analysis represented nearly 116,000 Grade 3 students in over6,900 classrooms in almost 3,300 schools. Tests were administered during April 1997 to assess the knowledge and skills that students had acquired in Grade 3 and earlier grades.

Achievement measure

The standardized test scores consisted of 14 performance assessments: 8 in mathematics, 3 in writing, and 3 in reading. The performance assessments were scaled using a logit transformation. The average achievement measure used in this analysis combines mathematics, writing and reading assessments into one score for each Grade 3 student.

continued on next page

The model

Student performance is thought to be influenced by numerous factors at different levels. Therefore, multilevel regression modeling was used to permit the simultaneous analysis of the influence of student, class and school characteristics on student achievement. The final model explains 21% of the variation in Grade 3 students' test scores, which falls into the typical range for this type of analysis.

1. A census subdivision is a geographic area representing a municipality or its equivalent, such as Indian reserves or settlements, or unorganized territories.

Experienced teachers and small classes are associated with higher test scores

After accounting for other variables influencing achievement, students scored 1 point higher when taught by teachers who had more than10 years of teaching experience in the lower elementary school grades or who were comfortable with the curriculum. Also, the more closely the teachers reported following the current curriculum, the better the students performed.

Smaller class size, proxied by the number of Grade 3 students in the class, can positively influence achievement.[7]

On average, 17.3 children were in each class, but class sizes were often much larger because nearly half of Grade 3 classes were split grades. By adding 8 more Grade 3 students to a class, students performed almost 1 point lower than students in classes of average size. Evidence about the relationship between class size and student performance in the United States has been mixed.[8] Research suggests that even though teachers do not change their teaching strategies in smaller classrooms, students are more readily engaged in the learning process.[9] While the size of a Grade 3 class was important in Ontario, having access to a computer in the classroom did not affect test outcomes. This mirrors results of a large U.S. study, which also found that computers in the classroom had no effect on student achievement at the Grade 4 level.[10]

Interpreting the meaning of the association between parental involvement and student achievement is not straight forward. It may be that parental involvement is a marker for parental enthusiasm and positive parenting style.

Being a boy reduces test scores by 3 points to 48

Base test score for reference group	51
Student-level characteristics	**Change in base test score**
Sex (male)	-3
English is the student's second language	-3
French immersion	0
No computer at home	-3
Less than 100 books at home	-3
Language other than English spoken at home	-1
Parents not actively or somewhat involved with school	-1
Class-level characteristics	
Teacher characteristics	
More than 10 years teaching experience	1
Comfortable with curriculum	1
Teaching practice[1]	1
Class environment	
Average number of Grade 3 students in class[2]	-1
Limited access to computer in class	0
No access to computer in class	0
School-level characteristics	
School environment	
Small school – less than 230 students	0
Large school – more than 471 students	0
School neighbourhood	
Rural[3]	-2
% of population with less than high school[4]	-1
Less than 0.6% of population are recent immigrants[5]	-1
More than 8.2% of population are recent immigrants[5]	3
Median income[6]	1

Notes
1. Change in student achievement when teachers followed the curriculum more closely by on standard deviation.
2. Change in student achievement when eight more Grade 3 students are added.
3. Rural schools include those in towns, villages and other populated places with less than 1,000 population, and rural fringes of census metropolitan areas and census agglomerations that may contain estate lots and agricultural or undeveloped land with a population density of less than 400 people per square kilometre.
4. Change in student achievement when the percentage of the population with less than high school graduation increases by 13 points.
5. Recent immigrants are those who entered Canada between 1991 and 1996.
6. Change in student achievement when median school neighbourhood income is increased by $10,000.
Sources: Education Quality and Accountability Office, 1996-97; and Statistics Canada, Census of Population, 1996.

Over half of Grade 3 students had parents involved with their school

	Sample size	%
Student-level characteristics	**115,712**	
Sex (female)		50
English is the student's second language		5
French immersion		4
Computer at home		54
More than 100 books at home		59
Language other than English spoken at home		24
Home language not reported		2
Parental involvement with school (actively or somewhat involved)		51
Class-level characteristics	**6,929**	
Teacher characteristics		
10 years or less teaching experience		63
Not comfortable with curriculum		25
Teaching practice (score)[1]		0†
Class environment		
Average number of Grade 3 students in class		17†
Split-grade with Grade 2		22
Split-grade with Grade 4		22
Other split grade		3
Limited access to computer in class		69
No access to computer in class		2
School-level characteristics	**3,285**	
School environment		
Public		69
Small school: less than 230 students		24
Large school: more than 471 students		25
School neighbourhood		
Urban		83
Population with less than high school graduation		31
Less than 0.6% of population are recent immigrants[2]		24
More than 8.2% of population are recent immigrants[2]		25
Median age under 33		23
Median age over 37		21
Median income ($ 000)		42.5†

Notes

† Numbers are not percentages

1. Teaching practice was a standardized measure of 68 items with mean 0 and standard deviation 1, representing how closely the teacher followed the suggested curriculum. The teaching practice scores ranged from -3.02 to 5.87.

2. Recent immigrants are those who entered Canada between 1991 and 1996.

Sources: Education Quality and Accountability Office, 1996-97 and Statistics Canada, Census of Population, 1996.

Students at urban schools and higher income neighbourhoods achieved higher scores

The location of a school and the socio-economic profile of its neighbourhood were also linked to student achievement on the tests. Students from rural schools scored 2 points lower than those from urban schools. This contrasts starkly with U.S. research showing that elementary students in urban schools perform below their non-urban counterparts, even after accounting for the higher concentration of low-income students in urban U.S. schools.[11] As expected though, students attending schools located in neighbourhoods with affluent and well-educated populations out performed those in less-advantaged neighbourhoods. A $10,000 increase in the neighbourhood median household income is associated with a 1-point increase in student scores. Also, after accounting for other characteristics, students living in a school neighbourhood with a high proportion of recent immigrants performed 3 points better than those who did not. Other studies have found that immigrant students perform as well as or better than native-born students.[12]

> The influences of schools and neighbourhoods on child performance are particularly important from a policy perspective because they are amenable to change through policy intervention.

Student characteristics account for two-thirds of variation in test scores

The variation in students' achievements may be attributed to a number of factors, such as student characteristics (67% of the variation), classroom environment (20%), and school environment or neighbourhood (13%).[13]

While factors that students "bring to the classroom" (i.e. their natural academic ability, their motivation) can explain the bulk of student achievement, a surprisingly large amount of variation was attributable to types of classes and schools. Variation at these levels was similar to that found in American studies, yet the popular perception is that Canada probably has smaller differences in school environments than the United States.[14]

Summary

Girls, students with computers and books at home, and students whose first language was English out performed their peers. Other important characteristics affecting test scores were not examined and may help to explain variations in test scores. These factors include students' past achievement, parents'/guardians' education levels, and students' use of cognitive resources in the home.

Tangible and intangible community resources can also have an effect.[15] Students from urban schools, in school neighbourhoods with high incomes and with many recent immigrants scored higher on the Grade 3 achievement tests after accounting for other factors in the model. The influences of schools and neighbourhoods on child performance are particularly important from a policy perspective because they are amenable to change through policy intervention.

Families and neighbourhoods can influence how well Grade 3 students perform in school. However, factors such as socio-economic status represent only one dimension of influence on achievement. General family functioning, parents' involvement with school-related issues, and strength of social ties among neighbourhood residents are not examined in this article and may be the subject of future research. ◖◗

Stéphane Tremblay is a senior analyst with Health Analysis and Measurement Group, Statistics Canada, Nancy Ross is an Assistant Professor in the Department of Geography at McGill University and an Associate of Health Analysis and Measurement Group, and Jean-Marie Berthelot is a manager with Health Analysis and Measurement Group, Statistics Canada.

This article is adapted from "Factors affecting Grade 3 student performance in Ontario: A multilevel analysis." Education Quarterly Review, Statistics Canada Catalogue no. 81-003, Vol. 7, no. 4, 2001 and was originally published in Canadian Social Trends, Summer 2002.

Notes

[1] Ryan, B. A. and G.R. Adams. 1999. "How do families affect children's success in school?" Education Quarterly Review (Statistics Canada Catalogue no. 81-003) 6, 1: 30–43; Sun, Y. 1999. "The contextual effects of community social capital on academic performance." Social Science Research 28: 403–426; Valenzuela, A. and S.M. Dornbusch. 1994. "Familism and social capital in the academic achievement of Mexican origin and Anglo adolescents." Social Science Quarterly 75, 1: 18–36.

[2] Willms, D. 1992. Monitoring School Per-formance: A Guide for Educators. Washington, D.C.: The Falmer Press.

[3] The reference group is defined as the group with the most prevalent charac-teristics. If the factor is continuous then the characteristic used to form the ref-erence group is the average. Otherwise, the mode (most common category of a factor) is the characteristic used to form the reference group. One exception to this rule involved girls, who represented a minority (49.7%) of the Grade 3 class but were defined as the reference characteris-tic in the model.

[4] Connolly, J. A., V. Hatchette and L. E. McMaster. 1999. "Academic achieve-ment in early adolescence: Do school attitudes make a difference?" Educa-tion Quarterly Review (Statistics Canada Catalogue no. 81-003) 6, 1: 20–29;Willms, D. 1996. "Indicators of mathematics achievement in Canadian elementary schools." Growing Up in Canada. (Statistics Canada Catalogue no. 89-550-MPE96001.) In national assessments of 9-year-olds in the United States, girls scored consistently higher in reading than did boys, but there was no significant difference between the sexes for mathematics. Federal Interagency Forum on Child and Family Statistics.1998. America's Children: Key National Indicators of Well-Being. Washington D.C.: U.S. Government Printing Office.

[5] Zellman, G. L. and J.M. Waterman.1998. "Understanding the impact of parent–school involvement on children's educational outcomes." The Journal of Educational Research 91:370–380; Brody, G.H., Z. Stoneman and D. Flor. 1995. "Linking family processes and academic competence among rural African-American youths." Journal of Marriage and the Family 57: 567–579.

[6] Zellman and Waterman. op. cit.

[7] Alexander, K.L. 1997. "Public schools and the public good." Social Forces 76,1: 1–30; Ravitch, D. 1999. "Student performance." Brookings Review. Win-ter:12–16.

[8] Class size was shown to have a large influence on achievement for children in the early grades: Finn, J. D. and C. M. Achilles. 1990. "Answers and questions about class size: a statewide experiment." American Educational Research Journal 27: 557–575; Mosteller, F. 1995."The Tennessee study of class size in the early school grades." Critical Issues for Children and Youths 5: 113–127.Others argue that there is no class size effect: Akerhielm, K. 1995. "Does class size matter?" Economics of Education Review 14: 229–241; Hanushek, E. A. and S.G. Rivkin, 1996. Understanding the 20th Century Growth in U.S. School Spending. National Bureau of Economic Research (NBER). Working Paper #5547NBER. Washington, D.C.

[9] Finn, J. D. and C. M. Achilles. 1999. "Tennessee's class size study: Findings, implications, misconceptions." Education Evaluation and Policy Analysis 21,2: 97–109.

[10] Johnson, K. A. , Ph.D. 2000. Do computers in the classroom boost academic achievement? A report of the Heritage Center for Data Analysis. www.heritage.org/library/cda/cda00-08.html. (Accessed August 13, 2001).

[11] U.S. Department of Education, National Center for Education Statistics. 1996.Urban Schools: The Challenge of Location and Poverty. Washington, D.C.

[12] Gibson, M. A. 1987. "The school performance of immigrant minorities: A comparative view." Anthropology and Education Quarterly 18, 4: 262–275.Ogbu, J.U. 1983. "Minority status and schooling in plural societies." Comparative Education Review 27, 2: 168–190.

[13] Variation accounted for by this model is in the typical range for this type of analysis. Gray, J. 1989. "Multilevel models: Issues and problems emerging from their recent application in British studies of school effectiveness." Multi-level Analysis of Educational Data. R. D. Bock (ed.). San Diego: Academic Press. p. 127-142; Organisation for Economic Co-operation and Development (OECD).1998. Education at a Glance: OECD Indicators 1998. France: Centre for Educational Research and Innovation.

[14] Ibid.

[15] Brooks-Gunn, J., P. Duncan, P.K. Klebanovand N. Sealand. 1993. "Do neighbourhoods influence child and adolescent development?" American Journal of Sociology 99, 2: 353–395;Kohen, D. E., C. Hertzman and J. Brooks-Gunn.1999. "Neighbourhood affluence and school readiness." Education Quarterly Review (Statistics Canada Catalogue no. 81-003) 6, 1: 44–52. Levanthal, T. and J. Brooks-Gunn. 2000."The neighbourhoods they live in: the effects of neighbourhood residence of child and adolescent outcomes." Psychological Bulletin 126, 2: 309–337.

The Ontario Grade 10 literacy test and the neo-conservative agenda

by Peter Lipman

N eo-conservativism arrived in Ontario in June 1995 with the election of a Tory government. An important part of their agenda was the restructuring of the public school system. Predictably, the result of a blizzard of heavy-handed "reforms" was that, by 2001, 59% of the public believed the province's public education system had deteriorated compared with 29% who believed it had improved.

Education Minister John Snobelen declared in July of 1995 that the Mike Harris Tories would "invent a crisis" in public education. They did this by amalgamating school boards, stripping their autonomy, and ridiculing the "educrats" who ran them. They slashed funding to public education by over $2 billion annually—a figure confirmed by Mordechai Rozanski in his Education Equality Task Force Report in December 2002.

In the name of "putting students first," they bashed teachers, educational workers and their union "bosses" and forced high school teachers to teach more classes while implementing a newly imposed curriculum without resources or training. Resources for special education, guidance, libraries, support staff, and professional development were cut. School administrators were forced out of their unions.

By 2001, having successfully created their crisis, the Tories offered generous tax credit incentives for parents to "go private" in the province's unregulated private schools.

Virtually every teacher and educational worker in the province walked off the job for two weeks in the fall of 1997 to protest the politically motivated agenda to undermine public education and harm students. By late 2002, a series of studies confirmed that the educators were right. The system had been starved financially, student achievement had not improved, a "harsh environment" for students was created, and the system lacked "spirit and energy." In one study, 88% of teachers said they were less likely to recommend their own children go into teaching.

Part of this deliberate destabilizing agenda was a complete overhaul of the elementary and secondary school curriculum and student assessment—without the resources or training to implement it. The American obsession with standardized testing was part of this neo-conservative agenda. The most pernicious component was the Ontario Secondary School Literacy Test (OSSLT).

In 1996, the Ontario Tories launched a consultation process, much of it non-negotiable, about high school reform. The plan was to reduce high school to four years, introduce an entirely new curriculum, more compulsory credits, dramatically cut the time for English courses, and allow students to create their own credits in the workplace—dismissed by the Ontario Secondary School Teachers' Federation (OSSTF) as "McCredits." There would be a rigid new system of streaming students, and, to a large extent, an effort to turn our high schools into job training centres.

Students had to pass both reading and writing components in order to achieve a passing grade. That grade was not established before the test was written.

Thousands of detailed written responses were submitted by an alarmed public. Some of the extreme reforms were dropped, but the Tories stubbornly maintained the neo-conservative focus on standardized testing despite widespread public opposition.

The firm Praxis tabulated 28,000 responses from the public in *What People Said About High School Reform (July 1997)*. It noted that the government did not even seek public input about its plan to implement a Grade 11 literacy test. Large numbers of respondents commented, anyway.

Almost all were opposed. It would be "extremely costly, time consuming, and of uncertain benefit to students." Specific opposition came from parents and educators of English As a Second Language and from exceptional students. There was general alarm about the misuse of the test results to rank schools, boards and teachers—another hobby horse of the neo-con movement.

But the concept of a credentialing graduation exam was too close to the hearts of neo-conservatives to be abandoned.

OSSTF and others argued that, if there must be a test, it should be diagnostic in nature "to ensure that appropriate remedial programs can be provided (for students) prior to graduation."

But when the government finally released its reform program in January 1998, the literacy test was moved to Grade 10, and was a mandatory graduation requirement. Students who were successful in all their course credits would not graduate without passing the literacy test.

This was particularly bizarre in that the government was advocating a more progressive assessment procedure, indicating that assessment should improve student learning, be fair to all students, and require even greater professional judgement on the part of educators. The decision to maintain the Grade 10 literacy test, then, was a purely political decision which ran counter to the government's own stated assessment philosophy.

But no details were available. What would be the standards and expectations? What would be the passing grade? What accommodations would be in place for exceptional students? How would students receive remedial assistance from boards which had no funding for it? How would ESL students cope with the test? How could there be one standard test when students were studying curriculum in several different streams?

All the questions were tossed to the Education Quality and Accountability Office (EQAO), an arms-length agency which believes the use of its test results to rank schools is misleading and inappropriate. But the "arms" were short—the EQAO was handed the parameters by the government. Students had to pass both reading and writing components in order to achieve a passing grade. That grade was not established before the test was written.

Only after intense lobbying from parents, boards and unions did the government agree to make the first administration in October 2000 a trial run so that it would not be a graduation requirement for the students who were guinea pigs for the government's rushed changes.

It was a five-hour test of reading and writing skills held over two days. Teachers signed a confidentiality agreement and could not help students in any way with the test. The test did not have a marking scheme for students to follow. All students wrote the same test, no matter what curriculum they were studying, whether they were ESL or special needs students, or had failed Grade 9.

Most objectionable, however, was the Tories' decision to prevent students from graduating because of a single test. According to U.S. expert Alfie Kohn, virtually all relevant experts and organizations condemn the practice of basing graduation or promotion on the results of a single test. A poll by Public Agenda in the U.S. in late 2000 found that 78% of parents believe standardized tests should be used in conjunction with teacher evaluation in making promotion decisions. But parents aren't making the decisions.

Cynics say the Tories' real non-conservative intent was to prevent large numbers of students from graduating, have them take a certificate at the end of Grade 10 and leave school. Costs are reduced. A pool of unskilled, cheap labour is available. As Doug Little's research in the Toronto Board made clear, those students will largely be from socio-economically disadvantaged areas.

The passing grade was probably lower as well, but the EQAO method of establishing the pass rate caused so much confusion that no one was sure.

Critics expressed a number of concerns following the October 2000 administration: the correlation of the first results to student socio-economic status; the government's leak of the results to prevent the EQAO from explaining the difficulties at a press conference; the fact that the passing grade was set at over 60% after the test was written (only 50% is required for any high school credit); the tests, which determine student graduation, were often marked by those with no teacher training; feedback to students was vague and unhelpful (students who passed got nothing back).

The first administration of the test to count was sabotaged in October 2001 when students posted it on a web site. The cost: $7 million.

It was estimated that, even if 15% of students failed (about the number who previously took their courses at the "basic" level), then approximately 20,000 students would be denied a diploma until they can pass the test. Even if 5% of students are absent on either day of the five-hour test, this adds another 7,000 students who must rewrite it. So, by the end of 2001, about 30,000 Ontario students would be denied a diploma.

This was an underestimate. Given the number of deferrals, failures and absentees, over 43,000 Grade 10 students became ineligible for a diploma when the first administration was completed in February 2002.

The results are tragic. Most shocking, however, was the response and spin put on these disastrous results by the government and by school boards. When only 61% of the students passed the field test, the government leaked the results and said the results were "a wake-up call" and "unacceptable."

Remarkably, when the results were marginally better on the first real test, the government was "pleased" and "excited" with the results and credited its new curriculum for the improvement, even though 32,000 students failed and another 12,000 did not write the test. Of course, an election was nearing and, having created a catastrophe, Mike Harris left the building and John Snobelen was roping cattle in Oklahoma.

Many school boards bought into the government's agenda and congratulated themselves if their results improved—even if huge numbers of their most vulnerable students were now going to be denied a diploma. One board was "cautiously elated" even though only 66% passed compared with a miserable 58% the year before. Another board was "celebrating" the outcome, even though in one school 56% of the students failed.

But now the province is spending $15 million simply to identify students who need remedial help (and millions more to create the new course in a matter of months) when the results of Grade 3 and 6 tests show which students needed assistance.

The provincial improvement of 8% pass rate was a travesty given that students knew the test would count and tried hard, and many schools had been drilling students on sample questions. The passing grade was probably lower as well, but the EQAO method of establishing the pass rate caused so much confusion that no one was sure.

OSSTF President Earl Manners said the failure rate was unacceptable and the test "seems designed to fail students and kick them out of school, rather than identify student needs and provide them with the resources for success."

Results showed that almost 90% of students studying at the academic level passed, compared with 44% of students studying the new "Applied" curriculum. For ESL students the failure rate was 63%. This, coupled with what government researcher Alan King called "disastrous" failure rates in Applied courses, will no doubt lead to many dropouts.

The EQAO and the government cancelled the planned second writing each April for students who had failed—due to costs.

With an election looming, and estimates that, after the 2002 results are released, 50-70,000 students will be ineligible for a diploma, the government finally admitted the neo-con agenda had to be abandoned and agreed that students who fail can take a remedial course in Grade 12 and still graduate. This will help thousands of students, but now the province is spending $15 million simply to identify students who need remedial help (and millions more to create the new course in a matter of months) when the results of Grade 3 and 6 tests show which students needed assistance.

Ontario now has a $15-million a year literacy test, Grade 3 and 6 tests which cost $6 million each, and a census Grade 9 math test which costs another $6 million. So the neo-con agenda now has the province spending about $33 million annually on testing, plus the costs of running the EQAO—the entire cost is estimated at $59 million annually—at a time when students lack textbooks and learning materials in classrooms, and the public system has been starved financially since 1996. A plan to introduce testing in subjects in every grade has, fortunately, been postponed.

There is, of course, no evidence that any of the provincial testing will actually improve student achievement. Meanwhile, because of the lack of a business plan, the government has not provided funding for enough textbooks to match the new curriculum, and is downloading the costs of its teacher recertification scheme to the teachers themselves.

But that is beside the point to neo-cons. It is more important to implement dogma than to actually provide the supports for student success. ❧

Peter Lipman is an Executive Assistant with the Ontario Secondary School Teachers' Federation.

Winners

In celebration of the Alberta achievement exams

by Jackie Seidel

They failed the test
Bottom of the heap
Junk on the scrap pile
Good for nothings
The newspapers said so
Who was best
Who was worst
Winners against losers
Must be those new-age, new-fangled teaching methods
Must be those bad awful kids
Must be someone's fault
Must be a reason
The government said so
Better test them more
Better test them lots
Get those results up up up
Maybe drill them harder
Maybe give more homework
Rows and Discipline! that'll work
Counting, counting, accountable teachers
Special guarantee:
Failures given repeat chances to fail again.
More tests! More fails! More wins! Hurrah!
Everyone in their places.

Jackie Seidel is a Ph.D. candidate in the Department of Secondary Education at the University of Alberta. Her interests include teacher education, language, ecology, and curriculum. She formerly taught with Calgary Public Schools.

Alberta Learning Achievement Testing Program

Alberta teachers express their opinions on achievement testing

by Charles Hyman

Each year the Alberta Teachers' Association (ATA) conducts a Member Opinion Survey. In 2001, the survey asked teachers for their impressions of the Alberta achievement tests. A total of 1,252 ATA members completed and returned surveys. A total of 34% of respondents to the survey reported a teaching assignment that included achievement testing. Of these, 12% taught Grade 3, 11% taught Grade 6 and 14% of respondents taught Grade 9.

What is the impact of achievement tests?

Teachers feel there is some negative impact of achievement tests on their approaches to teaching and little impact on the diagnosis of student needs, although teachers are divided in their opinion. Some teachers report a somewhat positive impact (20%) and others (20%) report a somewhat negative impact on the design of individual programs and decisions about instructional programming.

These opinions are the same as those found in the 1997 survey, in which similar questions were asked.

Tests should be changed

The majority of teachers indicated that a testing program is a reasonable idea but that it should be adjusted. The strongest push for abandoning the tests is at the Grade 3 level. When asked whether the tests should be abandoned or changed in specific ways, members said that the Grade 3 tests should be abandoned or replaced with diagnostic tests; that Grade 6 tests should be administered to samples or replaced with diagnostic tests; and that Grade 9 tests should be administered to samples, replaced with diagnostic tests or continued as is.

Although this question was worded slightly differently, the responses to the 1997 survey suggest that opinions have not changed much over time and are, if anything, more firmly held today.

Teaching Grades 3, 6, or 9

Some members have been asked to teach Grades 3, 6 or 9, and some have purposefully avoided Grades 3, 6 or 9 assignments.

- 33% of respondents have requested a grade assignment other than 3, 6 or 9; women are more likely to make this request than are men.
- 17% of respondents who answered the question were asked to teach Grades 3, 6 or 9.
- 11% of respondents who answered the question were pressured to take Grades other than 3, 6 or 9.

Have school programs suffered cutbacks to meet achievement test requirements?

A total of 50% of respondents do not feel that achievement tests have caused schools to cut back on other subjects. However, 25% feel that the testing program has influenced such cutbacks. This suggests that cutbacks do happen in certain circumstances. While those circumstances are not addressed directly in this survey, written responses suggest that principals and professional staff can significantly influence the approach taken.

We need tests to make teachers accountable!

Chill, mom. That's what principals, superintendents, locally elected school boards and departments of education do.

What teachers had to say about achievement tests

Members provided written comments regarding achievement tests. Responses to this write-in portion show the intensity of feelings that teachers have for achievement tests. Among the returned questionnaires 43% contained written comments.

When read with the responses to other questions about achievement tests, it is clear that the issue was given reasoned consideration. Respondents are not simply reacting to the issue but have thought about the best course of action from a professional perspective that puts the quality of education first.

The major conclusions of these written responses are that achievement tests are stressful for students and teachers, and that achievement tests, as currently structured at the Grade 3 level, are abusive and of little educational value.

A total of 2% of the comments state unequivocal opposition to the tests. Almost an equal number favour the tests. By far, the majority of

What teachers have written about achievement testing

"I am proud to be a male primary teacher. As a longtime Grade 3 teacher, I recall fighting and yelling that it is immoral to test Grade 3 students so rigorously. I've always maintained that it puts extreme pressure on seven-and eight-year-olds, even when the teacher tries to downplay the tests. What is to be served by testing Grade 3 students in this way? I want to cry each June when that pile of tests comes into the school, and I have to subject nearly all my students to these tests (as exemptions are difficult). I'm sick of being a statistic for the government. Testing Grade 6s at the end of elementary provides enough data for the counters. Leave my Grade 3s alone!"

"I teach a class of 25 students in a Grade 8/9 split. My biggest problem with achievement tests is that I am having an extremely difficult time getting my three special needs students exempted from the tests. They are not even studying the same courses as the regular Grade 9s. This is absolutely ridiculous! Another issue I have is that the tests are always targeted to the same grade. Perhaps they should rotate or pick random grades each year. I strongly believe that teachers, students and parents should be held accountable, but I am not sure achievement tests are a reasonable and accurate way of doing this."

comments are that the tests need more thought and need to be adjusted to meet the realities of today's classrooms.

Testing creates stress

More than a quarter of the comments relate to unusual stress for teachers, students, parents and administrators created by the testing program. A particularly heavy emphasis is placed on the inappropriateness of the tests for Grade 3 students.

Testing is inappropriate/problematic

A total of 39% of the comments suggest that the tests do not appropriately assess actual learning. Some teachers say that the tests assess reading and writing rather than subject content, or indicators of students' test-taking abilities. A number of people say they believe that the tests are politically motivated. Some complained that the administration of the tests is not consistent.

These comments include statements that the test results for specific classrooms can be skewed because of the inclusion of special needs students and because of difficulties encountered in applying for and receiving exemptions. Others mention concerns about the increased competition between schools resulting from publishing test results and inappropriate interpretations of test results. Teachers expressed concerns that high-needs schools can be at a disadvantage.

Teaching to the test

A total of 16% of the comments state that some critical aspects of the curriculum have been missed. They use the words "teach to the test," in other words, innovative and teacher-driven approaches to learning and teaching have been reduced.

Negative impact of tests

Another 8% of the comments state that the tests have negative impacts on students and teachers. These comments are particularly strong when it comes to special needs students and Grade 3 students. Words used to describe the test include "cruel," "destructive," "misused," "abusive," "immoral" and "extreme." ❧

Charles Hyman is the former ATA Executive Secretary.

This article was originally published in ATA Magazine, V 82, # 1, Sept 27, 2001. It has been slightly edited for length.

The Perils of Testing

by Margaret Stewart

R ecently I was asked to provide some information on standardized tests, with a view to explaining why so many educators
and teacher organizations are so opposed to this particular mode
of evaluating student learning and school success.

While I am no expert on this subject, I have done a good deal of
reading in the area, and have attended a couple of assessment and evaluation conferences. While proponents claim these tests increase accountability (of teachers, schools, systems), I have found virtually no philosophical support for them, a multitude of articles in opposition to them,
and a good deal of material designed and marketed to help teachers and
students prepare for them. There are several issues to consider:

1. The nature of the test

A standardized test is one that is given and scored in the same way, no
matter where or when it is given, so that scores of all students can be
compared, one against the other. Often the format is multiple choice,
so that they can be machine scored. Of these, norm-referenced tests are
used to evaluate the performance of one student in relation to the performance of others, or to compare individuals to a "norm". They are
designed so that results fit a "bell curve", with most in the middle, and a
few at the high and at the low end. (Questions are chosen on the basis of
how they contribute to spreading out the scores—those answered correctly 50% of the time).

Criterion referenced tests, on the other hand, are supposed to measure how well an individual has learned a specific body of knowledge or
set of skills, or how well a student has learned what is taught in a specific

course or grade. The passing or acceptable level of performance is often set by a panel of "experts", which might include teachers, members of the business community, etc. Tests are described as "high stakes" when the results are used to make decisions about placement, retention, graduation, etc. It is these high-stakes tests that have been most criticized by educators and teachers groups across the country, and indeed around the world.

In *Standardized Testing: Undermining Equity in Education*[1], Bernie Froese-Germain argues that while standardized tests may be useful in the sorting and ranking of students, they do not effectively measure student learning or development. The following are among the most common arguments (parentheses mine):

- While tests can be standardized, students can not. Without considering the characteristics of the students being tested, results may be misleading or misinterpreted.
- Many types of student ability which are clearly among the goals of education are not captured by standardized tests. Examples include sense of citizenship, ethics, aesthetic appreciation, respect for others, self-esteem, social competence, and intellectual curiosity. The reality of multiple intelligences is largely discounted.
- Tests which are to be used for a large number of students must be very general, which leads to frequent mismatches between test questions and curriculum—or what is taught and what is tested. (SAIP[2] tests are administered to a random sample of over 35,000 thirteen and sixteen year olds across Canada. PISA[3] involved 265,000 students in 32 countries). An international math and science assessment in 1996 (TIMSS) [4] reported test-curriculum matches ranging from 53% in one province to 98% in another.
- Standardized tests tend to measure what is easy to measure (lower-order recall), and penalize higher-order thinking—analyzing, synthesizing, forming hypotheses, and problem solving. (For example, there might be three logical answers to a multiple choice question, but only one will be marked right because there is no opportunity to explain one's answer).

2. How the results are used

While many are concerned with the nature of the tests, the greater concern is often with how the results are used. Standardized test results across the United States, and increasingly across Canada, are being used to place, retain, and track students; and to compare and rank students, teachers, schools, and school boards.

In Nova Scotia and New Brunswick, provincial exams in a number of Grade 11 and 12 courses account for 30% of the student's final mark. The Fraser Institute has used test results in Alberta and Ontario to produce and publish "report cards" which compare results and then rank schools throughout the province—currently an impossibility in PEI, which does not administer provincial exams. "Report Card 98", released publicly by the N.B. Department of Education Evaluation Branch, gave provincial exam results for each school and district in the province.

In the United States, results are regularly used to inform decision making about funding levels, with higher performing schools being rewarded with increased funding, and lower performing schools losing funding; and to select teachers for rewards such as enhanced salaries for high or improved test results.

While proponents claim these tests increase accountability, I have found virtually no philosophical support for them, a multitude of articles in opposition to them, and a good deal of material designed and marketed to help teachers and students prepare for them.

3. Negative impact on teaching and learning

Most opponents of standardized testing maintain that while results say little about the quality of teaching or learning, there are a number of ways in which their use may impact negatively on both. For example:

- In an attempt to raise test scores, teachers may teach to the test, and curriculum may become test driven. (At a recent meeting, I spoke to teachers from other provinces who admitted doing just that—even though they had previously thought they never would. Alberta publishes old achievement tests on the government website so that teachers and students may use them to get ready for the next round.)

- The curriculum may be narrowed, in order to make what is taught match more closely what is tested, and subjects which are not routinely tested may be relegated to second-class status. (Larry Booi, President of the Alberta Teachers' Association, in an interview with *Today's Parent*, expressed this very concern. "Fine arts, languages, practical arts, all these other areas—physical education, health— none of them factor into the schools' rankings, and so we've seen the deterioration of those programs because everyone's obsessed about what their school gets ranked on."[5])

- Methodologies which are meant to promote critical thinking, problem solving, analysis, hypothesizing, and synthesizing may give way to an emphasis on recall of facts and rote learning.

- Test preparation and administration take up valuable time which could be used for instruction. (The Grade 6 Language Arts Assessment in Newfoundland is administered over nine days: three days for the first component and 60-90 minute blocks each day for the next six).

- In extreme cases reported in the U.S., because jobs, reputations, schools, etc, are on the line, students have been encouraged to cheat, and/or results are doctored to make a school look better than it is.

4. Resource allocation

With parents and teachers in most jurisdictions feeling that education is underfunded, many are concerned that money spent on external exams, and standardized tests is necessarily money which is not spent on staffing, resource materials, teacher in-service and professional development. And there are large sums of money involved. For example, in June, 2001, the Ontario Ministry of Education estimated that a new, expanded testing program would cost $16,000,000 annually, in addition to $33,000,000 already spent on testing in Grades 3, 6, 9, and 10.

The last provincial exams were written in PEI in 1969. We have not administered any standardized test to all students at any grade level since we discontinued use of the Canadian Test of Basic Skills in 1991. A cursory look at the documentation around the elimination of both of these programs will show that they were dropped for many of the reasons that educators currently oppose standardized tests.

While the Canadian Teachers' Federation and its member organizations have expressed some concerns about SAIP and the interpretation of the results, PEI, along with most provinces and territories, has participated in this program, and in PISA. These tests have a multiple-choice component, but are not solely in this format. They are criterion-referenced tests, are administered to samples of students only, and are not high stakes. For these reasons, they are perceived as being more palatable than others.

There are some indications that there is a backlash beginning against standardized tests as a means of assessing teaching and learning, and a move toward what is generally called "authentic" or "performance-based" assessment. In PEI we are already there! By continuing to work with teachers to hone their assessment/evaluation skills, and working to ensure that assessment is closely linked to learning, as it should be, we can continue to lead the class!! [6] ◑◐

Margaret Stewart is the President of the Prince Edward Island Teachers' Federation.

A version of this article originally appeared in the PEITF Newsletter, June 2002.

Notes

[1] Froese-Germain, Bernie. *Standardized Testing: Undermining Equity in Education.* Canadian Teachers' Federation, 1999.

[2] SAIP—Student Achievement Indicators Program—a project of the Council of Ministers of Education Canada (CMEC).

[3] PISA—Program for International Student Assessment—a project of the Organisation for Economic Co-operation and Development (OECD). Co-ordinated in Canada by Human Resources Development Canada (HRDC), Council of Ministers of Education Canada (CMEC), Statistics Canada, and provincial ministries and departments of education.

[4] TIMSS—Third International Mathematics and Science Study—conducted under the auspices of the International Association for the Evaluation of Educational Achievement (IEA).

[5] Waytiuk, Judy and Steve Brearton. "Making the grade; Your child's success in school may depend on where you live." *Today's Parent*, September 2002. p.60.

[6] For those who would like more information on this topic, there is an abundance of material available. Look at several issues of almost any recently published educational journal and you are likely to find a number of articles. Check out the Fair Test site on the web (www.fairtest.org) as well as the Canadian Centre for Policy Alternatives (www.policyalternatives.ca) and the Canadian Teachers' Federation (www.ctf-fce.ca); read almost anything by Alfie Kohn (much of it online).

Coming to a school near you
Fraser Institute rankings of Canadian high schools

by Bernie Froese-Germain

T he Vancouver-based Fraser Institute is described by the British Columbia Teachers' Federation (BCTF) as a "right-wing think-tank, financed by business, which was established to undermine public support for public programs. The Fraser Institute budgets $250,000 annually to publishing research designed to influence Canadians to privatize education."[1] An example of such research is an Institute report entitled *The Case for School Choice: Models from the United States, New Zealand, Denmark, and Sweden.*[2] Ignoring the growing body of research on the negative impact of school choice on equity, the author concludes that "government schools" are failing and can only be saved through competitive market forces. In addition to charter schools and voucher programs, this translates into the ranking and publication of school assessment results to enable parents and students as 'education consumers' to make decisions in the education 'marketplace' regarding the best school 'product'.

Toward this end, the Fraser Institute has taken to publishing annual 'report cards' ranking secondary schools in B.C. since 1998 and in Alberta since 1999. The first annual report card on Quebec's high schools, co-published with the Montreal Economic Institute, received wide coverage in the media upon its release in October 2000. Similar report cards are planned for all provinces.

According to the Fraser Institute, the reports are designed to "measure [each school's academic] performance so that the schools will have an objective benchmark against which to improve"; enable parents and students to make "a more informed choice of an education provider"; and provide accountability for the expenditure of tax dollars for education. Exam results are a major component of the rankings.

In addition to being criticized by education ministers in B.C., Quebec and Alberta, the report cards have been roundly denounced by teacher organizations and other education stakeholder groups.

In B.C., key partner groups in the education community—representing school trustees, superintendents, district secretary treasurers, principals and vice-principals, and teachers—have challenged the report cards stating that "the simplistic rankings ... misinform the public about the complex and multi-faceted question of school performance and quality."[3] They effectively reduce education to preparation for, and performance on, provincial exams. A 1999 BCTF news release[4] notes that many of the rankings in the "pseudo-scientific study" are statistically insignificant and that "poverty is among the strongest predictors of student performance, yet the report ignores socio-economic status of school communities. It also fails to distinguish between private schools that select their students and public schools that serve all children, regardless of special needs." Amsden[5] remarks that the report cards reveal more about social status, personal financial success and neighbourhood property values than they do about school quality and effectiveness.

In Quebec, the Centrale des syndicats du Québec (CSQ) and the Fédération des syndicats de l'enseignement (FSE-CSQ) bluntly summed up the Quebec report as "an ideological project camouflaged with alleged scientific rigour." The president of the Quebec Federation of School Boards described it as, "Unproductive ... does no service to parents or students or staff .... How discouraging for people who are working their hearts out to help

Let's start with the good news. We need to pass one more student to keep our ratings up.

students from all kinds of backgrounds, in all kinds of conditions, to be told that they're 300th or 400th."[6]

Public comments by the Quebec report card's creators expose the underlying motivation for this initiative—to see the report cards used to fuel debate in Quebec about publicly-funded school vouchers. Michel Kelly-Gagnon, Executive Director of the Montreal Economic Institute, likens selecting a school to buying breakfast cereal: "You can choose a box of cereal because of the label and the advertising, but you don't have the same type of information when choosing a school .... You can't have school choice [including vouchers] without a rating system."[7] Responding to these and other comments, QPAT President Pierre Weber expressed strong opposition to the voucher idea and the use of school rankings to promote it.[8]

ATA President Larry Booi describes such rating exercises as "drive-by rankings", citing the following flaws in the Alberta report card:

- The basis of comparison for the rankings is extremely narrow and does not reflect society's expectations for the education of high school students. The rankings are based on a 10-point scale comprising five factors, all of which are derived only from diploma examination courses (1. Diploma exam marks, 2. Diploma exam failure rates, 3. Diploma completion rates, 4. Difference between school marks and diploma marks, 5. Diploma courses taken per student). All of the other courses in high school (second languages, fine arts, physical education, career and technology studies) are completely ignored.

- The five factors that make up the 10-point scale for the ranking are clearly inter-related and reinforce each other. A school that scores high on the first factor (diploma exam marks) will almost certainly score high on the second factor (that is, low diploma exam failure rates), as well as on the third factor (diploma completion rates). Positive results related to the factor of 'diploma courses taken per student' would also be expected in a high school with a strong emphasis on academic courses. Thus, while the rating is purportedly based on five factors, in reality it is based on five aspects of one factor—diploma examination courses.

- The rating system incorrectly suggests that the 222 [Alberta] schools mentioned in the report are in a 'fair competition,' which involves a 'level playing field.' It is not a competition and the playing field is most certainly not level.

- The rankings dramatically distort relatively small differences, with the result that some schools appear to perform far worse than they actually do.[9]

Booi concludes that:

> *Teachers agree that schools should be accountable to the public and that parents and others have the right to information about how well students are doing and how well schools are meeting students' needs. But these are complex questions that require a broad range of information about a considerable array of factors. Above all, there is a clear need to examine issues that go far beyond numbers related to diploma examinations. The Fraser Institute's rankings are an attempt to reduce complicated questions to simple numbers and to foster competition in the mistaken view that this "market method" will lead to school improvement. Rather than contributing to an informed discussion, their misguided approach leads to unfair criticism of schools and teachers, who instead should be supported in their crucial work in educating Alberta's youth.[10]*

This observation could apply equally to the other jurisdictions whose schools have been simplistically sorted and ranked in this manner. The Fraser Institute's ranking process does nothing to improve schooling and ultimately does more harm than good by undermining confidence in our public education system. ❧

Bernie Froese-Germain is a researcher with the Canadian Teachers' Federation.

Notes

[1] Flower, D. (2000, May 16). "What is the Fraser Institute?" [Editorial]. *ATA News*, 34(19), p. 2. Available online at: http://www.teachers.ab.ca/publications/news/_volume_34/v34n19/edit.html

[2] Hepburn, C. R. (1999, Sept.). *The Case for School Choice: Models from the United States, New Zealand, Denmark, and Sweden.* Vancouver, B.C.: Fraser Institute. Available online at: http://www.fraserinstitute.ca/publications/critical_issues/1999/school_choice/

[3] B.C. Teachers' Federation. (2000, Mar. 6). "Teachers caution parents not to rely upon Fraser Institute's rankings of B.C. schools." [News release] Vancouver, B.C. Available online at: http://www.bctf.bc.ca/Publications/NewsReleases/Archive/2000/2000-03-06.html

[4] B.C. Teachers' Federation. (1999, Mar. 25). "Teachers' concerns about ranking schools misunderstood, ignored by tabloid editors." [News release]

Vancouver, B.C. Available online at: http://www.bctf.bc.ca/Publications/NewsReleases/Archive/1999/1999-03-25.html

[5] Amsden, J. (1999, Mar.). "What colour are the collars in your neighbourhood? The Fraser Institute's ranking of schools." *Teacher Newsmagazine*, 11(5). Available online at: http://www.bctf.bc.ca/ezine/archive/1999-03/support/WhatColour.html

[6] "School ratings stir uproar." (2000, Oct. 28). *Montreal Gazette*, p. A1. Available online at: http://www.iedm.org/library/art49_en.html

[7] Lampert, A. (2000, Dec. 12). "Creators of school report card hope it spurs vouchers debate." *Montreal Gazette*, p. A3.

[8] Lampert, A. (2000, Dec. 13). "No place for vouchers here, teachers say." *Montreal Gazette*, p. A6.

[9] Booi, L. (2000, May 16). "More 'Drive-by Rankings' from the Fraser Institute." *ATA News*, 34(19), p. 3. Available online at: http://www.teachers.ab.ca/publications/news/_volume_34/v34n19/fraser.html

[10] ibid p. 3.

Additional background material

Alberta Teachers' Association. (1999, June 18). "School rankings by exam results invalid and misleading." [Media release] Edmonton, AB. Available online at: http://www.teachers.ab.ca/what/media/1999/media200.html

Centrale des syndicats du Québec. (2000, Oct. 27). "La CSQ et la FSE réagissent au lancement du bulletin des écoles secondaires du Québec de l'Institut économique de Montréal." [Communiqué de presse] Montréal, QC. Available online at: http://216.191.19.19/ceq/presse00/c001027.htm

Cowley, P., & Easton, S. (2000). *Second Annual Report Card on Alberta's High Schools*. Vancouver, B.C.: Fraser Institute. Available online at: http://www.fraserinstitute.ca/publications/studies/education/

Cowley, P., & Easton, S. (2000). *Third Annual Report Card on British Columbia's Secondary Schools*. Vancouver, B.C.: Fraser Institute. Available online at: http://www.fraserinstitute.ca/publications/studies/education/

Cowley, P., & Marceau, R. (2000). *Report Card on Quebec's Secondary Schools. 2000 Edition*. Vancouver, B.C.: Fraser Institute / Montreal Economic Institute. Available online at: http://www.fraserinstitute.ca/publications/studies/education/

Gaskell, J., & Vogel, D. (2000, Spring). "Encouraging cheating in BC: Fraser Institute's 'Report Card' flawed measure of school quality." *CCPA Education Monitor*, 4(2), p. 11.

Rotberg, I. C. (1998, June). "The trouble with ranking." *American School Board Journal*, 185(6), pp. 26-28.

Riding dead horses in Alberta

Contributed by Wayne Hampton, Principal,
Lacombe Upper Elementary (Grades 3 to 6),
Wolf Creek School Division No. 72, Alberta.

IN THE WEST, there's a fine old saying: "If the horse you're riding dies, get off!"

This advice continues to fall on deaf ears in Alberta government circles. Instead of getting off the horse, our government chooses from an array of alternatives to authentic school improvement which include:

- Buying a stronger whip.
- Trying a new bit or bridle.
- Switching riders.
- Moving the horse to a new location.
- Riding the horse for longer periods of time.
- Saying things like, *"This is the way we've always ridden this horse."*
- Appointing a committee to study the horse.
- Arranging to visit other sites where they ride dead horses more efficiently.
- Increasing the standards for riding dead horses.
- Creating a test for measuring our riding ability.
- Comparing how we're riding now with how we did ten or twenty years ago.
- Complaining about the state of horses these days.
- Coming up with new styles of riding.
- Blaming the horse's parents. The problem is often in the breeding.
- Tightening the cinch.
- Trying to resuscitate the horse.

And we continue to ride this dead horse in Alberta—all in the name of accountability.

An analysis of the Fraser Institute rankings of Ontario high schools

by Philip Nagy

On April 18, 2001, the Fraser Institute released a report ranking Ontario high schools on the basis of 1999 data obtained from the Ontario Ministry of Education and Training.[1],[2] The rankings were based on four criteria involving the subject choices and achievement of senior students:

- proportion of advanced[3] courses taken,
- proportion of courses passed,
- average number of core courses taken (mathematics, language arts, basic sciences), and
- the gender gap in average grade in mathematics and first language.

The method of ranking can be criticized both conceptually and empirically. Conceptually, the rankings are based on a narrow set of values concerning what is important about a child's education, along with a misapplication of basic conceptions of gender equity. Empirically, the rankings capitalize on small differences, and, through the weighting system used, give unjustified importance to some of the criteria. The report, written from a particularly narrow value system, is seriously flawed and damaging to education. It should play no role in judging the quality of schools.

Conceptual problems with the criteria

Proportion of Advanced Courses Taken. The Fraser Institute offers the argument that schools should encourage students to take the most difficult courses of which they are capable, and not let students take unchallenging courses. While this seems reasonable at first glance, it has serious flaws. Society is not well served if all students take academic university-bound courses. The skills taught in vocational programs, from auto repair to data processing, are essential to society. To penalize a school for offering such courses is inappropriate.

In addition, not all students are capable of passing university-bound courses. A school's reputation should not suffer because it serves the needs of such students. Do these schools have laissez-faire expectations of their students? We don't know. A system that labels a school as poor quality because of the clientele it serves is misleading.

There undoubtedly exists a group of students who find lower-level courses too easy, and who should be encouraged to attempt more advanced material. However, proportions of enrolment are invalid indicators of the extent to which a school is being "encouraging." Some schools simply do not offer non-academic courses. Being unable to accept a student into your school is not "encouraging." This criterion also ignores the realities of school organization. Facilities for vocational programs are expensive to build and operate. School district officials do not locate them in every high school. They are built selectively, and buses are used to move students substantial distances so that they may take advantage of such facilities. To penalize a school because it has been selected as the regional home of such facilities is wrong. The schools that benefit the most from this criterion are those that simply do not have the facilities to serve a substantial proportion of the school population. Those schools that offer only an academic program, mostly private schools and selective academies within the public system, are able to refuse admission to students they cannot serve.

If the intent of this criterion is to measure encouragement to try more advanced work, then it is inaccurate. A school with 30% enrolment in advanced courses might be more encouraging of students than a school that simply does not serve those who are unequipped to handle the advanced stream.

I have not been able to locate recent data, but historically, more than 90% of students have limited their course selection to one stream or the other. In other words, only a few students see themselves as possibly on the cusp between general and advanced courses. This places the burden of improving a school's score on this criterion on a small number of students. Thus, this seems the criterion score most difficult to change.

Proportion of Courses Passed. The Fraser Institute argues that higher passing rates are an indication of the school's effectiveness in helping students complete their programs. The most obvious criticism of this position is that the schools can improve their standing by simply passing students who may not deserve to pass. No mention is made in the report of the fact that schools have complete control of their passing rate. The point can be raised that, with provincial exams, this criterion might be more meaningful. However, Ontario's experience with such exams before 1967 revealed a further problem. Schools could, and did, refuse to allow some students to complete their exams under the school's name. Society is not well served by discouraging borderline students from attempting courses they find difficult. This indicator is ill-advised and contradictory to their first indicator.

Mean Number of Core Courses Taken. The Fraser Institute argues that choosing courses from among mathematics, first language, and basic sciences will equip students more adequately for their post-secondary careers. This makes some sense at first glance, but there are a number of problems. The definition of *core* is far too narrow. It rewards schools for offering a narrow curriculum, and penalizes them for offering a rich curriculum. Penalties accrue for offering history, geography, French (in English schools), and physical education, all of which are compulsory at some level of the high school curriculum. It penalizes schools for offering the wide range of courses we have come to expect of schools, including music, vocational subjects and computer education. Some of these courses that draw a penalty under this criterion are, in fact, compulsory at younger grades. Do we require history and French in Grades 9 or 10, and penalize them in Grade 12? More than the first two criteria, this reveals a value system rewarding only those courses of study judged utilitarian from the narrow value-base of the Fraser Institute.

Recently, the Ontario government announced a capital expansion program for university facilities. Their program, revealing the same narrow perspective as the Fraser Institute, was directed only to facilities in engineering and science. Liberal arts institutions were not granted any expansion funds.[4] A group of university presidents *and* corporate executives issued a statement to the effect that, although the high technology industry is a major creator of employment, not all jobs created call for high technology skills. Industry and society need graduates with a broader background than these expansion plans imply. This criterion is a redefinition of the purpose of school, and a denial of our culture.

In addition, is there not a limit to the number of scientists and mathematicians society needs? Are not our needs broader? In the days following September 11, 2001, to whom did we turn for an explanation of our changed world? Not to mathematicians and scientists, but to historians, social scientists and ethicists.

Gender Gaps in Mathematics and Language. These criteria are based on the assumption that boys and girls should score equally well in these two courses, and that if they do not, it is because schools are unjustifiably rewarding girls for characteristics that are not part of the curriculum. These characteristics for which girls are rewarded appear to be such things as working hard, doing neat work, and being well-behaved. The authors cite their own investigation of British Columbia school grades, where they found that girls do better on school-awarded marks than on marks from external exams. This is certainly true. This phenomenon is well documented in the literature, but the interpretation offered there is completely different. Rather than arguing that teachers reward girls unfairly, another interpretation could be that exam systems penalize girls unfairly.[5]

The method of ranking can be criticized both conceptually and empirically. The report, written from a particularly narrow value system, is seriously flawed and damaging to education. It should play no role in judging the quality of schools.

Which is the "true score," the one from teachers or the one from an external exam? The answer surely comes from an examination of the curriculum. Are schools charged with helping to produce people who work hard and behave well? Does society want such qualities from school graduates? The answer is obvious. Such characteristics are indeed part of the school's task, an important part that society expects. This is clear from an examination of any curriculum document. It is supported by the Conference Board of Canada[6] in their Employability Skills Profile. This gender gap criterion is, arguably, the most seriously flawed of the set.

The method of ranking

Before going on to an empirical examination of the rankings, I replicated the ranks of the Fraser Institute following their methods. I found two errors in their algebraic formulation. In these cases, I followed their described intent instead. My ranks correlated 0.997 with theirs. I attribute the small difference to the fact that they withdrew the data from a few schools that complained of inaccuracies, and did not re-calculate the ranks.

For a school to be ranked, the first three indicators had to be present; otherwise, the school was dropped before the analysis began. Each of the first three indicators, proportion of advanced course, proportion of courses passed, and average number of core courses, was standardized to a z-score. The report states that the gender criteria were treated the same way, but this is not the case, and if it were, it would run counter to the Fraser Institute description of the variable. The gender criteria in the database are mean score for males less that for females. To replicate their results, I took the negative of the absolute value of the gender gaps, and standardized these to z-scores. This gave a higher score to the smallest gender gap, ignoring direction of the gap, as is the authors' stated intention.

> I replicated the ranks of the Fraser Institute following their methods. I found two errors in their algebraic formulation.

These standard scores were then combined using a weighted average. The first three criteria were weighted 25% each, while the two gender were weighted 12.5% each, for a total of 25%. If either of the gender gap indicators were missing, then the gender gap component was dropped, but a mean z-score was produced using the remaining three indicators weighted one-third each.

These combined z-scores had a mean of .008, largely due to skewness in the gender criteria, and a standard deviation of 0.58 due to correlations among the scales. They were standardized again to mean 0 and standard deviation 1. As a method of dealing with outliers, z-scores above 2.0 were set to 2.0, resulting in the top 15 schools all being tied. The report states that scores below −3.29 were set to −3.29. In my calculations, there was only one such score, so all schools at the bottom of the distribution remained at different ranks. There may have been other such low outliers in the original full data set. No explanation is offered as to why different cut scores were selected for the ceiling and floor.

The report provides a formula presented as a calculation intended to put the normalized scores on a 0 to 10 scale. As reported, it appears to be in error. However, following the stated intentions of the authors, I re-scaled to scores so that –3.29 was set to 0, and 2.00 to 10. The resulting mean was 6.22. These scores were then converted to ranks. The almost perfect correlation (0.997) of my ranks with the originals indicates that the authors erred in the reporting rather than the calculations.

Empirical examination of the criteria

Table 1 gives values of the criteria at selected percentile points. Any discussion of the criteria should be prefaced by the fact that the Fraser Institute definition of school quality is correlated 0.56 with parental education, as obtained from the Canada census through student home postal codes. This value is higher than the result found by Nagy, Traub, and Moore,[7] whose work was with a younger sample from urban schools, using standardized achievement data. Nagy, Traub and Moore made no inference about school quality from their results. The issue addressed in the following analysis is what it takes to go from the 40th to the 60th percentile on each criterion.

Table 1: Selected percentiles of raw criterion variables							
Percentile (Variable)	1st	25th	40th	50th	60th	75th	99th
Proportion Advanced Courses (N=568)	33.8%	55.2%	62.7%	67.9%	72.5%	81.3%	100%
Proportion Passing (N=568)	43.5%	81.6%	84.5%	86.7%	88.5%	91.5%	100%
Mean Number of Core Courses (N=568)	1.5	2.4	2.6	2.7	2.9	3.2	5.1
Gender Gap— Language (N=539)	-15	-6	-5	-4	-4	-3	3
Gender Gap— Mathematics (N=542)	-13	-5	-2	-1	-1	1	13
Negative |gender gap| Language (N=539)	-15	-7	-5	-4	-4	-3	0
Negative |gender gap| Math (N=542)	-15	-5	-4	-3	-2	-1	0

Proportion of Advanced Courses. The proportion of advanced courses taken is calculated as the course enrolment for Grades 11, 12 and OAC (Ontario Academic Credit) in advanced (university-bound) courses over total course enrolment in the same grades. Some 47 schools (6.3%) have all their enrolment in the advanced stream. These schools accept only those students who can handle the advanced level courses. Most are private, with the remainder being elite academic institutions in the public system. All these schools received a "perfect" score for "encouraging" their students.

At the other end, 13 of schools (1999 data) have less than 40% of their enrolment in the advanced stream. Of the 13, one is labelled a technical school and six are labelled as "secondary schools," often an indication of a school designed for basic level (below general level) students.

We can put confidence intervals around the data in Table 1. Assuming an average of six credits per student, and using the median enrolment of 287, a 95% confidence interval for the proportion of advanced courses is about 5% near the middle of the distribution. This means that differences possibly due to chance could move a school 10 percentile points, or about 55 ranks on this one criterion.

It is interesting to note that only four of the top 20 schools, and only two of the bottom 20, have enrolments above the median. Ten of the top 20 schools and eight of the bottom 20 have enrolments under 100. At these low enrolments, 95% confidence intervals are over 10% of enrolment. However, because the data are more thinly spread on the shoulders of the distribution, the equating of 95% confidence intervals with about 100 ranks is more or less constant across the distribution.

Setting levels of chance error aside, and assuming six credits per student, a school would need to have 58% of the student body change one course from general to advanced in order to move from the 40th to the 60th percentile on this indicator. As noted, far fewer than 58% of students would be in a position to make such a change.

Proportion of Courses Passed. The proportion of courses passed is calculated, as above, using data from the three senior years. Some 34 schools fail no students at all. About eight of the schools are private, and it might be reasonable that a school composed entirely of students from families willing and able to pay tuition fees could see no need to fail any students. But this has nothing to do with school quality. However, most of this group is composed of schools in the public system that have had, in previous years, failure rates in the 15-20% range. Thus, the data seem highly questionable. Most of the schools that complained about their data were private schools, but errors may be more widespread than this small group. Some of these schools are now listed on the Fraser Institute website as having their data under review by the Ministry of Education, but the possibly incorrect data are still there, and the rankings have not been recalculated.

At the other end, 10 schools have passing rates under 50%. Only one is above the median enrolment. Two are in small, very isolated communities in Northwestern Ontario. I happen to have taught in one of these schools more than 30 years ago. One day, three students bought a car, packed their belongings, and headed off to Winnipeg to seek their fortunes. As a result, my Grade 13 Physics enrolment dropped by two-thirds, and my chemistry enrolment by half. This criterion includes such dropouts in the denominator.

Confidence intervals over most of the distribution are slightly narrower than those for the proportion of advanced courses. This is due to the highly skewed nature of the data. In contrast to the proportion of advanced courses, it would be quite easy for a school to improve on this criterion. Assuming classes of 25, if each teacher passed one more student in each class, the school could improve from the 40th to the 60th percentile, or about 110 ranks.

Mean Number of Core Courses Taken. Enrolment in language arts, mathematics, and basic sciences forms the basis of this criterion. The bulk of the distribution lies in a very narrow band. To improve on this criterion from the 40th to 60th percentile, about one student in three would need to drop a non-core course, such as history or French, in favour of mathematics. On the other hand, a good teacher in a non-core course can seriously damage the school's score on this criterion.

I know of an example. A new enthusiastic history teacher arrived in a quite large school (N=600 in this data base). After his first year, he increased the enrolment in the optional Grade 12 History course from one section per year to four. Assuming 25 students per section, I calculate that, if these additional students dropped a core course in favour of history, this teacher is responsible for dropping his school about seven percentile points, or 40 ranks. Admittedly, some of this number would choose history over other non-core courses.

The narrowness of this criterion can have serious consequences. Seven schools have a mean number of core courses, as defined, over 5.0. Are we not, as a society, concerned about a possible lack of understanding of the human consequences of technical decisions among our scientists and engineers? Do we not worry about bedside manner in medical students and doctors? What does it mean to a society to allow students at age 16 or 17 to become so narrow in their perspective? How many people regret that their education was too broad? How many wish that their education had been broader?

The Gender Gaps. The two criteria based on the gender gap reveal a serious misunderstanding of gender issues. Apart from the overwhelming conceptual flaws as outlined above, the data are only slightly more accurate than random numbers. The most obvious feature of the gender gap data in Table 1 is that schools do not vary much in this respect. Half the schools have an absolute gender gap of fewer than four marks. The weighting system used to arrive at the final criteria thus leads to a serious overemphasis on this criterion.

We can examine the accuracy of these mean differences with a few reasonable assumptions: equal numbers of boys and girls in the schools, a typical standard deviation of teacher-set marks of, say, 12, and that all students take English. At the median school size, 95% confidence intervals for the English marks would be ± 2 marks, and for the mathematics marks, slightly larger because not all students will take mathematics. Thus, at the median school size, the difference between the 40th and 75th percentile, almost 200 rankings, is no larger than chance. The overemphasis on this criterion means that a chance difference in average grades for boys and girls is given the same weight as, from the top row of Table 1, a change in proportion of advanced courses of more than 15%.

Investigation of the distribution of these two criteria leads to some interesting pieces of information. For example, it is interesting that 13 of the top 20 schools are exempt from this criterion, being single-sex private schools. All of the language gender gaps (N= 4 schools) favouring boys by more than three marks are from schools with enrolment under 100. Similarly, 14 of the 22 schools with language gender gaps greater than 10 favouring girls have fewer than 100 students enrolled.

Further examination

I did further investigation of other aspects of the data sets, involving stability of the quality indices over two years, the identities of low and high scoring schools, and alternate ways of looking at the data set.

Rank Stability. If school quality is a function of policy, staffing, and effort, then it should remain reasonably constant over time. I repeated the calculation done for the 1999 data on the 1998 information in the database. Without guidance as to how the Fraser Institute had truncated scores to deal with outliers, I did no such truncation. Data for both years were available from 459 schools. The correlation between rankings for the two years was 0.78, about 60% common variance. I recalculated the 1999 ranks of the schools remaining in this group to run without gaps from 1 to 459, rather than, with gaps, from 1 to 568. This allowed me to produce the information in Table 2. As can be seen, very large swings in scores occur in about half the schools. This argues against these criteria defining an enduring quality of the school.

Table 2: Summary of differences in ranks 1998 compared to 1999	
Difference from 1998 to 1999	Number of schools
Improved by more than 200 ranks	9
Improved by 100-200 ranks	39
Within 100 ranks in both years	252
Worsened by 100-200 ranks	50
Worsened by more than 200 ranks	9

Identity of Low and High Schools. I categorized the 20 lowest ranked and highest ranked schools as in Table 3. The distribution is strikingly similar to the distribution of wealth in the province. The schools labelled high quality are clustered around the centres of wealth in the province, while those labelled of poor quality are mostly in the disad-

Table 3:	Characteristics of low and high ranked schools, Fraser Institute rankings	
Top 20 ranked schools	**Lowest 20 ranked schools**	
Private, Greater Toronto (11)	Public, Greater Toronto (3)	
Private, Ottawa (3)	Private, Toronto, under review (1)	
Private, smaller cities (3)	Private, smaller city (1)	
Public, Greater Toronto (2)	Public, Northern Isolated (4)	
Public, smaller city (1)	Public, French Language (2)	
	Public, Eastern Rural (3)	
	Public, Central Small City (4)	
	Public, Central Small Town (2)	

vantaged rural and isolated corners of the province. I submit that this is not a definition of quality that most Ontarians would be comfortable with. If a school serving the poor and isolated inevitably has a poor index of quality, there is a flaw in the index. Nagy, Drost and Banfield[8] found that geographical isolation contributed to poor achievement beyond the influence of socio-economic conditions. They studied younger children in Newfoundland using standardized achievement data as the outcome variable.

An Alternative. As I was starting to think about this paper, a colleague asked me how else I would rank schools, under the assumption, I suppose, that schools need to be ranked. The database provides a measure of average parental education for each school, using data from the Canada census. The Fraser Institute use these data to provide a score adjusted for parental education, but these are added as an afterthought. The rankings are based on unadjusted scores.

I regressed the scores on the 10-point scale on parental education, and ranked schools on the residuals, that is, I ranked schools according to whether schools were higher or lower than would be predicted on the basis of parental education. The parental education variable, as noted, correlates 0.56 with the Fraser Institute rankings. It ranges from just over 11 to just under 18 years of education, with a median just under 14 years.

The resulting ranking is different, but not that different. It correlates 0.82 with the original Fraser Institute ranking, but, by design, it is uncorrelated with parental education. The resulting top and bottom 20 schools are quite different. Of the top 20, six were in the original top 20, while three did not rank in the original top 100. Of the bottom 20, 13 were in the original bottom 20. The greatest difference between

Table 4:	Characteristics of low and high ranked schools, alternate rankings	
Top 20 Ranked Schools	**Lowest 20 Ranked Schools**
Private, Greater Toronto (1)	Public, Greater Toronto (2)
Private, Ottawa (1)	Private, Toronto, (4) one under review
Private, smaller cities (5)	Private, smaller city (1)
Public, Greater Toronto (9)	Public, Northern Isolated (4)
Public, smaller cities (2)	Public, French Language (3)
Public small town (2)	Public, Eastern Rural (2)
	Public, Smaller City, (1)
	Public, Small Town (3)

Tables 3 and 4 is the better picture of Toronto area public (including Catholic) schools painted in Table 4. When parental education is taken into account, the schools that appear to do well change. Schools in less educated (and, presumably, less affluent areas) can aspire to be judged as higher quality.

The alternative ranking reported above is not offered as a serious alternative to the Fraser Institute rankings. Despite the differences between Tables 3 and 4, the input data for the alternative ranking is still seriously flawed.

A closing comment

Even setting aside the very serious conceptual problems with these criteria, they do not deserve to be equally weighted. Small differences in the gender gap criteria become as important as substantial changes in other criteria. A lower score on a criterion that is very difficult to change, such as the proportion of students taking advanced courses, can be balanced by simply passing a few more students. A school can "improve" by cancellation of optional courses. These scores are invalid, inaccurate, misleading, and potentially damaging. So seriously, in fact, that it is not enough to try to ignore the Fraser Institute rankings. ❧

Philip Nagy is Professor Emeritus, Measurement and Evaluation, Department of Curriculum, Teaching and Learning, The Ontario Institute for Studies in Education of the University of Toronto

This paper was presented at the Symposium on Large-Scale Assessment—Provincial Testing in Canadian Schools—Policy, Practice, and Research (January 31, 2002) Victoria, British Columbia.

Notes

[1] Although the database included 815 of Ontario's 883 high schools (809 public, 74 private), missing data resulted in ranks being produced for only 568 schools. The database also includes raw data, but not rankings, for the years 1994 through 1998.

[2] Within days, ten schools questioned the accuracy of these data, and the report was withdrawn. On April 26, the report was re-posted to the web, with a note acknowledging the concerns of these schools.

[3] At the time, Ontario secondary schools offered advanced level (university-bound) courses, general level courses, and basic courses. About 70% of enrolment was in the advanced stream in 1999.

[4] This policy has since been changed.

[5] American Association of University Women Educational Foundation (1998). *Gender gaps: Where schools still fail our children.* [Executive summary: Technical Report] Washington, DC: American Association of University Women Educational Foundation.

[6] Conference Board of Canada. (1992). Employability skills profile. Ottawa: Conference Board of Canada.

[7] Nagy, P., Traub, R.E. & Moore, S. (1999). A comparison of methods for portraying school demography using census data. *Alberta Journal of Educational Research, 45*, 35-50.

[8] Nagy, P., Drost, D.R. & Banfield, H. (1985). A path analytic study of the influence of community isolation on student achievement. *Alberta Journal of Educational Research, 31*, 209-227.

How to score high in school rankings

by Erika Shaker

In mid-April 2001, the Fraser Institute released—to a flurry of press coverage—the latest in its series of "report cards" ranking Canadian high schools. Previous targets had been B.C., Alberta and Quebec. This time Ontario's schools were drawn, quartered and rated, ostensibly in the name of accountability and school improvement.

From the results, we can conclude that the way to achieve a high ranking on this report card is quite straightforward:

- Choose your parents wisely—they must be affluent and speak English as a first language.

- Attend a highly academic, university-oriented school in a wealthy urban centre—but not too inner city.

- Better yet, get into a private school (if you can afford it and they admit you), preferably one that is single-sex.

- Avoid schools with a wide range of programs—vocational, arts, special education, technology, English / French as a second language.

And above all, stay out of isolated, rural communities.

Choice for whom?

It is more than a little ironic that the Fraser Institute, a vocal proponent of greater choice in education, has designed a ranking that effectively penalizes schools that have made a commitment to offering students a wide range of choice in programs and areas of study in an attempt to meet the diversity of student needs and interests.

Schools that cater to a broad range of students, many of whom may choose not to go on to post-secondary education, will not do well according to the Fraser Institute's narrow formula which in Ontario focused on core and advanced academic courses in the senior high school years. On the other hand, schools which offer excellent vocational, technology, arts and athletic programs; special education courses; or well-run day cares which allow young parents to complete their high school education will not be rewarded—in most cases, they will be penalized.

It is not surprising that private schools come out on top in such ranking exercises, in no small measure because selective admission policies allow private schools to choose those students most likely to succeed. Public schools by their nature serve a more diverse student body.

Research on school choice programs in the U.S. and elsewhere has found that it is affluent, well-educated parents who tend to take advantage of such initiatives (more choice for those who already have choices), and that wealthy schools in well-to-do neighbourhoods often do the choosing, with parents and students lining up before dawn on registration day.

Perhaps the more appropriate question should be "choice for whom?"

Gender and private schools

It is curious that private single-sex schools received a score of 10 when the gender gap in both math and language arts course marks was one of the indicators used in determining a school's results. This raises the issue of statistical validity given that two of the five indicators comprising the overall score cannot be measured for these schools and further, that single-sex schools are then compared with mixed gender schools.

Even the head of the Canadian Association of Independent Schools has written a letter advising that parents at private schools ignore the ratings, considering them invalid. Also fueling questions of validity is the fact that inaccuracies in Ministry of Education data obtained by the Fraser Institute—potentially affecting the rankings of a large number of schools—resulted in the report card being withdrawn from the Fraser web site, to be "re-posted upon resolution of these uncertainties". Unfortunately, this was discovered too late to withdraw the extensive *National Post* newspaper supplement listing all the schools and their respective ranking.

What's left out?

Critical factors not considered in the Fraser report card include class size, the quality and availability of educational facilities and resources (library, labs, studio, textbooks, etc.), the level of parental income, the presence of school clubs and other extra-curricular activities, opportunities for meaningful contact between students and teachers, a school climate which fosters a desire to pursue learning, and how a school meets community needs. Many of these factors can only be gauged through a school visit and discussions with teachers, principals and students. None of them are included in what the Fraser Institute calls "a detailed picture of each school that is not easily available elsewhere."

A total of 40% of graduates from Lake Superior High School in Terrace Bay will go on to higher education. This is an incredible result, especially considering the unique characteristics and challenges of schools in remote communities. Yet this school received a score of zero, coming last out of nearly 600 schools (approximately 250 schools were not included in the rankings at all). In no way does this reflect the remarkable job such schools are doing, not just for those kids in advanced courses who intend to go on to university, but for those students who will pursue other options including moving directly into the work force. Small wonder that the school principal felt "blindsided" by the low ranking—it simply isn't consistent with what she and others with intimate knowledge and experience of the school know to be true.

> Inaccuracies in Ministry of Education data obtained by the Fraser Institute – potentially affecting the rankings of a large number of schools – resulted in the report card being withdrawn from the Fraser web site... Unfortunately, this was discovered too late to withdraw the extensive *National Post* newspaper supplement listing all the schools and their respective ranking.

Public education—a monopoly?

The Fraser Institute's position on public education as a government-run monopoly, as well as its promotion of market-based reforms such as vouchers cannot be ignored, especially when one looks at the criteria used to rank Ontario's schools. It seems hardly coincidental that the Fraser Institute school rankings were released on the eve of the Ontario Throne Speech which called for more school "choice". Furthermore, the timing of the report comes shortly after results of the trial Grade 10 literacy test were made public. The Ontario government also recently announced its intention to expand province-wide standardized testing—from Grades 3, 6 and 9—to *all* grades in the areas of math, science and English. No doubt the Fraser Institute will look forward to factoring these test results into future versions of its report card, notwithstanding the documented problems with large-scale standardized testing programs. All of these ingredients—school choice, standardized testing, school rankings—add up to high-stakes, measurement-driven 'accountability'.

This is not about improving education for all students—it is about creating a measuring stick that ranks schools on narrow criteria in order to facilitate a move toward a market-driven education system which pits schools against each other and in which schools are "chosen" based on their position in the rankings. And in this system, schools catering to high-income families and university-bound students will do well, while others will not.

Remember the New Zealand experiment

This sort of school reform has been devastating in countries like New Zealand where all schools are charter schools. Parents flock to schools with the best reputations, the most affluent students and the highest test scores, leaving the poorer public schools with large numbers of at-risk students and few resources to address their needs. In 1998, top Education Ministry officials in New Zealand were admitting that market-based school reforms—using school rankings and tying school funding to student population—would never work for as many as 25% of schools. That represents a lot of students, families and communities sacrificed on the altar of school choice rhetoric. ❧

Erika Shaker is the Director of the Canadian Centre for Policy Alternatives Education Project

Reflections of a provincial achievement test marker and scorer

by Thomas Ryan

ABSTRACT: *This reconstruction illuminates several pitfalls of provincial achievement test marking and scoring. Marking and scoring error can be linked to the health, mood, and the motivation of a marker and scorer. The marking environment (room temperature, lighting, seating) needs to be comfortable, easily accessible (transportation, parking) and adult-oriented (professional) with limited interruptions (intercom, cell phone). Markers and scorers need to review grading skills through training, and the process needs to be transparent, collegial, and realistic to relieve marker and scorer anxiety. Setting marking and scoring targets too high creates fatigue, tension, and competition that can impact results. Markers need to follow, understand and apply directions as expected. Failing this, it is a matter of luck whether or not the marking and scoring is credible. Peer marking can positively support the marking and scoring process as item ambiguity often causes confusion not only for the student but also for the marker and scorer.*

The following is an effort to recover meaning via the reconstruction of lived experiences. The activities, thoughts, and feelings of an elementary teacher who became a provincial achievement test marker and scorer are detailed herein. Anecdotal records, notes, and artifacts aided the reconstruction. Henceforth, marking is defined as an activity where a person decides whether or not an answer is correct or incorrect, and scoring is the act of assigning value to an answer (level 1,2,3,4). These reflections, and the reconstruction, are now melded within my current role as an assistant professor of education. They are being made public for the first time.

In education, we often hear of teachers who point to experience as a place where most of their learning takes place. The following experiences have taught me a great deal. I have been moved by the contact and communication with others.[1] My ambition in this effort is to better understand my current stance concerning province-wide testing and to share what I have experienced in order to move others.

Context

In the midst of a doctoral program focused on assessment and evaluation, I was also teaching a Grade 4/5 split, full-time in a small rural school. On a typically frenetic day, I made a quick visit to my in-school mailbox and there I found an application to mark provincial assessments during the upcoming summer. At first I dismissed the possibility since it had been a busy day so far with several behavioural challenges confronting me. Later I studied the form with greater interest since I had learned from a colleague that it was possible to make an honourable sum of money for my services if I was selected. I began to fill out my application and dreamed about what I could afford if I were chosen. The more I dreamed, the more intense I became as I filled out the application carefully and completely. I selected Grade 3 Reading, Writing, and Mathematics, and faxed the application to the Education Quality and Accountability Office in downtown Toronto. I had very little idea of what lay ahead other than the additional pay-cheque and the fact that I would be marking student tests.

As the weeks passed, I began to become anxious about my possible destiny. I called the 1-800 number that put me in touch with a central information desk and asked if I had been selected. They replied that they were busy contacting people and I should wait another week or so to see if I am selected. That same day I was contacted by telephone. I said that I was still interested and with that response, I had obligated myself to a month of marking Grade 3 provincial achievement tests in Etobicoke, Ontario. My information package arrived soon after the telephone call.

The directions were clear. I was to be on-site July 5 through the 16th and mark from 8:30 a.m. until 4:30 p.m. each day, including Saturday. I had an option of staying at a local hotel or staying with friends. I drove down from a Central Ontario location where I lived to Etobicoke (Toronto) and arrived at a local high school ready to mark on July 5. What immediately struck me was the number of cars that overflowed the parking lots. It seemed very congested and I eventually learned first-hand that parking was a daily problem. There was not enough of it. Each day we would have announcements concerning vehicles that needed attention (parked illegally, lights-on). This was a distraction for many of us, and I heard numerous complaints from fellow markers concerning the inadequate parking.

Each morning I walked from my car, parked several blocks away, to the high school that would become my home six days a week from 8:30 a.m. to 4:30 p.m. I was an elementary teacher who had come from a rural school of less than 200 and now I was in a large urban secondary school that could easily seat 1500 or more students. Many times, I felt as if I was a student, with many questions concerning my tasks and daily agenda. I made sure to have my identification tag around my neck. This allowed me to enter each day, past the security guards who were often too assertive. My new routine was not easy to adjust to. Sleeping in strange surroundings often meant uneasy nights and sleepy days. The travel to the marking site each day was through morning rush hour on one of Toronto's major arteries. Daily parking confusion and security entrance (nametag) requirements usually resulted in humorous stories when the group of teachers with whom I worked arrived in our class.

Each day our group of 25 (team-members) teachers arrived, some late, some early, to settle in for a day of marking. I would estimate that there were about 1,200 teachers marking that summer. Each class in this large high school was full of teachers doing a similar task. The morning routine included a visit to hospitality tables that were loaded with fruit, muffins, and drinks. All markers seemed to appreciate this gesture and those few minutes before 9:00 a.m., which became a time to share marking concerns, events, and insights.

During our first two days (orientation), our group leader took us through the "holistic" marking process. We were to use an HB pencil only, and fill in the bubbles on the scoring cards completely. Some of us had previously administered the test. Others were learning for the first time what this assessment involved. I was learning a great deal since I was a Grade 4/5 teacher and I had not spent any time examining the Grade 3 math test.

The leader's central message was that this enterprise was a high-stakes, high-security exercise that would be closely monitored by a team of leaders who were connected by an intercom and walkie-talkies. No material was allowed to leave the building. The tension increased as our classroom-based leader took us through detailed explanations of the test booklets, which contained sections on measurement, number sense and numeration, patterning and algebra, data management and probability, and geometry and spatial sense. From some of the questions asked I could tell that there was anxiety and uncertainty among our group of teacher/markers. One teacher/marker asked: What would happen if a marker made numerous errors—would they be asked to leave? Our leader responded that all of us would be quite good after a few days of training. We learned that we had to record our identification number on each booklet marked so that a marker could be linked and ultimately held accountable for any situation that arose concerning questionable marking. Each test booklet had a bar code and they were bundled into groups of 12. I felt the pressure to perform as expected and this heightened my attention to detail.

Reliability

I knew from my doctoral studies that a test by itself is neither reliable nor unreliable.[2] However, "when a test is used to assign scores to individuals, the scores that are obtained may be reliable or they may be unreliable; it is the scores that have the property of reliability, and not the test itself."[3] During our two orientation days, we slowly and carefully scored a couple of questions. As a large group, we compared our judgments and discussed the rationale for our decisions. To do this we plotted our decisions on a blackboard. Each teacher moved from their seat, with test booklet in hand, to the blackboard to place an 'x' in one of four levels. I felt tremendous pressure to conform. At times, I had been at odds with the majority of the group in my head, but I decided to remain silent and plot my 'x' within the groups. I believe this resulted from the fact that those of us demonstrating judgments different from the group were counseled openly by referring to an "anchor book" to illuminate our errors in judgment.

Anchor books contained exemplary level answers that had been marked by leaders and were available for each of the four levels of performance. A Level 1 anchor book was well below the expected performance standard, Level 2 was one level below, and Level 3 was the expected level of performance. A Level 4 anchor book contained answers that exceeded the provincial standard. I found myself checking anchor books when I lost my focus or was uncertain about the evidence in a test booklet. It was amazing to see the group establish inter-rater reliability levels, which often approached 100% over a period of two days. We had consensus and agreement, something which often is hard to find within a group of educators. It was difficult to argue for your point when the criteria for a decision were presented in a clear manner by leaders who consistently referred to a posted rubric. To me it sometimes felt as if we were being programmed/brainwashed because even veteran teachers, firm in their judgments, became less sure when a number of leaders presented an anchor booklet and assertive stances concerning their judgments. We used a few simple criteria (rubric) rather than a complicated marking scheme. Hence, our group marking reliability was uniform and high throughout our two-week session.

> I felt tremendous pressure to conform. At times, I had been at odds with the majority of the group in my head, but I decided to remain silent and plot my 'x' within the groups.

One of my greatest fears was to be erratic and draw attention to myself, since it has been suggested that "the single most important characteristic of the grading process is its dependence upon teacher judgments."[4] Our leader would check our first few booklets carefully and report to us any irregularities found. I believe it made our group more focused, motivated and serious. The odd booklet had to be examined by a central leader who could be summoned by intercom, walkie-talkie, and telephone. The central leader seemed to be very serious and decisive, as it took only minutes to pronounce judgment upon a puzzling test answer within a booklet.

Test booklets often contained evidence that was incomplete (missing/insufficient), illegible (unintelligible), profane, irrelevant, or humorous. We learned how to deal with each situation as it arrived before our eyes. We found out that, if half of the questions were complete, that section could be marked. I felt that my judgment sometimes vacillated between guessing and uncertainty,[5] since there simply was not enough evidence for me. Illegible answers were sometimes studied by leaders and deemed useful or not. Profanity was generally ignored, yet I wondered if it might influence certain judges either negatively or positively.

Irrelevant material might include doodles and graffiti, but there were times when the evidence seemed to be mixed in with the graffiti. Often a fellow teacher/marker would break the tension in our classroom by offering a humorous answer found in a test booklet. I appreciated this break in the silence.

Validity

To me, the term validity and its definition are best understood by embracing both traditional views and a current reality."[6] The traditional view that there are several different "types of validity" has been replaced by the view that validity is a single, unitary concept that is based on various forms of evidence. My marking and scoring involved judging forms of evidence. I was being asked to judge whether the evidence in front of me was adequate enough to suggest that a student was Level 1,2,3,4 in areas such as measurement, number sense and numeration, patterning and algebra, data management and probability, and geometry and spatial sense.

I was informed that, if the students completed over 50% of the questions in that area, that this was enough evidence and I was to judge. If less than 50% of the questions were completed in one area or in the entire book, I was to indicate, accordingly, that there was not enough evidence. However, even at 50%, or sometimes 70%, I do not believe that there always was enough evidence (content-related) to judge as required. Therefore, I believe this to be one of several factors that lowered the validity of this achievement testing exercise.

Other features noted in the marking and scoring process that illuminated validity concerns were tasks (questions) that were not functioning as they should. While marking and scoring, many of us discovered that students had demonstrated a lack of understanding or a misunderstanding of the clues which led many of the markers and scorers to conclude that the directions and/or the item seemed ambiguous or too difficult. When we tried to bring this up with a central leader, we were quickly reminded of our reason for being here and our specific task at hand. Still, the directions were unclear, even to us. Again, these factors lower the validity of the results.

Therefore, in sum, "a valid interpretation of the assessment results assumes that the assessment was properly prepared, administered, and scored. Validity can be lowered by inadequate procedures in any of these areas."[7] It is my belief that validity was problematic and lowered in light of the concerns and observations noted.

Pace

Eventually, as we became familiar with test questions, answers, and the sequence of events within a marker's day, each of us began to mark more test booklets. The problem with efficiency is that routines created boredom and it was hard to remain focused. As a group we tried to lighten the burden through humour and occasional social activities each morning and noon-hour. I found my ability to mark quickly, accurately, and reliably increased with practice. For the first few days, I completed approximately 50 test booklets. Each of our booklets had to have our identification number placed on it in order to scan it later in another area of the school (marking site). However, during the first day I recall that I had forgotten to do this. I had to retrieve the books that were packed away in a box, ready to be transported to the data input centre, and place my identification number on these. It was a minor embarrassment, but, had it gone unchecked, there would be no way to link a marker to a set of 10 test booklets.

It sometimes felt as if we were being programmed/brainwashed because even veteran teachers, firm in their judgments, became less sure when a number of leaders presented an anchor booklet and assertive stances concerning their judgments.

Our leader talked to us about marker "output" and the possibility of leaving early on the last day if we increased our work-pace. By day four, I was completing almost 100 booklets a day and I was feeling competent. Our leader checked our test booklets by randomly selecting the odd one. I was surprised that more of my test booklets were not questioned because many of my judgments were questionable; some answers could have fit into either one or the other level. By the second week of marking, I was completing over 110 booklets each day. I believed I was doing a good job in spite of error-inducing variables such as fatigue and mood.

Partner marking

During our orientation, we were told that we would partner (collaborate) with another marker in our group. This paired comparison method[8] would be used only if you were very uncertain about questionable evidence contained in a test booklet. We learned that a partner was a person we could quickly communicate with concerning any aspect of our marking. Partners changed daily so that by the end of two weeks we had worked with everyone. I found it useful to have another marker beside me to either offer a comment or remark on material I was uncertain of. While occasional paired comparisons were completed, it slowed your marking pace. It was interesting to discover that most of my partners were non-competitive and didn't seem to keep track of how many booklets were marked per hour, morning, afternoon or day. I often did keep track of how many I had marked. Our leader informed us that there were over 150,000 test booklets marked that summer at three Ontario marking sites.

Outcomes

I believe the experience provided me with perspectives that caused me to review large-scale province–wide assessment and evaluation in a more informed manner. I learned how to score (evaluate), even though the only evidence I had in front of me was often a poorly written short answer that was usually confusing and difficult to decode.

I continued to ask myself throughout this process about issues related to fairness. My fellow markers also verbalized concerns that centred on test bias in general and "test item bias" specifically. I recall one of my peers asking, "Could students from minority groups answer this question?" Our group of markers refocused on the question and we decided that our concern was really a false alarm after one of my peers cited the research findings of Sattler [9] who found, "items that might appear on the surface to be biased against minorities are not necessarily more difficult for minorities to answer correctly." The depth and breadth of knowledge of my fellow markers, many of whom were engaged in post-graduate studies, was impressive. During our discussion I recalled for our group how Hills discovered, in a study of test items that most . . . items flagged as potentially biased in all the studies done to date have turned out to be unbiased after all.[10] Our impromptu discussions were both stimulating and motivating for us as we learned from one another.

In addition, due to the nature of this experience, I grew professionally via systematic and strategic activities, which often resembled action research. I had an opportunity to voice concerns, questions, exchange observations, insights, and strategies for self-improvement as a teacher, marker, and scorer. I now realize that all assessment and evaluation is prone to errors,[11] and that in order for educators to change they need to seek professional development opportunities outside of the classroom.

Limitations

As I reflected on my marking experiences, I began to become increasingly uncomfortable with several aspects of large-scale testing. First, the testing marked and scored was limited to written responses. Therefore, items not fitting that format were not considered and were, in fact, ignored. I marked test booklets that represented huge variations in performance between one student and another. I question the validity of each performance-based written exercise since "validity is not a property of the test or assessment as such, but rather of the meaning of the test scores. These scores are a function not only of the items or stimulus conditions but also of the persons responding as well as the context of the assessment."[12]

> Many of us discovered that students had demonstrated a lack of understanding or a misunderstanding of the clues which led many of the markers and scorers to conclude that the directions and/or the item seemed ambiguous or too difficult.

In addition, this testing program will, and has, led to ranking and unfair comparative analyses between schools, boards of education, provinces and countries without consideration of contextual elements such as the rate of secondary school completion, ethnicity, or linguistic background.[13] Headlines in local papers often read: "County students test short of norm; Board launches training of teachers,"[14] or "Students have bleak future,"[15] or "Local Catholic Board exceeding Alberta Learning Standards."[16] These types of messages can only create tensions between stakeholders and will not promote either positive or open relationships.

Summary

In sum, my efforts have been limited to the reconstruction of my lived experiences as a marker and scorer. This contextualized reconstruction was necessary to further examine my current beliefs as a university educator who teaches courses in evaluation. The process of recovering memories was challenging and the resultant product, this paper, was satisfying and moving. These reflections now become a means to guide future research efforts and experiences.

As an elementary teacher, I believe that I was somewhat isolated and assessment illiterate[17] before I decided to become involved in provincial achievement test marking and scoring. I now see my efforts not so much as a moneymaking effort but more of a professional development experience. Within the first few days of training, I learned a great deal about assessment and evaluation practice and theory. I experienced the process of nurturing reliable judges (markers/scorers). My learning continued as I marked more and more test booklets (pace) and interacted with other teachers who were concentrating on assessment and evaluation dilemmas and problems. Partner marking produced new insights and outcomes. I realized that many of the limitations encountered could be named and discussed by referring to my doctoral studies which complemented this process as it provided me with the necessary theory to inform my marking and scoring practices.

Finally, I suggest some sources of marking and scoring error can be linked to the health, mood, and the motivation of a marker and scorer. The marking environment (room temperature, lighting, seating) needs to be comfortable, easily accessible (transportation, parking) and adult-oriented (professional) with limited interruptions (intercom, cell phone). Professional educators who opt to mark and score need to learn or at least review test-marking/scoring skills through training. Assuming there is a general ability to mark or score is problematic and naive.

A sense of marker and scorer bias can be illuminated and discussed if time is taken to focus on individual and group knowledge, understanding and reasoning skills (preview). However, care must be taken to relieve anxiety by making the process transparent, collegial, and realistic. For instance, setting marking and scoring targets too high creates fatigue, anxiety, and competition that can lead to unfortunate results for all stakeholders. Yet, markers need to follow, understand and apply directions as expected. Failing this, it is a matter of luck whether or not the marking and scoring is credible and reliable (validity). Peer marking, a welcome necessity, can positively support the marking and scoring process as item ambiguity often causes confusion not only for the student but also the marker and scorer. Marking and scoring differences can be reduced to a point; however, the goal of homogeneity is unrealistic given the diverse teaching populations in Canada. ❧

Dr. Thomas G. Ryan is Assistant Professor of Education at Nipissing University in North Bay, Ontario. He was formerly Assistant Professor of Education in the Faculty of Education, University of Lethbridge, Lethbridge, Alberta. His teaching areas are assessment, evaluation, classroom management and research methods. Previously, he was a secondary school teacher and has also taught at the elementary level.

*This paper was presented at the Symposium on Large-Scale
Assessment—Provincial Testing in Canadian Schools—Policy, Practice,
and Research (January 31, 2002) Victoria, British Columbia.*

Notes

[1] Dewey, J. (1938). Experience and education. New York: Collier Books

[2] MacMillan, J. H. (2001). Classroom assessment: Principles and practice for effective instruction. Toronto, ON: Allyn and Bacon.

[3] Traub, R. E., & Rowley, G. L. (1991). Understanding reliability. Educational Measurement: Issues and Practice. 10 (1), p.42.

[4] Airasian, P. (2001). Classroom assessment: Concepts and applications. (4th ed.). New York: McGraw-Hill. p. 298

[5] Airasian, P. (2001). Classroom assessment: Concepts and applications. (4th ed.). New York: McGraw-Hill.

[6] Gronlund, N. E. (1998). Assessment of student achievement. (6th ed.). Boston, Allyn and Bacon.

[7] Ibid. p. 203).

[8] Popham, J.W. (1993). Educational evaluation. (3rd ed.). Boston, MA: Allyn and Bacon.

[9] Sattler, J. (1992). Assessment of children. (3rd ed.). San Diego: Jerome M. Sattler. p.87

[10] Hills, J. R. (1989). Screening for potentially biased items in testing programs. Educational Measurement: Issues and Practice. 7 (3), 5-11.

[11] MacMillan, J. H. (2000, September 23). Fundamental assessment principles for teachers and administrators. Practical assessment, research and evaluation, 7(8). Retrieved September 30, 2000, from http://ericae.net/pare/getvn.asp?v=7&n=8

[12] Messick, S. (1995). Standards of validity and the validity of standards in performance assessment. Educational Measurement: Issues and Practice. 14 (5), 5-8.

[13] Earl, L. & Nagy, P. (1998). Assessment and accountability. ORBIT, 29 (1), 23-28.

[14] Skelton, E. (1997, December 02). County students test short of norm; Board launches training of teachers. The Orillia Packet and Times, p. 01.

[15] Dyck, H.V. (2001, October 15). Students have bleak future/Local Catholic Board exceeded Alberta learning standards. Brooks and County Chronicle, p. A3.

[16] Ibid

[17] Stiggins, R. J. (1991). Relevant classroom assessment training for teachers. Educational Measurement: Issues and Practice. 10 (1), 7-11.

5
PART

Can't take
it any more?
Join the resistance

Challenging the testing
regime in Alberta

by Wayne Hampton

I. Some background on testing in Alberta

Alberta is a rich province with a strong economy based largely on rev-
enue from oil and gas, agriculture, forestry and technology. Alberta is,
and always has been, a small and large "c" conservative province. The
present party in power, the Progressive Conservatives, was first elected
in 1971. Since that time, we have had three premiers—Peter Lougheed
(14 years); Don Getty (7 years) and the incumbent Ralph Klein, (10
years).

Premier Klein's election (1993) came at a time when oil and gas rev-
enues had fallen drastically and the province was running a debt of around
$30 billion. Mr. Klein was elected on the promise that government debt
and government waste would be eliminated and "accountability" for all
government services, including education, would be guaranteed.
Through what has become known as the "slash and burn" process of
governing, department budgets were reduced by 20% and a plethora of
"accountability" measures were introduced. For schools, that meant a
drastic increase in externally imposed tests.

Prior to 1971, Alberta had followed a testing program in which students in Grades 9 and 12, myself included, were required to write de-
partmental exams in the core subjects of math, science, social studies

PASSING THE TEST | The false promises of standardized testing 217 and language arts. These counted for the full year's mark. When Peter Lougheed became premier, he completely eliminated externally imposed testing. When Premier Getty's government took over, testing was reinstated under two programs. The first was the Provincial Achievement Testing Program which required students in Grades 3, 6 and 9 to write a test in a different core subject each year (rotated every four years). The tests did not count as part of a student's final grade. The second was the reintroduction of Grade 12 diploma exams which counted for 50% of the student's final grade.

To "guarantee" accountability, the Klein government introduced annual testing in language arts and math at the Grade 3 level, and language arts, math, science and social studies at the Grades 6 and 9 levels, the results of which may be used by teachers as part of a student's final grade. Grade 12 diploma exams continued as introduced by the Getty government.

In May 2002, in an acceptance speech for the *Canadian Principal of the Year Award*, I discussed my concerns with the testing regime. To my surprise, the house nearly came down with a standing ovation of support! This is definitely not an issue that is unique to Alberta. It is a concern right across the country and internationally. My position is that it's not a question of accountability, but rather a question of what types of measures are appropriate, used by whom, on whom and when, and what the results are used for. The question must be asked, "To what extent do we want accountability measures to drive practice?"

II. Alberta testing instruments and how the results are used

Good assessment is a natural part of good teaching and learning. It takes time and it doesn't come cheaply.[1] Other than for reasons of efficiency and economy, there is little educational justification for using easily scored tests, and only those tests, to make decisions about the educational well-being of children in our schools.[2] What business would rely on one indicator to judge the worth of its operation? No sensible hospital director would mandate more frequent temperature-taking to cure patients. Yet, we find the governments in Alberta, in other parts of Canada, and around the world doing just that: mandating more and more external testing of students and expecting this practice to result in better teaching and learning.

I am concerned about the culture of testing that has developed in our province over the past 10 years. I am also concerned about what I call the "widget" syndrome—the move in our world to standardize everything, including learning, with the intent of producing an identical product or "widget." Children develop at differing rates and have different learning styles. Children's social and emotional maturation, which is not measured by achievement testing, is every bit as important as their intellectual growth. A "one size fits all" approach to teaching, learning, assessment, and accountability is doomed to failure.

Writing on the impact of standardized testing in the December/January 2001 issue of *Education Leadership*, Carl Glickman says: "A democracy flourishes only when it protects the marketplace of ideas and a diversity of perspectives."[3] The Provincial Achievement Testing Program does just the opposite. By imposing standardization, achievement testing narrows learning. Using one-shot instruments like these to measure student and system success assumes that learning occurs in a neat, tidy, linear fashion—in a lockstep progression with all student "widgets" moving forward in the same way at the same time. In fact, learning is anything but standard. Learning is a messy, gooey, often coincidental and accidental process. Some of our most famous inventions have occurred accidentally.

My position is that it's not a question of accountability, but rather a question of what types of measures are appropriate, used by whom, on whom and when, and what the results are used for. The question must be asked, "To what extent do we want accountability measures to drive practice?"

Research clearly demonstrates there is no correlation between how well students perform on standardized achievement tests and how successful they will be later in life. They not only measure a very narrow set of skills, but skills that are easily memorized and, hence, readily measured by a multiple-choice question. They measure what's easy to measure rather than what's important. Many questions are designed as "trick" questions. Few of the questions challenge the intellectual capacity of students. In the words of American testing critic Alfie Kohn, it amounts to nothing less than the "dumbing down" of learning.[4]

This doesn't seem to bother policy-makers in Alberta Learning, which has recently suggested that achievement test and diploma exam results could be used to develop a "value added accountability" rating system. This would be very damaging to the system. If school and school system success is largely determined by these test results, the implied threat of sanctions for those that don't make the grade can only lead to a huge push to "get those numbers up." This is usually accompanied by a strong classroom focus on "teaching to the test."[5] To make sure the students perform well on "the test," many rich, meaningful learning experiences, experiences identified by the Conference Board of Canada as essential for success in the world of work, will be passed up.[6] As a school principal, I see it happen every day.

The process of standard setting for these tests is another major area of concern. Few Albertans realize that the standards (acceptable and excellence) are determined after the tests are scored. For example, in 2002, the standard of excellence in Grade 6 math was set at 91%—15% of our Grade 6 students achieved at or above that level. However, if we use the traditionally accepted 80% mark for the standard of excellence, which is used for the Grade 12 diploma exams, 47% of our students achieved excellence. This seems to indicate that the results are being manipulated to make sure the government achieves its 15% (excellence) and 85% (acceptable) standards, as well as to ensure that there were no drastic swings in results from year to year. How long would I survive as a teacher if I told students (and parents) that the standard is determined after a paper, assignment or test is marked?

Alberta Learning rationale for setting the standards after tests are administered and marked is to allow for year-to-year comparisons to compensate for the possibility of a test being easier or harder from one year to the next. This assumes students and learning conditions are the same from year to year. No matter what the rationale, this clever play with numbers shortchanges students and the community. Parents want much more information about their children than what can be measured by provincial achievement tests.

As educators, we strive to develop positive, caring, contributing citizens. To that end we endeavour to make learning in the classroom as "real world" as possible. Keeping this in mind, I wonder when was the last time any of us, as adults in the working world, wrote an externally imposed exam, or any exam for that matter, as part of the performance appraisal process. As a school principal, I have seen first-hand the stress these tests cause students and parents. It's simply not good enough to say "The stress prepares the student for the real world!"

III. Challenging the Provincial Achievement Testing Program

With the Klein revolution came the accountability movement and our government's love affair with provincial achievement testing. Annually in our province, Grade 3 students write two tests in language arts and two tests in math; Grade 6 and 9 students write tests in the four core subjects for a total of six tests (two each in math and language arts)—unless they are in French immersion where students write eight tests. Some $12 million dollars is being spent annually on testing while only $4 million is spent on curriculum development! I fully support standards and accountability. However, those accountability measures should be left in the hands of the professionals. Who's in a better position to know how a child is achieving?[7]

In February 2001, along with one of our school trustees, I attended a session by Alfie Kohn, the guru of gurus on the vices of standardized testing. We then embarked on a process to begin challenging the Provincial Achievement Testing Program. Having the unwavering support of an elected school trustee has been essential at all stages of this process. We also worked very closely with our supportive school council, staff and administrator colleagues to review the abundance of literature that conclusively demonstrates what is wrong with standardized testing.

> Using one-shot instruments like these to measure student and system success assumes that learning occurs in a neat, tidy, linear fashion — in a lock-step progression with all student "widgets" moving forward in the same way at the same time. In fact, learning is anything but standard.

In June 2001, I chose to honour the wishes of a small number of parents who wrote letters to me directing that their child be exempt from writing the provincial achievement tests, although their child would be present at school on the days the tests were to be administered. This did cause some dismay, consternation and confusion with my superiors and in the ranks of Alberta Learning. I have always been up-front with all officials throughout this process, reported on all actions, and have been careful to never violate any laws or policies. However, it appeared that some people felt honouring parent directives to exempt their child from writing the tests was a violation of Alberta Learning policy.

Consequently, in 2001-2002, I pushed Alberta Learning for a clarification of the policy. I was informed that parents could exempt their child from writing the achievement tests if, on ideological grounds, they disagreed with the tests. All a parent needed to do was write a letter to the principal. This was good news!

At the moment, the exemption rate is growing fast and furiously throughout the province—much to the chagrin of Alberta Learning. At Lacombe Upper Elementary School, approximately 30% of the students were exempted from writing the Grade 3 and 6 provincial achievement tests in June 2002.

In the spring of 2002, I worked very closely with our local MLA (Member of the Legislative Assembly), a member of the Progressive Conservative party, on a Private Member's Bill asking for the complete elimination of the Provincial Achievement Testing Program. In the process, this became a Private Member's Motion requesting that the government undertake a thorough and complete review of the Provincial Achievement Testing Program. The motion was introduced after careful consultation with constituents about concerns with the program. It passed easily in the Legislature on April 22, 2002, with strong support from all parties, including the ruling Progressive Conservatives. There were hundreds of letters from parents supporting the motion.

Unfortunately, because this initiative ended as a motion rather than a bill, the government is not required to act upon it. This is exactly what our Learning Minister has decided to do. So we still have plenty of work ahead of us, but I believe, as school leaders, through perseverance, we can effect a positive change in the area of assessment and externally imposed testing.

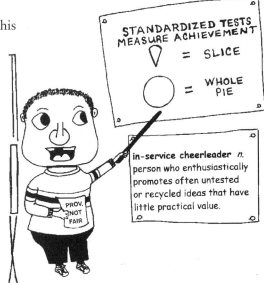

"Tests designed to be a slice of the pie have been made into the whole pie by test vendors, politicians, and the in-service cheerleaders of education."

IV. What would be a suitable alternative?

For an accountability system to be meaningful, it must encompass all aspects of students' learning. Hence, I am proposing a *responsible accountability system* for education in Alberta. To achieve this, we must stop thinking about "testing" and start thinking about "learning and meaningful assessment." We need to stop regarding expenditures in education as an expense and start viewing expenditures as an investment in our future and in our most precious resource—our children.

We need to start spending our money wisely by spending it on those things that are important—i.e., the people in the schools. We need to spend the money and provide the time to create and develop the context to allow deep, rich, meaningful teaching, learning and assessment to take place. Externally imposed tests will not ensure improved student learning.

In February 2001, along with one of our school trustees, I embarked on a process to begin challenging the Provincial Achievement Testing Program. Having the unwavering support of an elected school trustee has been essential at all stages of this process.

The Conference Board of Canada (of which Alberta Learning is a member) in its *2000+ Employability Skills* identifies the skills that students require to enter the work force and progress in the world of work—whether they work on their own or as a part of a team. According to the Conference Board, students must be able to demonstrate:

- Teamwork skills—ability to work with others, participate in projects and tasks.
- Personal management skills—positive attitudes and behaviors, be responsible, be adaptable, have a commitment to lifelong learning, work safely.
- Fundamental skills—communicate (orally and written), manage information, use numbers, think and solve problems.[8]

A *responsible accountability system* that would address these skills must be based on professional judgement, using multiple indicators and assessments—both quantitative and qualitative—over an extended period of time. Such a system must employ authentic performance-based assessments to measure a wide variety of skills such as reading, writing, speaking, presenting, problem-solving, collaborating, contributions in a team setting, flexibility, experimenting, inquiring and creativity.[9]

Assessment instruments would include student portfolios containing artifacts and work-samples of teacher-and-student-created assessments and assignments—including group and individual projects, written assignments, oral and multi-media presentations, closed-book and open-book teacher prepared tests, quizzes and exams. The portfolio should contain artifacts that demonstrate true on-going performance and growth, understanding of learning, evidence of reflection, self-examination, self-evaluation, sound decision- making, personal growth, goal-setting and goal realization, teacher-guided comments and suggestions for growth.

Teacher-administered diagnostic instruments for all grade levels, such as the CAMP (Classroom Assessment Materials Project) materials, should be available to teachers. Portfolios and diagnostic assessment results would be shared with students, parents and professionals on a regular, ongoing basis.

The bottom line is:

> *externally imposed assessments are not necessary and in their present form are ineffective and harmful to learning!*

As Seymour Sarason reminds us, "We often labour under beliefs and views that are so deeply rooted that they remain unformulated and unchallenged." I would submit that this is what is happening with the culture of testing that has developed in Alberta over the past 10 years. Accountability for education in Alberta relies on test scores collected from students in sufficiently standardized fashion that they can be analyzed (to death) in terms of individual students, schools and districts. So much so that, when a Private Member's Motion passed in the Legislature last spring with the support of Members from all parties, the response from the Minister of Learning was that "Alberta Learning's testing program is reviewed regularly," and he saw no need for any further review.

This is sheer arrogance! ❧

Wayne Hampton is the Principal at Lacombe Upper Elementary (Grades 3 to 6) in Wolf Creek School Division No. 72. He was selected Principal of the Year for Alberta in 2001 by the ATA (Alberta Teachers' Association) Council for School Administrators and Canadian Principal of the Year in 2002 by the Canadian Association of Principals.

This is an edited version of a presentation to the International Confederation of Principals meeting in Ottawa, Ontario, Feb. 13, 2003.

Notes

[1] Elmore, Richard, "The Price of Accountability", *Results*, November 2002.

[2] Guskey, Thomas R., "Computerized Grade Books and the Myth of Objectivity", *Phi Delta Kappan*, June 2002, pp. 775-780.

[3] Glickman, Carl D., "Holding Sacred Ground: The Impact of Standardization", *Education Leadership*, December 2000/January 2001, pp. 46-51.

[4] Kohn, Alfie, *The Schools Our Children Deserve: Moving Beyond Traditional Classrooms and "Tougher Standards"*, (Houghton Mifflin Company, 1999); Kohn, Alfie, *The Case Against Standardized Testing: Raising Scores, Ruining the Schools*, (Heinman Portsmouth, NH, 2000).

[5] Popham, James W., "Teaching to the Test", *Education Leadership*, March 2001, pp. 16-20.

[6] *Employability Skills 2000+*, (The Conference Board of Canada, www.conferenceboard.ca/nbec).

[7] Popham, James W., *The Truth About Testing: An Educator's Call to Action*, (Association for Supervision and Curriculum Development, Alexandria, Virginia USA, 2001).

[8] Ibid.

[9] Coladarci, Theodore, "Is It a House…. Or a Pile of Bricks? Important Features of a Local Assessment System", *Phi Delta Kappan* June 2002, pp. 772-774.

Alberta teachers boycott marking

Alberta teachers are being urged not to mark provincial achievement tests, the latest blow to the exams for Grades 3, 6 and 9 students. Teachers representing all areas of the province decided on the weekend to refrain from marking the tests, based on a philosophical opposition to the high-stakes exams. The move follows a boycott of the tests by more than 500 parents in Calgary, Lethbridge, Banff, Canmore and Exshaw…

Grade 3 students across Alberta write provincial achievement tests in language arts and math, while those in Grades 6 and 9 write language arts, math, science, and social studies exams… Some parents who have vowed to pull their children from the exams are protesting what they call a chronic underfunding of education. Others are opposed to the tests as a measure of student success.

Dee Dee Hibbert, parent of a Grade 6 student at Banff Trail Elementary School, said 13 students out of 37 in her daughter's class will not write the exams.

"The tests are a bad idea," she said. "They are not measuring our system effectively.

Alberta Home and School Councils' Association calls for an end to Grade 3 testing saying it is too stressful for the children. "They're learning how to do the test," said Marilyn Fisher, president of the association.

Fine, Sean. "Putting public education to the test." Globe and Mail, September 3, 2002. p. A3

This year, in particular, when education dollars are so limited, to see money put towards these tests—which are such a bad idea in the first place—is something I am not prepared to do," said Hibbert.

Parents have said as many as 25 schools in Calgary have talked about participating in the boycott, although the province has reminded school districts participation is mandatory. Noel Jantzie, president of the Calgary public teachers' union local, said the boycott by parents and the refusal to mark the exams are related in principle.

"That is a parent initiative coming from parents," he said. "We have tried to be very cautionary to our members that the decision to keep their child out of exams is really a parental decision."

The decision not to mark achievement tests is also up to individual teachers, added Jantzie. "We are required to administer the tests, but beyond that, we have profound disagreements with the provincial government on the achievement tests," he said. "Multiple choice evaluation is inappropriate…"

Colette Derworiz . "Teachers consider test boycott."
The Edmonton Journal, Tue 21 May 2002

Students take action for education

Opposing standardized testing in Ontario

by Justin Woza Goldenthal-Walters

S ome people view students who oppose the provincial changes in education as troublemakers who just want to protest to skip school. The fact is that, due to recent cutbacks in education, students are organizing. The notion that "we're not gonna take it any more" is embodied by a rebellious group called the "Flying Squad."

The Flying Squad was established in September 2001 and is comprised of 70 high school students representing schools across the GTA [Greater Toronto Area]. About a quarter of them get together, usually every Thursday, to find new and constructive ways to get the student message out to the public and to see what they can do to undo the mess the province has created with education. Their goal is to create a broad-based high school movement to fight the power.

Their first action was to occupy the Education Quality and Accountability Office, the corporation that the Tory government contracted to administer standardized testing. The action disrupted office activities and peacefully ended with the Flying Squad presenting a list of demands. This was followed by a day of walkouts across the city. The 500-student protest led to the steps of the Ministry of Education, where students listened to speakers and spoke out against standardized testing. The point of the protest was to show that youth have the power to come together and rebel against injustices in the education system.

The government then had to strike back. Instead of negotiating with the group to address student concerns around standardized testing, the government blamed last fall's theft of the tests on the Flying Squad. One of the members of the Flying Squad, Karen Silverman, was falsely arrested and charged with possession of stolen goods under $5,000. That arrest temporarily derailed the activities of the group.

On February 6, 2002, the Flying Squad collaborated with other student groups to promote the National Day of Action against tuition increases, the "Freeze Tuition Fees" campaign, by encouraging students at local high schools to participate. Many high school students were present among the 10,000 students who chanted and sang out against the deregulation of tuition fees in front of the Ontario legislature. The activities of the National Day of Action have inspired other high school groups to mobilize.

Currently, the Flying Squad is collaborating with a new group called "Stir it Up." The group is dedicated to mobilizing high school students to join with university students in their campaign to "freeze the fees."

In the words of Joel Duff, chairperson of the Canadian Federation of Students, who spoke at the National Day of Action, "Get organized and get out! Don't let tuition fees get in the way of your post-secondary pursuit. Take a stand against educational injustices. The future is yours, get involved."

Why the Flying Squad says no to standardized testing

The Ontario provincial government has drained $2.4 billion from education since 1995; Bill 160 increased class sizes, and decreased teacher prep time; Bill 45 gave tax credits to private schools, making good education dependent upon how rich you are.

This year Grade 10 students in Ontario were subjected to rigorous standardized testing processes. These tests play a fundamental role in the Tory government's plan for privatizing education. The rationale goes like this: decrease funding for schools, bring in a new curriculum without teaching materials, test the crap out of the students who have suffered from funding cuts. Make the case for the privatization of education based on the poor grades of tests that were fabricated for students to fail.

To get in touch with the Flying Squad, e-mail fighting_kids @hotmail.com.

News update: On April 15, 2003, *The Toronto Star* reported that all charges were dropped against Karen Silverman and Laura Shilliday. Ms. Shilliday had been accused of stealing the test, while Ms. Silverman allegedly had a copy when she and other students held a rally against the test one-and-a-half years ago. A witness who claimed to have spotted Ms. Silverman tearing up the exam at the Education Quality and Accountability Office, which administers the test, later recanted, according to a court document. The Crown's case dried up after police learned the test had been posted on the Internet, where it could be accessed by anyone with a computer. Ms. Silverman has accused Toronto police of illegally strip-searching her following her arrest in October, 2001. ◖◗

Justin Woza Goldenthal-Walters is a student at Toronto's Ursula Franklin Academy.

This article originally appeared in the Tuesday, April 7, 2002 edition of Catch da Flava, an online and print newspaper produced by young people involved in the Regent Park Focus Media Arts Program. http:// www.catchdaflava.com/

More pockets of resistance to testing in Ontario

Ontario elementary teachers vote to boycott marking

At the ETFO (Elementary Teachers' Federation of Ontario) 2001 Annual Meeting held in August 2001, delegates passed the following resolution:

> That ETFO encourage members not to participate in any EQAO marking exercise.

Delegates informed the annual meeting that the results of these assessments have been misused to undermine the teaching profession and the students on Ontario. As such, if teachers continue to participate in marking of these assessments they may be perceived as condoning and supporting the inappropriate use of assessment results.

The emerging trend within the media of ranking schools by assessment results has been unfair to students and is potentially destructive to the education system.

Elementary Teachers' Federation of Ontario. Advisory to members. August 2001.

http://www.etfo.ca/documents/EQAO_Marking_Update.PDF

Ontario school board chair speaks out on testing

After watching his other children suffer from the stress of Grade 3 provincial tests, Ron Motz, chairman of the Bluewater School Board in Central Ontario, refused to permit his daughter to write the Grade 3 provincial test. After taking a close look at the tests and their impact, he came to believe that the tests were pointless. "We don't know what goes into good test scores. I really don't think that we do," says Mr. Motz.

Fine, Sean. "Putting public education to the test." Globe and Mail, September 3, 2002. p. A3

Kingston parents struggle to challenge high stakes testing

by Marita Moll

"There are times when we are powerless to prevent injustice, but there must never be a time when we fail to protest," said Nobel laureate Elie Wiesel. In that spirit, a group of parents in Kingston, Ontario have worked at the school level to raise awareness and objections to the high stakes tests faced by their children in Grades 3 and 6. Last year, when process trumped protest, Kingston parents Karl and Wendy Flecker sent the following letter to school authorities and the local press:

> *Sue Rawson, Principal*
> *Central Public School*
> *Kingston, Ontario*
> *May 2, 2002*
>
> *Just a few days ago we received a school memo from you, sent home with our children stating the Grade 3 and 6 high stakes testing will begin on Monday, May 6. As you are aware, we do not support these tests nor do we intend for either of our children to participate in them.*
>
> *The EQAO (Education Quality and Accountability Office) Parent Update newsletter that came with your undated memo states, "...this year's assessments will take place between May 6 and May 23, 2002." It goes on to say the exact dates for the 2.5 hrs/day test will be determined by you and the school teachers, who will in turn let parents know the exact dates well in advance.*

Clearly, this has not happened.

Over the past year we have petitioned the School Advisory Council to hold a balanced dialogue, involving experts on the topic of testing, to increase everyone's understanding of the issues. In March, the School Advisory Council opted to avoid holding an information session despite policy and legislative obligations empowering them to do so.

Until your notice was sent home this week, exact dates the tests would appear at Central Public School had not been communicated to concerned parents. Thus, you may appreciate how disappointing it is to receive such short notice.

We are writing to advise you, the School Board, EQAO and the local media of the following:

1. Receiving only a few days' notice of the high stakes test schedule is not consistent with EQAO's April newsletter message that parents will be advised "well in advance."

2. The EQAO flyer continues to misinform parents that "students are required by law" to participate in these tests.

We do not want to conclude the short notice and the false legal intimidation messages are calculated efforts to leave parents with few options and make them feel they must acquiesce their children to participate in educationally irrelevant, expensive tests. We would prefer to engage in dialogue with the local Board officials and Central School staff aimed at establishing meaningful assessment and educational experiences for next week.

With this in mind, please advise us what arrangements the school is prepared to put in place for children who will not take the test. Will Central provide meaningful educational activities for the 2.5 hrs/5 day portion of next week's high stakes test schedule? We would be willing to discuss our children's participation in educationally relevant and constructive assessment activities, useful participation in other classes or noteworthy independent studies. Isolated or segregated activities that can be perceived as punitive would naturally not be acceptable.

Finally, we encourage EQAO to attempt to have the "law" applied to our decision that our children will not participate in their destructive high stakes tests.

Karl & Wendy Flecker
Kingston, Ontario

The letter was copied to the Director of Education at the Limestone Board of Education, EQAO, the Canadian Centre for Policy Alternatives (CCPA) Education Project, the *Kingston Whig Standard*, and *Kingston This Week*. Mr. Flecker, when contacted a year later, reported that efforts to challenge the testing agenda continue to be met with stubborn resistance:

- The response to the letter was a phone call from Pat Warren Chappel, a school board employee. "I can confidently say the school board made no effort to answer questions posed in the letter—not even to the extent of 'pretending' to recognize a parent's concerns about late notice nor to follow up on our persistent efforts to have a dialogue about high stakes testing," reported Mr. Flecker.

- The 2.5 hours/day was spread over the entire day in such small blocks that it was quite impossible to withdraw children for that portion of the day when the test was administered—even if parents had been given adequate notice. "We ended up pulling our daughter for the entire week."

- The School Advisory Council that had opted against holding a forum on this topic did so by sending out a "survey" to parents to gauge interest. The process was cramped for time and even though a number of parents responded, the Council and Principal interpreted the results as "too low" to warrant organizing such a discussion. "There were no adequate responses to our questions about why a 'survey process' was required, what the bench marks for 'too low' were, and exactly what the response rate was." Later in the year, when the issue of fund-raising to finance replacing aging playground equipment came up, the same council immediately organized a forum to discuss the issue. "The precedent of sending out surveys to gauge interest level was conveniently forgotten."

"The HST (high stakes testing) mantra continues, and we now discover that the Limestone Board is introducing its own versions of 'standardized tests' in all class levels, in addition to the tests provincially dictated" says Mr. Flecker.

But he remains determined to continue opposing the tests. In his words, "The struggle continues." ❧

PEI rejects school ranking; sticks to fair testing principles

"We support good educational research opportunities which help us to improve quality in our schools," [PEI Education Minister Chester] Gillan said Wednesday. "However, we choose not to participate in this particular study because we didn't have the required data readily available and we don't support the ranking of schools."

"Ranking schools against each other serves no educational purpose, and particularly when it is done using insufficient and inconsistent data it can do a serious disservice to students, teachers and the many people who are dedicated to improving quality in our schools."....

Gillan said he didn't necessarily have a major problem with [the criteria Atlantic Institute for Market Studies (AIMS) uses to assess schools—class size, socio-economic factors, the number of overall students and standardized testing] but AIMS doesn't take into account factors his department feels are also important, such as internal testing which includes exams that students write and the feedback students get from teachers and that parents receive in parent-teacher interviews.

Ken Gunn, senior director of public education on PEI, said concerns have been expressed by ministries of education in Nova Scotia, New Brunswick and Newfoundland and Labrador that the study was statistically and methodologically weak and the data analysis was flawed.

Gunn said the authors acknowledged there were serious shortcomings in the data yet went ahead and ranked the schools anyway.

"One of our big problems with AIMS is that they were going to rank the schools," Gunn said. "We're against ranking a set of teachers against a set of teachers . . . they don't have the resources to do a comprehensive analysis. They knew they didn't have enough data and they went ahead and did it anyway and that says something about them."

Stewart, Dave. "Minister defends not participating in school rankings: Think tank criticizes Binns government for not knowing what's happening in own high schools, but Gillan says study weak, flawed." The Guardian (Charlottetown), Thu 20 Mar 2003

Bird's eye view of recent international anti-testing activities

United Kingdom—national teacher boycott

Next month's national tests for children aged seven, 11 and 14 will almost certainly be the last after a unanimous decision yesterday by the biggest teaching union to ballot its 250,000 members on an immediate and permanent boycott.

Doug McAvoy, the general secretary of the National Union of Teachers, said a survey had shown that support for the boycott would be overwhelming. So, from next January, primary and secondary school teachers would stop preparing children for the tests and refuse to administer them.

Primary school league tables would cease and the government's target-setting regime, on which teachers' pay and promotion partly depend and by which the performance of schools and education authorities are largely judged, would be destroyed.

Mr McAvoy said there was "absolutely no doubt" that a boycott would be legal because the tests prevented teachers from teaching effectively. He conceded that staff who boycotted the tests, which two million pupils take every year, would be breaking their contracts. But schools and education authorities "foolish" enough to dock their pay would face strikes and other action.

Delegates to the union's annual conference in Harrogate twice voted unanimously, with the executive's backing, for motions calling for the tests to be abolished on the grounds that they distorted teaching, narrowed the curriculum and caused stress to children and parents. The votes were greeted by a standing ovation, with many delegates rhythmically clapping and chanting "No more SATs" (School Assessment Tasks, the original name for the tests).

Moving the first motion, Mick Harrington, from Westminster, a primary school teacher for 30 years, said the tests in English, maths and science stifled creativity and lowered self-esteem. The £2.2 million they cost every year ought to be spent on teaching.

Clare, John. Teachers Threaten to Wreck School Testing. London Telegraph, April 21, 2003.

Washington State—political candidates asked to submit to standardized tests

A group of Washington State educators has filed an initiative that requires any candidate running for any local or state-wide office in Washington to take the same high stakes test required of all tenth grade students, and to post their scores in the Voter's Pamphlet and on the Secretary of State's web site. The details of the initiative, filed on January 9, 2002, are as follows:

Anyone running for any local or state-wide office in the state will take all sections of the tenth grade WASL, (the Washington Assessment of Student Learning) at their own expense. The tests will be offered in proctored sites around the state and will be scored by the office of the Superintendent of Public Instruction.

Scores will be posted in Voter's Pamphlets provided before elections and on the Secretary of State's web site. There are no requirements that candidates must pass all or any sections of the test, but they must post their scores.

FairTest
Press Release
http://www.fairtest.org/arn/washington%20press%20release.html

Illinois—teachers refuse to administer tests; veteran teacher leaks pilot tests

A dozen teachers from Curie High School are refusing to administer a controversial achievement test called the CASE this January, even if it means losing their jobs.

Ten English teachers and two history teachers wrote Chicago school board officials last month to say they will not give the next Chicago Academic Standards Exam—developed by Chicago teachers and administrators—because they view it as flawed and invalid. Representatives of the new movement, called the Curie Teachers for Authentic Assessment, are scheduled to meet today with Chief Education Officer Barbara Eason-Watkins to discuss the reasons behind their protest.

The teachers could face disciplinary action if they refuse to give the test, but "we're hoping it won't get to that point," said Peter Cunningham, a spokesman for the Chicago public schools. "We are aware there are issues with the CASE and we're always working to improve the test."

Teachers from 30 Chicago public high schools have voiced support for the new movement, and as many as 100 may refuse to give the CASE, said Curie English teacher Martin McGreal. The core group of 12 all have master's degrees or are working on them, and they include four with master's from the University of Chicago or Stanford University.

Rossi, Rosalind. "Teachers refuse to give 'bad exam'"
Chicago Sun Times, October 16, 2002.

Illinois

Veteran Chicago teacher and journalist George Schmidt has paid the highest price for resisting high-stakes tests. Schmidt was fired from what even his antagonists admit was a distinguished career of 29 years teaching in the public schools of Chicago. He is also being sued for $1.3 million for publishing six of 22 Chicago pilot tests in *Substance*, an investigative and analytical newspaper about Chicago schools. Independent experts, including Gerald Bracey, have declared these tests unprofessional, simplistic, and error-ridden, but Schmidt, not the testmakers, is on the firing line. A group of teachers and parents has established the Committee to Recognize Courage in Education and offers the Emperor's Clothes Award. George Schmidt will be the first recipient of the group's award.

Ohanian, Susan. "News from the test resistance trail." Phi Delta
Kappan vol. 82, no. 5. January 2001.

California—school board opposes exit exams

The Los Angeles Unified School Board voted unanimously Tuesday to oppose the state's requirement that students pass an exit exam before graduating from high school, a move that some educators hope will influence the state to postpone or drop the test.

"We should be working with the State Board of Education so that this whole thing gets stopped," said board member Genethia Hudley-Hayes, who co-sponsored the motion with board member Jose Huizar.

"If we use the California Exit Exam to determine whether or not a student receives a diploma, and yet we're not giving youngsters what they need to pass, then we're holding students accountable for something that we're not holding the institution accountable for," she said.

More than 100,000 teenagers have failed the California High School Exit Exam at least twice and must retake it. Students across the state have held rallies and protests in recent months to urge to state to delay or drop the graduation requirement, which takes effect for the class of 2004."

Moore, Solomon and Erika Hayasaki. "L.A. School Board Votes to Oppose State Exit Exam; Opponents of the high school graduation requirement hope the action will persuade California to drop or delay the test." LA Times, April 9, 2003.

Massachusetts—students sue, claiming test discrimination

In the first legal challenge to Massachusetts' high-stakes tests, lawyers representing students who have failed the state graduation exam have filed suit in federal court claiming that the state has not adequately prepared students for the assessments, and that the tests discriminate against minority students.

A group of lawyers filed the complaint Sept. 19 in U.S. District Court in Springfield, Mass., on behalf of six unidentified students attending public schools in Holyoke, Northhampton, and Springfield who have not passed the Massachusetts Comprehensive Assessment System exams in mathematics and English.

Beginning this school year, all students must pass the MCAS in those subjects in order to graduate from high school. Students have five chances, beginning in 10th grade, to pass. Lawyers are seeking class-action status for the case and are challenging the use of the MCAS tests as a graduation requirement.

The suit lists six sub-groups of students that it says have been disproportionately affected by the exams: African-Americans; Hispanics; students with limited English proficiency; students with disabilities; students attending vocational and technical education schools; and students attending schools in the Holyoke school district.

Gehring, John. "Massachusetts Sued Over Graduation Tests." Education Week, October 2, 2002. http://www.edweek.org/ew/ewstory.cfm?slug=05mcas.h22

High stakes are for tomatoes, say resisters

California Educator

While the sun rises and sets on standardized tests at many public schools, there is a growing teacher and parent backlash to the account-ability movement. The resisters assert that basing student achievement on test scores is extremely unfair and a pointless political exercise. They maintain that high-stakes testing stresses out children, miscalculates their abilities, limits school curriculum and takes the joy out of learning.

"The API [Academic Performance Index] stands for Affluent Parents Index," says Susan Harmon, a resource specialist at Lake Elementary School and a member of the United Teachers of Richmond. "Or maybe it stands for Ambitious Politicians Index." To express her views, Harmon has designed and sold T-shirts printed with "High Stakes are for Tomatoes."

"The resistance movement is definitely growing, no question," says Judi Hirsch, an algebra teacher at McClymonds High School in Oakland and a member of the Oakland Education Association. "It's growing because people in the profession are being asked not to teach. Instead, we're drilling for the test. It's really sad."

Harmon and Hirsch are co-founders of California Resisters and Bay Area Resisters, groups with hundreds of subscribers to their e-mail lists. The movement does not have a membership organization, but it does hold meetings attended by teachers, administrators, parents and the media.

The message is being taken to heart at some school sites. Parents, who have the right to exempt children from SAT-9 tests, are doing so in growing numbers. At a Saratoga school, 90% of second-graders were exempted from state testing last spring. At a San Jose school, a third of all students were kept home by parents.

The school that ranked dead last in the previous API scoring, Saul Martinez Elementary in Mecca, received headlines for raising its API dramatically this year from 302 to 490. However, it was soon reported that the increase was attributed to the fact that parents of half the students decided to keep their Spanish-speaking children from taking the test, which is given in English.

"Teachers are not allowed to encourage parents to keep kids home, but we can inform them of this right," says Harmon. "The district has a model letter parents can sign, saying they don't want their child to take the test, as is their right under the law. These letters were handed out at parent conferences last year."

Resisters object to the way the test is constructed. Because it is a norm-referenced test with a bell curve, it is designed so half of all kids who take it will fail. "I work with poor kids who are immigrants, special ed kids and minorities," says Hirsch. "These kids are already feeling bad due to classism and racism. When they take the test they feel worse. It humiliates children. What is the point of that?"

"Approximately 89% of scores are explained by non-school issues, such as parent income, parent education ,and whether the student lives in a single-parent home," says Harmon. "The test is irrelevant at best and discriminatory. It offers no useful information, such as how to help children learn."

"More and more is riding on these tests," says Harmon. "Social workers say they are seeing psychosomatic illnesses in kids based on test fear, including physical ailments, throwing up and nightmares."

In addition, says Harmon, "You hear more and more stories about teachers quitting, saying this is not the profession they thought it would be.

"For these reasons, I'm urging people to join the fight against standardized testing."

This article was published in the California Educator, Vol. 5, Issue 5, February 2001
see: http://www.cta.org/CaliforniaEducator/

High stakes t-shirts are available through:
http://www.fairtest.org/Testing%20T-Shirts.html

MCAS 2003

A call for mass refusal

From New Democracy

The MCAS (Massachusetts Comprehensive Assessment System) test has been imposed on public school children from the 3rd through the 10th grades (except the 9th). Beginning with the Class of 2003, 10th graders have to pass MCAS to graduate. In spite of dramatically higher scores, more than 33% still failed to pass this test in 2001. Approximately 41% of urban students failed either the English or math tests; 54% of vocational students failed.

This high stakes test is very destructive. It tests children on materials above their grade level and puts far too much stress on children as young as eight years old. It is gutting school curricula, reducing education to a pursuit of performance and "coverage" rather than thoughtful exploration of issues, and imposing a climate of fear. It will drive many students out of school without a diploma, as has already happened in Florida and Texas.

Despite the claims of its supporters, MCAS is designed to lower young people's expectations so that they will accept their place in a more unequal, less democratic society. Abigail Thernstrom, member of the Mass Board of Education, recently made the point clearly: "a thriving economy depends on a lot of unskilled people." (Boston Globe, 1/7/01) Similar tests have been imposed in 27 states.

Public education needs substantial change, but MCAS and other corporate-led education reforms move in the wrong direction. They intensify the competition and inequality already at the heart of the educational system. Real education reforms must begin by providing a high level of support for all our children to succeed, not set them up for failure.

We cannot rely solely on our legislators or political figures to solve the problem of MCAS. We have to rely on our own individual and collective strength. MassRefusal will help build the deep and powerful movement we need to stop MCAS and to make the schools all they should be to meet the needs of our children.

- **We call on all teachers and teacher union locals** to refuse to administer the MCAS in 2003.

- **We call on all parents and parent organizations** to support teachers' refusal to administer the MCAS.

- **We call on all people** to copy and distribute this "Call for MassRefusal" as widely as possible.

- **We call on all people** to ask that any organization of which they are members—teacher unions, PTOs, school councils, trade unions, faith-based groups, civil rights, civic, and professional organizations, political groups, etc.—endorse this "Call for MassRefusal" and publicize their endorsement.

It will take time to organize an effective mass boycott of the tests. In the coming year we need your help circulating literature exposing MCAS, organizing parents, recruiting teacher union locals to engage in MassRefusal, inviting speakers to your local or organization, holding house meetings about MCAS, raising money for printing and other costs. Please contact us if you can help in any way.

Visit New Democracy
www.newdemocracyworld.org
Contact: Dave Stratman, Carol Doherty —Newdem@aol.com
From: http://www.massrefusal.org/index.html

Why so many exams?

A Marxist response

by Bertell Ollman

I

The psychologist, Bill Livant, has remarked, "When a liberal sees a beggar, he says the system isn't working. When a Marxist does, he says it is". The same insight could be applied today to the entire area of education. The learned journals as well as the popular media are full of studies documenting how little most students know and how fragile are their basic skills. The cry heard almost everywhere is, "The system isn't working." Responding to this common complaint, conservatives—starting (but not ending) with the Bush Administration—have offered a package of reforms in which increased testing occupies the central place. The typical liberal and even radical response to this has been to demonstrate that such measures are not likely to have the "desired" effect. The assumption, of course, is that we all want more or less the same thing from a system of education, and that conservatives have simply made an error in the means they have chosen to attain our common end. But what if students are already receiving—more or less—the kind of education that conservatives favour? This would cast their proposals for "reform" in another light. What if, as Livant points out in the case of beggars, the system *is* working?

The 17th century French philosopher, Pascal, noted that, if you make children get on their knees every day to pray, whatever their initial beliefs, they will end up believing in God. It seems that a practice repeated often enough, especially if it includes particular movements and emotions, can exercise an extraordinary effect on how and what we think.

Didn't Marshall McLuhan warn us in the early years of TV that "the medium is the message?" What applies to praying and to watching TV applies as well to taking exams. If you make students at any rung of the educational ladder take lots of exams, this will have at least as much influence on what they become as the kind of questions that are asked. In short, exams, especially so many exams, teach us even more than they test us. To grasp what it is they teach us is to understand why our system of education already "works" and in what ways conservative proposals for reform would make it "work" still better.

II

Before detailing what young people learn from their forced participation in this educational ritual, it may be useful to dispose of a number of myths that surround exams and exam-taking in our society. The most important of these myths are—

- *that exams are a necessary part of education.* Education, of one kind or another, however, has existed in all human societies, but exams have not; and the practice of requiring frequent exams is a very recent innovation, and still relatively rare in the world;

- *that exams are unbiased.* In 1912, Henry Goddard, a distinguished psychologist, administered what he claimed were "culture-free" IQ tests to new immigrants on Ellis Island, and found that 83% of Jews, 80% of Hungarians, 79% of Italians, and 87% of Russians were "feeble-minded," adding that "all feeble-minded are at least potential criminals." IQ tests have gotten a little better since then, but given the character of the testing process, the attitudes of those who make up any test and the variety of people—coming from so many different backgrounds—who take it, it is impossible to produce a test that does not have serious biases;

- *that exams are objectively graded.* Daniel Stark and Edward Elliot sent two English essays to 200 high school teachers for grading. They got back 142 grades. For one paper, the grades ranged from 50 to 99; for the other, the grades went from 64 to 99. But English is not an "objective" subject, you say. Well, they did the same thing for an essay answer in mathematics and got back grades ranging from 28 to 95. Though most of the grades they received in both cases fell into the middle ground, it was evident that a good part of any grade was the result of who marked the exam and not of who took it;

- *that exams are an accurate indication of what students know and of intelligence in general.* But all sorts of things, including luck in getting (or not getting) the questions you hoped for and one's state of mind and emotions the day of the exam, can have an important affect on the result. Here, readers only have to think back to exams where you were well prepared and did poorly, or where you knew very little and did extremely well;

- *that all students have an equal chance to do well on exams, that even major differences in their conditions of life have a negligible impact on their performance.* There is such a strong correlation between students' family income and their test scores, however, that the radical educational theorist, Ira Shor, has suggested (tongue-in-cheek, I think) that college applications should ignore test scores altogether and just ask students to enter their family income. The results would be the same—with relatively few exceptions, the same people would get admitted into college, but then, of course, the belief that there is equality of opportunity in the class room would stand forth as the myth that it is;

- *that exams are the fairest way to distribute society's scarce resources to the young, and hence the association of exams with the ideas of meritocracy and equality of opportunity.* But if some students consistently do better on exams because of the advantages they possess and other students do not outside of school, then directing society's main benefits to these same people merely compounds the initial inequality. Between members of this educational elite, of course, a degree of meritocracy and equality of opportunity does exist— though George W. Bush's emergence as President should tell us something about its limits. What is unfair are the material benefits won by the whole of this educational elite by doing better on exams than the rest of the people in their age cohort when it is not the exams but differences in their conditions of life that have determined most of the outcome. Perhaps this is what former President and millionaire, Jimmy Carter, meant when he said, "Life is unfair";

- *that exams, and particularly the fear of them, are necessary in order to motivate students to do their assignments.* Who can doubt that years of reacting to such threats have produced in many students a reflex of the kind depicted here? The sad fact is that the natural curiosity of young people and their desire to learn, to develop, to advance, to master, and the pleasure that comes from succeeding—which could and should motivate all studying—has been progressively replaced in their psyches by a pervasive fear of failing. This needn't be. For the rest, if the only reason that a student does the assignments for a particular course is that he/she is worried about the exam, he/she should not be taking that course in the first place;

- *that exams are not injurious—socially, intellectually and psychologically.* This is a big one, and I prefer to deal with it in connection with my analysis of what exams actually do.

III

Complaining about exams may be most students' first truly informed criticism about the society in which they live, informed because they are its victims and know from experience how exams work. They know, for example, that exams don't only involve reading questions and writing answers. They also involve forced isolation from other students, prohibition on talking and walking around and going to the bathroom, writing a lot faster than usual, physical discomfort, worry, fear, anxiety (lots of that), and often guilt.

They are also aware that exams do a poor job of testing what students actually know. What student hasn't griped about at least some of these things. But it is just here that most of their criticisms run into a brick wall, because most students don't know enough about society to understand the role that exams—especially taking so many exams—plays in preparing them to take their place in it.

Up to this point, my main effort has gone into debunking our most widespread beliefs about exams as so many myths. But if exams are not what most people think they are, then what are they? The short answer, as indicated above, is that exams have less to do with testing us for what we are supposed to know than teaching us what the other aspects of instruction cannot get at (or get at as well). To understand what that is, we must examine what the capitalist class, who control the main levers of power in our society, require from a system of education. Here, it is clear that capitalists need a system of education that provides young people with the knowledge and skills necessary for their businesses to function and prosper. But they also want schools to give youth the beliefs, attitudes, emotions, and associated habits of behaviour that make it easy for capitalists to tap into this store of knowledge and skills. And they need all this not only to maximize their profits, but to help reproduce the social, economic, and even political conditions and accompanying processes that allow them to extract any profits whatsoever. Without workers, consumers ,and citizens who are well versed in and accepting of their roles in these processes, the entire capitalist system would grind to a halt. It is here—particularly as regards the behaviourial and attitudinal prerequisites of capitalist rule—that the culture of exams has become indispensable.

Well, what does sitting for so many exams, together with the long hours spent and anxiety involved in studying for them, and the shame felt for the imperfect grades obtained on them, "teach" students?

Here's the short list:

- The crush of tests gets students to believe that one gets what one works for, that the standards by which this is decided are objective and fair, and therefore that those who do better deserve what they get; and that the same holds for those who do badly. After awhile, this attitude is carried over to what students find in the rest of society, including their own failures later in life, where it encourages them to "blame the victim" (themselves or others) and feel guilty for what is not their fault.

- By fixing a time and a form in which they have to deliver or else, exams prepare students for the more rigorous discipline of the work situation that lies ahead.

- In forcing students to think and write faster than they ordinarily do, exams get them ready—mentally, emotionally, and also morally—for the speed-ups they will face on the job.

- The self-discipline students acquire in preparing for exams also helps them put up with the disrespect, personal abuse and boredom that awaits them on the job.

- Exams are orders that are not open to question—"discuss this," "outline that," etc.—and taking so many exams conditions students to accept unthinkingly the orders that will come from their future employers. As with the army, following lots of orders, including many that don't seem to make much sense, is ideal training for a life in which one will be expected to follow orders.

- By fitting the infinite variety of answers given on exams into the straitjacket of A, B, C, D and F, students get accustomed to the standardization of people as well as of things and the impersonal job categories that will constitute such an important part of their identity later on.

- Because passing an exam is mainly good for enabling students to move up a grade so they can take a slightly harder exam, which—if they pass—enables them to repeat the exercise ad infinitum, they begin to see life itself as an endless series of ever more complicated exams, where one never finishes being judged and the need for being prepared and respectful of the judging authorities only grows.
- Because their teachers know all the right answers to the exams, students tend to assume that those who are above them in other hierarchies—at work and in politics—also know much more than they do.
- Because their teachers genuinely want them to do well on exams, students also mistakenly assume that those in relation of authority over them in other hierarchies are also rooting for them to succeed, that is, have their best interests at heart.
- Because most tests are taken individually, striving to do well on a test is treated as something that concerns students only as individuals. Cooperative solutions are equated with cheating, if considered at all. Again, the implications of this for how students should approach the problems they will confront later in life are usually taken as obvious.
- Because one is never quite ready for an exam—there is always something more to do—students often feel guilty for reading materials or engaging in activities unrelated to the exam. The whole of life, it would appear, is but preparation for exams, or doing what is required in order to succeed (as those in charge define "success").
- With the Damocles sword of a failing (or for some a mediocre) grade hanging over their heads throughout their years in school (including university), the inhibiting fear of swift and dire punishment never leaves students, no matter their later situation.
- Coupled with the above, because there is always so much to be known, exams—especially so many of them—tend to undermine students' self-confidence and to raise their levels of anxiety, with the result that most young people remain unsure that they will ever know enough to criticize existing institutions, and become even physically uncomfortable at the thought of trying to put something better in their place.
- Exams also play the key role in determining course content, leaving little time for material that is not on the exam. Among the first things to be omitted in this "tightening" of the curriculum are students' own reactions to the topics that come up, collective reflection on

the main problems of the day (like the war), alternative points of view and other possibilities generally, the larger picture (where everything fits}, explorations of topics triggered by individual curiosity, and indeed anything that is likely to promote creative, cooperative, or critical thinking. But then our capitalist ruling class is not particularly interested in dealing with workers, consumers and citizens who possess these qualities.

- Exams also determine the form in which most teaching goes on, since for any given exam there is generally a best way to prepare for it. Repetition and forced memorization, even learning by rote, and frequent quizzes (more exams) leave little time for other more imaginative approaches to conveying, exchanging and questioning facts and ideas. Again, creative and critical thinking are discouraged.

- Finally, multiple exams become one of the main factors determining the character of the relation between students (with students viewing each other as competitors for the best grades), the relation between students and teachers (with most students viewing their teachers as examiners and graders first, and most teachers viewing their students largely in terms of how well they have done on exams), also the relation between teachers and school administrators (since principals and deans now have an "objective" standard by which to measure teacher performance), and even the relation between school administrations and various state bodies (since the same standard is used by the state to judge the work of schools and school systems). In short, exams mediate all social relations in the educational system in a manner very similar to the way money—that other great mystifier and falsifier—mediates all relations between people in the larger society, and with the same dehumanizing results.

Without workers, consumers, and citizens who are well versed in and accepting of their roles in these processes, the entire capitalist system would grind to a halt. It is here — particularly as regards the behaviourial and attitudinal prerequisites of capitalist rule — that the culture of exams has become indispensable.

Once we put all these pieces together, it is clear that the current craze for increasing the number of exams for students at all levels has less to do with "raising standards," as the popular mantra would have it, than with developing more extensive control over the entire educational process, control that will allow the ruling class to streamline its necessary work of socialization. Control, then, rather than education, as this is ordinarily understood, is the overriding aim of the government's current passion for more exams, and it must be understood as such, and not as a misguided effort to "raise standards" that is unlikely to work.

IV

The question that arises next is: Why now? For it is clear that, while exams have been with us for a long time, socializing students in all the ways that I have outlined above, it is only recently that the mania for exams, for still more exams, has begun to affect government policies. The short answer to the question, "Why now?", is probably something we can all agree on. It is: globalization, or whatever it is one chooses to call this new stage at which our capitalist system has arrived. But to which of its aspects is the current drive for more exams a carefully fashioned response? The proponents of such educational "reform" point to the intensified competition between industries, and therefore too between workers world-wide, and the increasingly rapid pace at which economic changes of all kinds are occurring. To survive in this new order requires people, they say, who are not only efficient but have a variety of skills (or can quickly acquire them) and the flexibility to change tasks whenever called upon to do so. Thus, the only way to prepare our youth for the new economic life that awaits them is to raise standards of education, and that entails, among other things, more exams. On this view, exams are there to help students get and keep good jobs.

A more critical approach to globalization begins by emphasizing that the intensification of economic competition world-wide is driven by capitalists' efforts to maximize their profits. It is this that puts all the other developments associated with globalization into motion. And it is well known that, all things being equal, the less capitalists pay their workers and the less money they spend on improving work conditions and reducing pollution, the more profit they make. Recent technological progress in transportation and communication, together with free trade and the abolition of laws restricting the movement of capital, allow capitalists today to consider workers all over the world in making their calculations. While the full impact of these developments is yet to be felt, we can already see two of its most important effects in the movement of more and more companies (and parts of companies) out of the U.S. and a roll-back of the modest gains in wages, benefits and work conditions that American workers have won over the last 50 years of struggle. There is no question but that capitalists are simply following the goose that lays the golden egg wherever it takes them; they have always done so and will always do so, no matter the social costs, so long as we allow it.

Thus, while capitalists in this new age of globalization certainly need workers with the right mix of skills and knowledge to run their businesses, they need every bit as much—and I believe even more—people across the society and particularly in the working class who will accept their worsening conditions and accompanying fears and anxieties without making waves. Naturally, if changes in education alone (with the main focus on exams) could produce the desired effect, the capitalists would be very pleased. But if—and where—it can't, the capitalists and their government (and their media, and their cultural, educational and social institutions) are quick to supplement it with other tactics. The current rage for more exams, therefore, needs to be viewed as part of a larger strategy that includes the obscene stoking of patriotic fires and the chipping away of traditional civil liberties (both rationalized by the so-called "war" on terrorism), the promotion of "family values," restrictions on sexual freedom (but not, as we see, on sexual hypocrisy), and the push for more prisons and longer prison sentences for a whole range of minor crimes. Simply put, the "Man" is worried about loss of control at a key turning point in the development of capitalism when the disruption in people's lives is going to require more control than ever before.

Control, then, rather than education, as this is ordinarily understood, is the overriding aim of the government's current passion for more exams, and it must be understood as such, and not as a misguided effort to "raise standards" that is unlikely to work.

Is there also a connection between the explosion in the number of exams and the current drive toward the privatization of public education? They appear to be quite separate, but look again. With new investment opportunities failing to keep up with the rapidly escalating surpluses in search of them (a periodic problem for a system that never pays its workers enough to consume all the wealth that they produce), the public sector has become the latest "last" frontier for capitalist expansion. And given its size, and therefore potential for profit, what are state prisons, or utilities, or transport or communication systems, or other social services next to public education? But how to convince the citizenry that companies whose only concern is with the bottom line can do a better job educating our young than public servants who are dedicated to the task? Yet, what seems impossible could be done if—somehow—"education" were redefined to emphasize the qualities associated with business and its achievements. Then, of course—by definition—business could do the "job" better than any public agency.

Enter exams, especially standardized exams, especially so many of them. Businesses exist to make a profit, a sum of money that can be quantitatively measured at the end of the year, and all their activities are organized accordingly. Increasingly, the forces most responsible for the system of education in our society have begun to treat exams and the grades students receive on them on this model. Standardization, easily quantifiable results, and the willingness to reshape all intervening processes to obtain them characterize the path to success in both exams and in business.

How long does it take for what is still a model for how to deal with education to become a new definition of what education is (and can only be) about? When that happens (and to the extent it has already happened), putting education in the hands of businessmen who know best how to dispense with "inessentials" becomes a perfectly rational thing to do. In this manner, whether undertaken consciously or not (and I suspect it's a bit of both), does the introduction of more and more exams prepare the ground for the privatization of public education.

If there is any reader out there who still believes that exams have more to do with education than with control (and possibly privatization), and that increasing the number of exams is motivated by a sincere desire to help people learn, a recent story in the *New York Times* (Mar. 7, 2002) has something just for you. Poverty, it seems, plays a major role in lowering students' grades on exams. According to studies cited in this story, the prevalence of lead in the homes of poor children produces lower IQs and interferes with children's ability to concentrate. Frequent moves because of the lack of a permanent home also makes it very hard for the young people effected to prepare for exams. Persistent toothaches, due to inadequate dental care—another byproduct of poverty—is another problem related to poor exam results. After listing several such factors (simple hunger from not eating enough is not mentioned), the author concludes, "it is *curious* (my emphasis) that when we see poor children with lower test scores, we fail to consider if improving conditions of poverty, sometimes at relatively little cost, might also have an impact". Well, it would be "curious" (and more, and worse) if raising test scores and providing a good education were the goals of the exercise. But if the main goal of tests is maximizing control and learning how to accept being controlled, then the special handicaps under which some students suffer in taking tests is completely irrelevant. Which is it? Examine the evidence, then you decide. (Here's an exam worth taking).

V

"What Is To Be Done?" Or, more to the point, what should students do about all this? Well, they shouldn't refuse to take exams (unless the whole class gets involved), and they shouldn't drop out of school. Given the relations of power inside education and throughout the rest of society, that would be suicidal, and suicide is never good politics. Rather, they should become better students by learning more about the role of education, and of exams in particular, in capitalism. Nowhere does the contradiction between the selfish and manipulative interests of our ruling class and the educational and developmental interests of students stand out in such sharp relief as in the current debate over exams. Students of all ages need to get more involved in this debate, therefore, in order to raise the consciousness of young people regarding the source of their special oppression and the possibility of uniting with other oppressed groups to create a truly human society.

Beyond this, just remember that THEY are few and WE are many, but the power that comes from our greater numbers only becomes operational when people get organized and work together toward agreed-upon goals. Everything depends on the youth of today doing better on this crucial test than my generation did, because the price for failure has never been so high. Will they succeed? Can they afford to fail? ◆

Bertell Ollman is a professor of Politics at New York University and author, most recently, of How to Take an Exam . . . and Remake the World and Ballbuster? True Confessions of a Marxist Businessman.

This article was published in Our Schools/ Our Selves, Vol. 12 #2 Winter 2003.

Allies and resources

Compiled by Marita Moll

There are many individuals and organizations working against the standardized testing agendas now plaguing schools across the continent. The fastest place to find them is on the web. Following is a short list of sites that serve as good starting points:

ALFIE KOHN—Alfie Kohn was recently described by *Time* magazine as "perhaps the country's most outspoken critic of education's fixation on grades [and] test scores." His criticisms of competition and rewards have helped to shape the thinking of educators—as well as parents and managers—across the country and abroad. He is the author of eight books, and lectures widely at universities and to school faculties, parent groups, and corporations. http://www.alfiekohn.org/standards/standards.htm

CALIFORNIA COALITION FOR AUTHENTIC REFORM IN EDUCATION —a site dedicated to fighting standardized testing in California. The site asks two basic questions: "Does California's new system for testing all students in grades 2-11 move us toward higher achievement?" and "Is there a crisis in achievement in the first place." http://www.calcare.org/oldsite/whatsnew/whatsnew.htm

CANADIAN CENTRE FOR POLICY ALTERNATIVES (CCPA) undertakes and promotes research on issues of social and economic justice. CCPA produces research reports, books, opinion pieces, fact sheets and other publications, including *The Monitor*, a monthly digest of progressive research and opinion. Information about *Passing the Test; The False Promises of Standardized Testing*, as well as some the content is available on the website as well as in the CCPA education quarterly *Our Schools/ Our Selves*. http://www.policyalternatives.ca

MARITA MOLL is an educational researcher and research associate with the Canadian Centre for Policy Alternatives. She is the editor of *Passing the Test: The False Promises of Standardized Testing*. She manages a website on standardized testing in Canada with detailed information on who tests and how, with extensive links to research, national and informational information and other resources on the issue. http://www.maritamoll.ca

MASSREFUSAL is an anti-testing movement that started in Massachusetts and is growing vigorously around the country as more people become aware of how devastating these tests can be for students, and how destructive they are to the idea of a democratic public education system. The presidents of several local teacher unions in Massachusetts have joined with *New Democracy*, calling on teachers and teacher union locals to refuse to administer MCAS, the high stakes test in Massachusetts, in 2002, and they are calling on parents to organize mass support for the teachers' actions. http://www.massrefusal.org

THE NATIONAL CENTER FOR FAIR & OPEN TESTING (FAIRTEST) is an advocacy organization working to end the abuses, misuses and flaws of standardized testing and ensure that evaluation of students and workers is fair, open, and educationally sound. FairTest places special emphasis on eliminating the racial, class, gender, and cultural barriers to equal opportunity posed by standardized tests, and preventing their damage to the quality of education. http://www.fairtest.org/

STUDENTS AGAINST TESTING (SAT) was created to be a force against the score-obsessed education machine known as standardized testing. At the same time, SAT also exists as an advocate for bringing positive, creative and real-life learning activities into the schools. SAT believes that for the reasons stated below urgent action from the student body itself is the most direct way to counteract the boredom and petty competition that currently plagues the schools. http://www.nomoretests.com/

SUSAN OHANIAN is a longtime teacher and the author of *Caught in the Middle: Nonstandard Kids and a Killing Curriculum* and *One Size Fits Few: The Folly of Educational Standards*. She is media consultant for the John Dewey Project on Progressive Education at the University of Vermont, Burlington. She is the author of numerous articles on standardized testing, many of which are posted on this site along with cartoons, letters from resisters, resources, news stories, etc. This is a very rich resource on standardized testing activities in the U.S. and beyond. http://www.susanohanian.org

Statements of concern

THE ALLIANCE FOR CHILDHOOD is an international partnership of individuals and organizations committed to fostering and respecting each child's inherent right to a healthy, developmentally appropriate childhood. *High-Stakes Testing: A Statement of Concern and a Call to Action* http://www.allianceforchildhood.net/news/index.htm

AMERICAN EDUCATIONAL RESEARCH ASSOCIATION (AERA) is the largest professional organization devoted to the scientific study of education. *Position Statement Concerning High-Stakes Testing in PreK-12 Education.* http://www.aera.net/about/policy/stakes.htm

CANADIAN ASSOCIATION OF PRINCIPALS (CAP) Valid Uses of Student Testing as part of Authentic, Comprehensive Student Assessment, A Statement of Concern from Canada's School Principals. http://www.cdnprincipals.org/news.htm

CANADIAN PSYCHOLOGICAL ASSOCIATION A Joint Position Statement by the Canadian Psychological Association and the Canadian Association of School Psychologists on the Canadian Press Coverage of the Province-wide Achievement Test Results. http://www.cpa.ca/documents/joint%5Fposition.html

ELEMENTARY TEACHERS' FEDERATION OF ONTARIO (ETFO) Adjusting the Optics: Assessment, Evaluation and Reporting. A Response from the ETFO. http://www.etfo.ca/documents/adjusting theoptics.pdf

ONTARIO STUDENT TRUSTEES' ASSOCIATION A Road Map For Success; Testing in Our Schools. http://www.osta-aeco.org/framee index.html

Measuring school and school system effectiveness

by Wayne Hampton

If we were to impose a moratorium on achievement testing in schools, then what might we pay attention to in order to say that a school/school system is doing well? Research and experience lead me to suggest that the school, as a community of learners with superior principal leadership, needs to gather data that answer the following questions:

- What kinds of learning activities and challenges do students engage in? Are students encouraged to wonder and raise questions about what they have studied? We should be less concerned with whether students can answer our questions than with whether they can ask their own.

- What is the intellectual significance of the ideas that students encounter? Are they important? Do they lead to meaningful learning experiences?

- Are students introduced to multiple perspectives? Are students asked to provide multiple perspectives?

- Do students have the ability to raise challenging questions?

- What connections (transfer of learning) are students encouraged to make between what they study in class and the world outside the school? What students do with what they learn, once they have choices and decisions to make, is the real measure of educational achievement.

- What opportunities do students have to become literate in the use of representational forms – music, poetry, prose, pictures, verbal/oral, written, multi-media, etc.?
- Do students have the opportunity to set their own goals and design ways to achieve them?
- What opportunities do students have to work cooperatively? Is cooperating and working together as a team part of what it means to be a student?
- To what extent are students given the opportunity to work in depth in domains that relate to their aptitudes (multiple intelligences)?
- Do students participate in the assessment of their own work (reflections and self-evaluation)?
- To what degree are students genuinely engaged in what they do in school? Do they find satisfaction with their involvement and participation in the school? As a school, are we paying attention to the joy of the journey?
- Are teachers given the time to observe and work with one another?
- Are parents encouraged to understand the educational importance of what their child has accomplished? Are support mechanisms in place to assist them?

In order to measure the effectiveness of schools and school systems, we need to ask specific and meaningful questions and gather precise, accurate data that demonstrate whether or not we are succeeding. We must widen, far beyond one-shot testing results, what educators know, and what the government, parents and the public believe to be important in judging the quality of schools and school systems. We need to think about public education not only as the education of the public in the schools, but also the education of the public outside our schools. A substantial and complex understanding of what constitutes good schooling by the public is essential if we are to survive as a public education system. ❧

Wayne Hampton is the Principal at Lacombe Upper Elementary
(Grades 3 to 6) in Wolf Creek School Division No. 72, Alberta.
Excerpted from remarks on standardized testing programs in Alberta
made to the International Confederation of Principals meeting, Ottawa,
Ontario, Feb. 13, 2003.

References

Coladarci, Theodore, "Is It a House.... Or a Pile of Bricks? Important Features of a Local Assessment System", *Phi Delta Kappan* June 2002, pp. 772-774.

Eisner, Elliot W., "What Does It Mean To Say a School Is Doing Well?", *Phi Delta Kappan*, January 2001, pp. 367-372.

Kohn, Alfie, *The Schools Our Children Deserve: Moving Beyond Traditional Classrooms and "Tougher Standards"*, (Houghton Mifflin Company, 1999).

Kohn, Alfie, *The Case Against Standardized Testing: Raising Scores, Ruining the Schools*, (Heinman Portsmouth, NH, 2000).

Popham, James W., "Teaching to the Test", *Education Leadership*, March 2001, pp. 16-20.

Popham, James W., *The Truth About Testing: An Educator's Call to Action*, (Association for Supervision and Curriculum Development, Alexandria, Virginia USA, 2001).

Raywid, Mary Anne, "Accountability: What's Worth Measuring?", *Phi Delta Kappan*, February 2002, pp. 433 – 436.

Sirotnik, Kenneth A., "Promoting Responsible Accountability in Schools and Education", *Phi Delta Kappan*, May 2002, pp. 662-673.

Stiggins, Richard J., "Assessment Crisis: The Absence of Assessment FOR Learning", *Phi Delta Kappan*, June 2002, pp. 758-765.

Tice, Lou, "Investment in Excellence for the 80s"; "Investment in Excellence for the 90s" and "Imagine 21: Fast Track to Change", *The Pacific Institute*.

Thompson, Scott, "The Authentic Standards Movement and Its Evil Twin", *Phi Delta Kappan*, January 2001, pp. 358 – 362.

How's my child doing?

Can a standardized test score answer this question?

by Elaine Decker

"**Is** my child all right?" is reportedly the first question asked in the delivery room by the new parent(s), and parents continue to ask that question as they follow their child's growth and development to adulthood. They frequently ask that question of the school. If the reply is comprised exclusively of the child's score on standardized tests, the answer is certainly insufficient, possibly misleading, or even downright meaningless.

"How's my child doing? (HMCD)" is a big question about a big question. Its top-level meaning is most likely, "Is my child building repertoire to thrive in the world, now, and later?" but it subsumes many subsidiary questions such as: "Are there problems?" "Is she making friends?" "Does he have good work habits?" or even "Is she having a good time at school?"

Just as we teach our students when they confront complex problems to break the problem into pieces, it may be useful to break this big question down into its key elements so that we can forge more honest and meaningful answers. There are at least five separate inquiries that parents (or guardians) are typically making with the global HMCD question:

- Is my child making progress over time?
- Is my child making appropriate or sufficient effort?

- Is my child performing within normal parameters for the age group?
- What is my child's rank in the peer cohort?
- Are there talents or trouble spots of which I should be aware?

Information gleaned from standardized test results can contribute to the answers to some of these questions, but is clearly inadequate to the entire task. Let's examine an appropriate response to each of the five elements of the HMCD question.

1. Progress over time

How can we show parents what the child can do *now* that she/he could not do when the school term began? Samples of work in a portfolio that document *then* and *now* will be helpful; naturalistic assessment data gathered in classroom observations will add evidence; student self-assessment using heuristics like charts, graphs, and sentence completions (One thing I learned in this science project is ...) can contribute. Class test scores and standardized test scores that show a change over time can be included. Note, however, that we need at *least* two scores on tests to show progress over time. Based on a single test result, we cannot claim that the child has changed over time. It could well be that she/he arrived in the class months earlier already capable of achieving a particular standard. We cannot claim that her performance was in any way influenced by class lessons or activities, or even the simple passage of time in the class. If, when tested again in a year's time, a child achieves the same results as she did on an initial test, that's obviously not progress over time. It tells us we ought to look for greater detail to help us understand this child's "steady state," whether the test result itself is high, medium or low.

Clearly, to show progress over time we need to provide evidence of *change*, evidence that simply cannot be shown by a single snapshot, a single conversation, or the score on a single test.

2. Appropriate effort

Some accomplishments in school or in life are as a result of special genetic endowment, what we typically call a gift, or a talent. Some accomplishments are as a result of focused and dedicated effort, what we typically call practice or hard work. Elite accomplishments of every kind appear to require *both* talent and effort. As teachers and parents, we may become anxious when we see a talented child failing to build habits of focus and dedication, because we fear that her/his gift will be squandered, never developing to its full, never enriching the individual nor contributing its richness to our common world.

Again, through naturalistic observations, and peer and self-evaluation, we can get a better picture of *how* a child is working, and also *how hard*. Teachers who use cooperative learning strategies for group work typically ask their students to evaluate not only their final product, but how they accomplished it, making judgments on their individual contributions as well as the efforts of their team members. With experience, students can make sophisticated comments about the appropriateness of their levels of concentration, data gathering, problem solving, turn taking, brainstorming, note making, openmindedness, listening skills, supporting others, summarizing. These are among the tools that they will need to get them through the tough, complex assignments that life presents, the novel situations likely to require both talent and tenacity, gifts and guts.

Novel problems, performances and projects, or what Grant Wiggins calls "authentic assessment" opportunities, can provide data about effort, especially if they require students to document their preparation for the performance or event. Likewise tests, even standardized tests, can reveal effort *if* the student is required to "show her/his work" *and* that work is part of the grade given to each question. If only the answer *count*s, we can't obtain any reliable information about effort. The answer could simply be a guess, the result of luck, which is even less useful as a life skill than is an undeveloped gift!

3. Functioning within normal parameters

When asked by Captain Picard *(Star Trek: The Next Generation)* to assess the state of various technical systems of the Starship Enterprise, Commander Data would typically reply that the system was "functioning within normal parameters," something we might translate to mean, "no worries." No worries is definitely a worthy, though elusive, goal in both parenting and teaching. Observers of children, including Benjamin Spock, Jean Piaget, Lev Vygotsky, Maria Montessori and others, have helped us to understand child development and developmental readiness, and to accept that, while each individual is unique, there are some patterns or typical ranges of function (usually contextually or culturally influenced) that we call *normal*, often bounded by age markers around indicators of achievement. For instance, we may say children typically begin to walk unassisted between the ages of 10 months and 18 months.

Typical is not identical, and any family with more than one child will attest to the fact that siblings do not demonstrate acquisition of motor, intellectual and social skills at exactly the same time, though each may be functioning within normal parameters.

If a child demonstrates a level of achievement at something we value, say, speaking in sentences, at an earlier age than is common, we are usually pleased; if he or she is approaching the late side of the normal parameters range, we usually worry and possibly look for both reasons and remedy. Over time, as lay people and experts, individuals and members of cultures, we re-examine and adjust the parameters of what we call normal and we readjust our worrying. Understanding developmental readiness and normal parameters (fluid as they are and should be) and providing evidence to parents that for particular learning outcomes their child is functioning within the normal range are important contributions to that elusive parental state, "no worries."

4. Rank in cohort

Any kind of judgment about rank requires a standard; when one is asked to rank an object, experience, or individual, one typically asks, "Compared to what?" Complex judgments also require criteria which work together with standards to enable us to determine what is acceptable performance. For example, "Is this the best vehicle?" may be answered against the criteria of gas consumption and price. In each case we typically seek the lowest value. If we add the criterion of passenger and/or cargo capacity, we would be looking for a high standard. We rank or compare the vehicles against others that are "in the running" and, in the end, we make a judgment based on the array of available data.

> To show progress over time we need to provide evidence of *change*, evidence that simply cannot be shown by a single snapshot, a single conversation, or the score on a single test.

Standardized test promoters tell us that they are providing similar data. For example, they claim that they have a test mechanism that provides a standard of achievement – say, the ability to correctly answer questions of long division using a two-digit divisor – that they can apply to all students in British Columbia in Grade 4 in the year 2002. They claim that the results of this test can tell parents, teachers, and policy makers who is better able to do long division than whom. Bearing in mind that the manufacture and delivery of these tests consumes a great deal of money and time, we should question just how reliable this ranking claim is, and just how important or useful it is to have this ranking information.

This result could be useful information if correctly doing long division were a public priority (the topic for another paper entirely!) *and* if the various jurisdictions and cohorts of students within them were comparable in significant and reliable ways *and* we could aggregate the data with confidence, *and* the test conditions were comparable, *and* so on. Problems creep in when we leap to the conclusions that, if the majority of students *do* get the right answer, the schools are a) solely responsible for that, b) good, and c) we have no worries. Problems creep in, too, when we conclude that, if the majority of students *don't* get the right answer, the schools are a) solely responsible for that, b) bad, and c) we need to test the students more, and more often so that they *will* get the answers right! I'll say more about these dangerous conclusions later. For now, we must admit that the long division test question results really only allow us to compare the student against the standard of correct or incorrect – and even some mathematicians balk at the "single answer = mathematics" equation! And, as mentioned in the progress-over-time argument, this result could be evidence of a bad day or a good guess. Much more than standardized test data is necessary to make an honest adjudication of student success, pedagogical success, policy success, or the general goodness of our schools.

Rather than comparing all Grade 4 students in B.C. to one another, it is more sensible to compare all students in our Grade 4 class in East Vancouver this year. This comparison contributes richer detail because these students share a school, a neighbourhood, a teacher, and a learning experience. It will help parents conceptualize the cohort – conditions here, now – which in turn creates an understandable context for information about rank. When the teacher says, "Your 10-year-old daughter is articulate and entertaining; she is among the top three public speakers in our class," parents can draw an informed conclusion. They are likely to sense that in another cohort at another time, or even another cohort at this time, (theatre, sports, a Toastmaster's Club for adults, a university moot court), the ranking data might change. Or it might not!

Common to the work of Howard Gardner, Daniel Goelman, Caine & Caine, and Belenky et. al is the recognition that human beings are intelligent in many different ways, we learn different things in many different ways, we communicate in many different ways. The profile of any individual's "intelligence" might look like a mountain range, with a peak in kinesthetic awareness, a valley in verbal skills, a plateau in emotional intelligence. As the child grows and moves about in different social and physical spheres, that profile will undoubtedly shift. When comparing students to each other, we are best to remember former U.S. child advocate Marian Wright Edelman's advice about getting the wrong answer by asking the wrong questions. She said, "Don't ask 'How *smart* is this child?', but rather, 'How is *this* child smart?'" If we were all smart in exactly the same ways, society would be dull indeed!

5. Talents or trouble spots

The last aspect of the HMCD question is driven by the awareness that each child is "special," especially to her/his parents. If a child has demonstrated unusual interest in music or intense curiosity about dinosaurs, it makes sense to share this observation with parents so that they can join the child in exploring or developing this interest. Likewise, if a child is struggling with language development, or is not functioning within normal parameters with handwriting or other fine motor skills, it makes sense to engage with parents to develop a plan for close observation, support, and possible remediation. Two cautionary notes are in order. While "the sooner the better" seems sensible when reporting a child's possible developmental lag, we know that the developmental path is not a straight line, and raising concerns too soon can put unreasonable pressure on a child who is simply a late bloomer. Secondly, just as a competent physician would not announce a diagnosis without an accompanying treatment plan, a caring teacher does not just deliver the "problem," handing it off to the parents to worry over themselves. Some strategies to support the child should be proposed, which can be discussed and implemented jointly, to the extent possible.

> "Don't ask 'How *smart* is this child?', but rather, 'How is *this* child smart?'"

Definitive statements, threats, or warnings about the child's "failure to achieve her potential" are neither humane not productive. There is ample evidence that, when a physician tells a patient he has three months to live, the patient lives three months. Another patient with the same medical condition, who is invited by her physician to participate in a program of healing, is likely to live a great deal longer. Our work as teachers and parents is to help our children prepare for their future; it is not our work – nor even an option, if we are honest – to tell them what that future is.

Other considerations

As a parent, I long for that "no worries" state of mind, partly engendered by knowing that my child is all right in the world, or will likely become an adult who is all right in the world. Rationally, I know that "no worries" is unrealizable because the world is neither perfect nor stable, just as the child or the adult is neither perfect nor stable. No worries now doesn't mean no worries later! Helping my child to be "all right" requires as much my constant effort to work on and in the world, as it does to work on and with the child. No report from a teacher at any time should suggest that the learning story is finished. We simply can't know what will be next, for ourselves, for our students, for our children, and we must treat any data as small elements in a grand scheme comprised of individuals, collectives, and physical and social contexts, all shifting in and around each other in some causal, some chaotic, and some downright accidental relationships. Humility is in order.

Secondly, both parents and teachers need to realize that each has intelligence to offer the other about the progress of the child. Parental observations about work habits at home are equally valid as teacher observations about work habits at school. Parents and teachers should build, through dialogue, a deeper understanding of the contributions and requirements of their joint charge. If the parent is sitting as a silent receiver of teacher wisdom, or the teacher is sitting as a silent receiver of parental demands, any data about the child's behaviour has diminished utility because the probing, revising, expanding, and confirming contributions of conversation are missing.

Finally, using aggregated data about individual student performance to make conclusive statements about the performance of classes, schools ,or school systems is not only silly, it is dangerous. It can lead us in entirely inappropriate directions. Columbia University Professor Linda Darling-Hammond once remarked that this process is akin to taking the basal temperature of every hospital patient and, upon finding that the majority were in the "normal" range, concluding that the health care system was itself OK! We need to recognize the fact that it isn't easy to live a good life, it isn't easy to walk gently in the environment of Earth, it isn't easy to create social communities that forge common purpose while accommodating differences. Given that failure to meet these difficult challenges results in sadness, loneliness or pain; fouling our nest so that we can't survive; or solving our conflicts in violent and destructive ways, our individual and collective good lives depend on our embracing the challenge. In the shadow of that enormous realization, looking for a report card or a standardized test to capture the complex past or the promising future of a child seems silly indeed.

"How is my child doing?" is a fundamental question that ought to be asked regularly and often, by all of us in the human family, not just about our own biological children. It ought to be answered in the broadest, most hopeful, most respectful ways. We should seek the answer not just of our schools, but of ourselves. We are, after all, the people who set the standards, for the tests, for the children, for the schools, for the world. 🕮

Elaine Decker is the Director, Office of Continuing Professional Education, Faculty of Education, University of British Columbia.

PEI keeps its focus on classroom assessments

by Bob MacRae

Teachers are often asked for quick, articulate responses to questions about what a test really tells us about our education system. How do our schools stack up compared to others, not only regionally but globally? Or more significantly, how is his or her child doing in school? Many people are looking for the impossible – a "quick fix", a simple, yet conclusive answer. The wisest answers really must be complex and conditional. Unfortunately, starting a response with "It depends" or a reference to the philosophy of public education in our province is not likely to get the questioner's attention, or get quoted by the local journalist looking for a story.

The release of test scores such as the Programme for International Student Assessment (PISA) highlights this frustration. What gets reported may make a sensational "sound bite" but what gets ignored is often the most compelling, cogent part of the story.

The mania for accountability and the mercurial rise in standardized tests and assessments – PISA, SAIP (Student Achievement Indicators Program) and other "high-stakes testing" – in most jurisdictions in the developed world has been mind boggling. The media has been full of rankings, comparisons, and treatises by policy makers seeking accountability. Even teachers are now being tested to determine their suitability to teach. Last year, I along with others, met with a group of visiting teachers to discuss our educational system and specifically our slate of professional development programs. The first eight questions posed by these visiting teachers dealt with assessment and accountability, not the programs themselves. It soon became clear that nothing happens in their jurisdiction without measurement and that this mania for accountability has overwhelmed the system. It is not just important, as anyone will concede, but has become all that is important in many cases.

To its credit, the PEI Department of Education has bucked the trend towards expensive "quick fix" tests to demonstrate accountability and has maintained a focus on more informative measures:

- classroom assessments, tests, class exams;
- oral and written reports;
- journals;
- group activities;
- portfolios;
- and good old observation.

Now, other jurisdictions looking for improved forms of accountability are starting to notice the benefits of classroom assessments. The May 22, 2002 edition of *Education Week on the Web* suggests that classroom assessments teachers use daily provide one of the most powerful tools available for improving student achievement. In Lincoln, Nebraska, the Director of Evaluation has said that "Large scale assessment programs are never going to provide teachers with the information they need because by the time teachers get the information back, they've already moved on". The school board is now emphasizing classroom assessments.

As educators, we are interested in being able to accurately explain to a parent how his or her child is achieving. Continuing to improve our knowledge about good classroom assessment practices, clarifying learning goals and providing effective feedback, and giving challenging classroom assignments will all be positive steps in this process.

It's ironic that, in other jurisdictions bitten by the mania for high stakes testing, classroom assessment is re-emerging as possibly the most useful measure or test. In PEI, classroom assessment has always been the major form of assessment. While there is no question that we must continue to strive to find more and better "classroom assessment strategies", there now appears to be some evidence that we have been correct to avoid the craze for large scale testing. ❧

Bob MacRae is the Executive Assistant, Professional Development Services, Prince Edward Island Teachers' Federation.

(A version of this article originally appeared in the PEITF Newsletter, June 2002.)

Education Quality Indicators Project (EQUIP)

A project of the Education Quality and Accountability Office (Ontario)

EQUIP has identified seven themes, 21 indicators of education quality at the elementary school level and 13 indicators at the secondary school level. These indicators were chosen based on research findings that show a correlation between the selected indicators and student achievement and consultations with education stakeholders in the province.

1. Community, student and family demographics
   - Student enrolment (E&S)
   - Socio-economic status.
   - Parents' educational attainment (E&S)
   - Language background (E&S)
   - Categories of students with special needs (E&S)
   - Student mobility (E)

2. Preparedness to learn and early-learning support
   - Attendance in nursery school or kindergarten programs (E)

3. School leadership
   - School Leadership, planning and decision making (E&S)

4. School climate
   - Safety in Schools (E&S)
   - Class size and organization (E&S)
   - Support Personnel (E&S)
   - The types of special education programs available (E&S)

5. Community-school relationships
   - Community-school relationships (E&S)

6. Teaching and learning environment
   - Time allocation. (E)
   - Accessibility of instructional materials. (E)
   - Availability of assessment materials (E)
   - Availability of computers (E&S)
   - Teacher professional-development, planning and collaboration (E)
   - Parental involvement. (E)
   - Teacher qualifications and experience (E&S)

7. Student achievement
   - Student Achievement (E&S)

For full version of this document see: http//www.eqao.com.

A 10 step alternative to high stakes testing in Ontario

High stakes test providers say that this is the only way to make schools, teachers and school boards accountable for student learning. Testing does not ensure that students have the schooling they need to learn.

1. Eliminate the Grade 10 literacy test as a graduation requirement; replace it with ongoing evaluations and appropriate remedial assistance.

2. Use random standardized testing in certain subjects, grades and schools, followed by an analysis of the test results and intervention to improve areas of weakness before testing again.

3. Provide time and resources to ensure that all students have success in school.

4. Provide on-the-job training for teachers in curriculum delivery and use of performance-based tests that measure not just the ability to memorize facts but also the capacity for original thinking, real-world problem-solving, perseverance, and social responsibility.

5. Support students at risk with full service school teams, including counselling and support from educational assistants and professional student services personnel.

6. Ensure the comparison of exam results across the province by implementing a consistent template for the content and marking of Grade 12 examinations.

7. Implement a curriculum renewal cycle, beginning with a systematic review and revision of each grade and course that has been offered in the new Ontario curriculum.

8. Recognize the value of subject expertise by pilot testing Grades 7 to 12 schools with qualified subject specialists.

9. Develop a self-evaluation process for schools and school boards every five to seven years and implement improvements subject to provincial supervision.

10. Measure and publicize accountability using a number of indicators. The Education Quality Indicators Project (EQUIP) collects data on nine indicators including school climate, student achievement, education financing, community characteristics and stakeholder satisfaction.

From the Ontario Secondary School Teachers' Federation web site
http://www.osstf.on.ca/www/issues/studenttesting/tenstepalternative.html

Cooperative testing

A review of How to Take an Exam... and Remake the World, *by Bertell Ollman. Montreal, Black Rose Books, 2000, viii/ 191 pages, $19.99 (paperback), ISBN 1-55164-170-4.*

reviewed by Paul Leduc Browne

Bertell Ollman once made headlines as the inventor of the world's first Marxist board game, *Class Struggle*. In *How to Take an Exam... and Remake the World*, he offers us a Marxist self-help book for students, indeed for all those willing to think critically. The book is intriguingly written and very intelligent. Ollman has a wonderful sense of humour and the book is also extremely funny.

A noted philosopher who has taught at a number of American and European universities for thirty-five years, Ollman has "acquired an enormous exam lore" during his career, but doesn't feel any strong urge to share it with his readers. Rather:

> *What I really would like to do is to tell you about capitalism, the system by which we produce and distribute the wealth of our society, but I suspect that most of you couldn't care less about what I have to say on this topic. Yet you'd probably like to hear my exam advice. So: Let's Make a Deal. That's the catch. I'll tell you what you need to know in order to write the best possible exams if you lend an ear to my account of capitalism.*

In the nearly 200 pages that follow, Ollman intersperses a montage of brief reflections on the disparities and contradictions of capitalist society with practical (and often sardonic) tips on preparing for exams and passing them.

The logic by which Ollman's thought unfolds is not linear. The book at first appears as a collection of little snippets pasted together almost randomly. It helps to know that he first made his reputation with a book entitled *Alienation* (Cambridge University Press, 1971), which expounds Marx's philosophy of internal relations, and has recently published *Dialectical Investigations*. Dialectical thinking "is the ongoing effort to grasp things in terms of their interconnections and this includes their ties with their own preconditions and future possibilities as well as with whatever is affecting them (and whatever they are affecting) right now." But Ollman gives us all the tools we need in *How to Take an Exam...*

In a marvellous passage, Ollman recalls Oliver Sacks's brain-injured patient, who could perceive all the discrete aspects of things, but couldn't understand how they related to each other to form a whole. In Ollman's eyes, we all suffer from such blindness; only, most of us do so for sociological, rather than neurological reasons: "the socialization that we all undergo in capitalism inclines us to see the particulars that enter our lives but to ignore the ways they are related and, thus, to miss the patterns that emerge from these relations."

We can see much of what goes on in capitalist society; but the system, capitalism,that underpins and unites all these experiences and relations, remains invisible to most of us. *How to Take an Exam... and Remake the World* aims first to show us the many different particulars, then to give us to tools to relate them to each other, and finally to make the whole – capitalism – visible in all its contradictions.

You will have guessed from this that the topic of exams is more than incidental here, more than a mere gimmick to gain an audience. Indeed, a punning cartoon right at the beginning of the book tells us as much. A teacher lectures a student: "Pass the exam! Your future is at stake!" To which the student retorts: "Examine the past! Your present is at stake!" (Incidentally, the book's hilarious political cartoons alone would make it worth reading.)

Ollman regards exams as part of the process of moulding individuals' hearts, minds and bodies to the needs of the labour market in the interest of employers. In his words, exams "are the chain that binds students to their desks and to the *status quo*, the treadmill that prepares them for the still bigger rat race to come, the gun at the head that threatens to go off should they try to move away, and, maybe worst of all, the drug that so befogs students' minds that they take this mad scene for normal." Exams condition us to sit still, to endure abuse, stress and boredom, to cope with speeded-up work, to accept orders and imposed tasks without question, to live in fear of failure, to feel always inadequate, and to believe in the greater wisdom and intelligence of those administering the tests. "Is it any wonder," Ollman asks, "that life itself is often experienced as a series of exams for which one is never quite prepared, never quite in time, and never quite finished?"

Yet it need not be thus. In a metaphor for a broader process of social change, Ollman describes an "alternative to the typical exam, where each individual is thrown into a deadly competition with others," namely the *cooperative exam*, "where students work together to produce a common product." Anyone who has tried cooperative ventures within the school system knows that the results are uneven. Some always feel that they are doing all the work or contributing all the brains, while others just aren't pulling their weight. As Ollman recognizes, the cooperative approach requires students to display a strong sense of responsibility; but as he also points out, it fosters such qualities in turn.

Georg Lukács once pointed out that there can be no such thing as a blessed island of socialism in an ocean of capitalism. The competitive system tends to overwhelm isolated attempts to live and work cooperatively. True and lasting change can only be systemic. Systemic change requires knowledge. Like Hegel, who defined freedom not as the absence of necessity, but as its recognition, Ollman believes that freedom "is not simply doing what you want, but includes knowing how to do it, when to do it, why you should do it, and, sometimes, why you shouldn't."

How to Take an Exam... demystifies the context in which exams are administered. But it also offers the student a wealth of excellent advice on how to approach exams. By suggesting ways to prepare for exams and achieve the best results, while putting the whole process in perspective, Ollman aims to give us "the mental distance and the moral right to manipulate them back (...) to ace an exam without losing [our] soul[s] in the process." In so doing, he arms us intellectually to take on the challenge of remaking the world of alienation in which we live. ❧

Paul Leduc Browne teaches political science at l'Université du Québec en Outaouais. He has endured many exams on both sides of the divide.

This article was originally published in Our Schools, Our Selves Vol.11 #1, October, 2001.

What is the relation between grades and money?

by Bertell Ollman

In ancient Greek mythology, Procrustes was an inn keeper who made sure that guests fit perfectly into the bed he prepared for them. Those who were too short were stretched, while guests who were too tall had their legs trimmed to the size of the bed. Both money and grades serve our society as Procrustean beds. Money enables us to compare very different things on the basis of their price. Grades enable us to compare very different people on the basis of a letter. Once we attach a monetary value to something, its other qualities become much less important and are often ignored altogether. The same thing happens to the distinctive qualities of each person once we view him or her as an "A," "B," or "C" student.

"Commodification" is the process by which things acquire a price. What is made to be eaten, worn, lived in, etc. finds its way into the market and is hereafter thought about and valued largely in function of its price. Grades represent the commodification of the learning process. They stand in for many different kinds and levels of knowledge much like money does for the different kind of products it can buy. Grades reduce the enormous variety of human talent and achievement to a single dimension (which gets tested), then measures it, and eventually replaces it in the eyes of students, teachers and the general public alike. No wonder the grade consciousness of many students often reaches demented proportions, very much like the greed for money.

Grades could only acquire this power, because – as in the case of money – the activities they represent have become separated from and turned against the very people who are engaged in them. As we saw in the discussion of alienation above, everything students do as part of getting educated is controlled by those who run the universities and used primarily for their own benefit. Thus, exams break down students, viewed as a group of people who share a common interest in acquiring an education, into so many atomistic individuals competing for a limited good; while grading recombines the now isolated individuals into new, artificial groups ("A" students, "B" students, etc.), whose most distinctive qualities are of greatest interest to their future employers. More than a simple instrument of control, grades are the sign that academic servitude has arrived full circle. It is the form in which the relation of domination itself has passed into the hands of its victims, who are encouraged to treat the yellow star sown onto their jackets as if it were an Olympic gold medal.

Excerpted from How to Take an Exam... and Remake the World

Educational accountability
...as if education mattered

by Bernie Froese-Germain

As someone who has spent his entire career doing research, writing, and thinking about educational testing and assessment issues, I would like to conclude by summarizing a compelling case showing that the major uses of tests for student and school accountability during the past 50 years have improved education and student learning in dramatic ways. Unfortunately, that is not my conclusion. Instead, I am led to conclude that in most cases the instruments and technology have not been up to the demands that have been placed on them by high-stakes accountability. Assessment systems that are useful monitors lose much of their dependability and credibility for that purpose when high stakes are attached to them. The unintended negative effects of the high-stakes accountability uses often outweigh the intended positive effects. (R.L.Linn[1])

If 2000 was the year that testing went crazy, 2001 was the year it went stark raving mad. (G.W. Bracey[2])

As an education researcher and parent, I harbour serious apprehensions about many of the so-called "reforms" imposed on the education system in the name of "accountability" over the past 10 to 15 years. Perhaps my biggest concern lies with the growing use of large-scale standardized testing, whether provincial, national or international in scope.

A perusal of the contemporary education literature tells a revealing story in this regard:

- cash awards being offered to teachers and schools for improved student test scores – and sanctions imposed on those schools whose scores do not improve;

- schools eliminating student recess in favour of additional preparation for tests;
- paying students as an incentive for obtaining high test scores;
- students dropping out of school due to pressure from high-stakes testing;
- excluding students with disabilities or with limited fluency in English from taking tests to ensure their scores don't bring down school averages;
- using scarce instructional resources to purchase test preparation materials;
- incidents of test cheating on the increase;
- testing very young children to assess "readiness" for kindergarten and imposing standards-based reform on early childhood education;
- having Grade 8 students take college preparation tests for practice;
- replacing teachers and administrators or revoking a school's accreditation for poor test performance;
- distributing "pacing charts" to teachers spelling out what is to be taught on a given day; and
- requiring "accountability contracts" between school districts and education ministries which set targets for improvement based on student achievement data.

This is a sampling of the numerous practices that have bubbled out of our test-obsessed culture, symptoms of educational accountability gone badly wrong. Some researchers have described these phenomena as a demonstration of Heisenberg's Uncertainty Principle (social science version) which states that:

> The more important that any quantitative social indicator becomes in social decision-making, the more likely it will be to distort and corrupt the social process it is intended to monitor.[3]

So, what does this have to do with testing? Amrein and Berliner explain:

> When applied to a high-stakes testing environment, this principle warns us that attaching serious personal and educational consequences to performance on tests for schools, administrators, teachers, and students, may have distorting and corrupting effects. The distortions and corruptions that accompany high-stakes tests make inferences about the meanings of the scores on those

*tests uncertain. If there is uncertainty about the meaning of a
test score the test may not be valid. Unaware of this ominous
warning, supporters of high-stakes testing, particularly politicians, have caused high-stakes testing to proliferate.*[4]

Testing costs – financially and otherwise

Ontario – where the testing agenda is out of control – is a good case in
point. The province currently tests all Grade 3 and 6 students in reading, writing and math; all Grade 9 students are tested in math; and all
Grade 10 students must now take a literacy test as a graduation requirement – arguably one of the most high-stakes tests in the country. With
further testing planned in the areas of science and technology (Grades 4
and 7) and social studies (Grades 5 and 8), testing will soon take place
every year in Grades 3 through 10. If nothing else, students are sure to
become good, if not anxious, test-takers.

It is estimated that the Education Quality and Accountability Office
(EQAO), the government agency that administers province-wide testing, spends $50 million annually in direct costs for the program. This
figure does not begin to capture the indirect or "buried soft costs" ex-
pended on testing by school boards and individual schools.[5] At the same
time, fundraising in Ontario schools for basic items like textbooks and
school supplies is on the increase. One parent recently told me that her
local school board is planning to introduce a board-wide testing program in response to, and to prepare students for, the expanding provincial testing program – a classic case of testing begetting testing. Testing
can always be justified as a way to verify the results of other testing
programs.

In addition to financial expenditures (both direct and indirect), there
are of course real educational, social, and other costs associated with
high-stakes testing.

Testing, for example, exacts a high price on educational equity. Ample evidence exists to demonstrate that high-stakes testing is especially
harmful to those students with the greatest needs, including poor and
minority students and those with limited English proficiency.[6] Describing accountability as a "creative new form of discrimination," Bartlett
states that race and poverty are consistently good predictors of test score
differences, largely due to "racially and class-biased notions of what
constitutes knowledge, how it should be taught, and how it should be
assessed."[7]

Alfie Kohn, an outspoken critic of the obsession with high-stakes testing and its negative impact on education, raises a host of other issues: educators becoming defensive and competitive in a high-stakes environment; pressure to raise test scores leading to cheating; testing contributing to teacher over-specialization in those subject areas targeted by high-stakes tests (such as math and science); and testing narrowing the conversation about education with respect to the overall goals of schooling.[8]

Children's very health and well-being are also suffering as a result of high-stakes testing. In spring 2001, several prominent U.S. psychologists, psychiatrists and educators, through the *Alliance for Childhood*, issued a statement of concern and a call to action on high-stakes testing, citing evidence of harm to children's health. It states that

> ...*children's levels of stress and test-related anxiety are showing up as headaches, stomach aches, sleep problems, attendance problems, acting out, and depression. The political push for even more standardized testing ... has ignored the adverse health consequences of such policies.*[9]

Further, it notes that high-stakes testing "may undermine the development of positive social relationships and attitudes towards school and learning."[10] Canadian mental health professionals have also expressed concerns with the growing incidence of large-scale testing. It is hard to imagine a more disastrous outcome of the accountability movement than turning young minds off learning.

One parent recently told me that her local school board is planning to introduce a board-wide testing program in response to, and to prepare students for, the expanding provincial testing program.

Unfortunately, the health and psychological impacts of high-stakes testing – only beginning to receive some attention – are likely to increase dramatically now that the U.S. testing agenda has switched into overdrive. The adoption in January 2002 of the revised Elementary and Secondary Education Act – ESEA (also called the "No Child Left Behind" Act) requires states to test all students in Grades 3-8 in reading and math by 2005-2006; mandates additional annual tests in science beginning in 2007; and requires that all districts and states use these tests "to plot a path from current levels of achievement to 100 percent proficiency within 12 years" (e.g., by

2013-2014) with sanctions imposed on schools which don't meet their "adequate yearly progress" goals.[11]

The profit-making potential of the legislation, given the general fixation on test-based accountability, is not lost on the education industry. According to McVety, testing, tutoring and test preparation are among the "key segments of the K-12 marketplace that stand out as potential boom markets as a result of ESEA appropriations."[12] With state-wide testing programs mandated in only nine states at present, McVety says this "opens the door" for testing companies (such as Harcourt Educational Measurement, Riverside Publishing, Educational Testing Service, NCS Pearson, and the CTB division of McGraw-Hill, to name the major players) to access nearly $400 million in federal funds.

On the market potential for tutoring and test preparation services, he is even more blunt:

> *Already close to a $4 billion industry, the surge in high stakes testing will have students focused on test results more than ever before. And, states and districts, with an eye towards account-ability, are already willing to spend to get results.*[13]

Private companies like Sylvan Learning and Kaplan are counting on the "fear factor" – benefiting from academic failure or merely the fear of failure – to boost their profits. In fact, McVety claims that something like 3,000 U.S. schools are ripe for the picking, having been "identified as underachieving, indicating that the market opportunity could be readily available at the start of the 2002-2003 school year."[14] Aiding and abetting increased corporate involvement in public education is another potential cost associated with the high-stakes accountability movement that cannot be ignored.

Whither the joy of teaching?

Test-driven accountability is also taking its toll on the ability of the teaching profession to recruit and retain good teachers and principals, particularly at a time of anticipated shortages. South of the border, teacher attrition and retirement combined with increased student enrolment are predicted to create a demand for approximately 2.4 million teachers over the coming decade.[15]

Bracey reports that in Virginia, tests "have created a new class of drop-outs: teachers. Some have taken early retirement, some have fled to private schools, and some have requested transfers to grades that are not tested."[16] Another poignant example of the unintended consequences of testing comes from New York where high-stakes testing in Grade 4 is resulting in less experienced teachers teaching that particular grade as tenured teachers choose to teach the untested 'lower-stakes' grades.[17,18] In some cases, principals are reported to be making decisions about who should teach "high-stakes grades" on the basis of how well teachers will prepare students for the mandated tests.

Kohn states that

> many educators are leaving the field because of what is being done to schools in the name of 'accountability' and 'tougher standards' ... Prospective teachers are rethinking whether to begin a career in which high test scores matter most, and in which they will be pressured to produce these scores.[19]

Hardest hit by this consequence of high-stakes accountability will be teachers and students in the poorest schools, which are often under the greatest pressure to boost their test scores.

Teacher supply and demand issues are also high on the Canadian education agenda. With approximately 120,000 full-time elementary and secondary teachers employed in Ontario's public schools, the Ontario College of Teachers predicts that, between 1999 and 2010, the province will lose nearly half – about 56,000 teachers – to retirement.[20]

It is hard to imagine a more disastrous outcome of the accountability movement than turning young minds off learning.

Any examination of teacher shortages and the related issues of recruitment and retention needs to carefully consider teachers' professional working conditions, among other factors. Such analyses cannot underestimate the importance of intrinsic motivators for teachers – perhaps best captured in the expression, the "joy of teaching." Such job "satisfiers" attract many to the profession in the first place. Most teachers polled in a recent teacher workplace survey by the Canadian Teachers' Federation[21] indicated that the major factor influencing their decision to enter the profession was their love of children and teaching.

Hargreaves has examined what he describes as the "emotional practice of teaching," observing in one study that "teachers valued emotional bonds formed with students and appreciated the purposes of educating their students as emotional, social, and intellectual beings. Their emotional commitments and connections to students energized and articulated everything they did."[22] Drawing on the research base, Leithwood tells us that "the most often cited goal motivating the professional work of teachers is intrinsic – helping students learn and seeing them achieve."[23] He argues that current accountability policies – such as the use of large-scale standardized test results to compare and rank students, schools, districts and provinces – fail because, among other reasons, they erode these fundamental intrinsic goals and distract teachers from doing their best teaching. There is a need for more analysis of the impacts of accountability and other education policies on the emotional and other intrinsic factors motivating Canadian classroom teachers.

Such studies also need to address diversity issues – both in terms of the capacity of teachers to address the needs of diverse classrooms, and with respect to the "colour of the teaching profession" itself, particularly the situation of Aboriginal and visible minority educators. Low Aboriginal representation in the teaching workforce is contrasted with the fact that, in places such as Saskatchewan and Manitoba, Aboriginal children account for a rapidly growing proportion of the total population of children. The representation of visible minorities in elementary and secondary school teaching, particularly in urban settings, is also significantly below average, resulting in large gaps in racial and cultural diversity between students and their teachers. Another important issue relates to the growing "feminization" of the profession.

What are the implications of high-stakes accountability policies, including teacher testing of the variety adopted in Ontario, for diversity in the teaching profession? Will they have a disproportionately negative impact on equity-seeking groups? In the U.S., teacher competency testing is among the barriers preventing minority teacher candidates from entering the profession.[24] This issue also needs to be examined in the Canadian context.

Threats to teacher professionalism are coming on several fronts, not the least of which is standards- and test-driven accountability. On the subject of standards-based reform and deprofessionalization, Hatch observes that:

> *Across the education landscape, the movement toward standards is a movement away from teacher responsibility and agency. As curricula, teaching strategies, outcomes, and evaluation techniques are standardized, teachers' opportunities to make decisions based on their professional judgement are systematically reduced. The implementation of standards-based programs signals students, parents, and society at large that teachers are not to be trusted or respected and that technical/managerial control is what is needed to fix problems that teachers helped create.*[25]

This general tendency of decision-makers to address complex educational issues with standardized, technical policy responses contributes to teacher de-skilling.

Accountability – where we're at

Brawdy and Egan summarize the major accountability measures implemented in the U.S. over the past 25 years: tight curriculum control by governments, increased resources being spent on testing programs, and the use of rewards and sanctions attached to test performance.[26] The ranking and publishing of test results is a critical component of the latter measure. This has come to be known as the "shame and blame" approach to accountability because it attempts to embarrass schools to improve their rankings on the assumption that, as Kohn puts it, "...teachers and students *could* be doing a better job but have for some reason chosen not to do so and need only be bribed or threatened into improvement."[27]

The idea of improving the quality of education by spelling out what schools should teach (in the form of highly specific demanding academic standards), measuring performance in meeting these standards and holding schools accountable for the results by applying rewards and, more often, sanctions has taken hold with a vengeance. To understand where the preoccupation with test-driven, high-stakes accountability is coming from, it is important to understand the prevailing corporate mindset regarding education's role in the "new economy," summed up in this quote by former Chairman and CEO of BCE Inc., Jean Monty:

> *Education is now the main barometer of competitiveness among countries – more than capital and more than technology. More than ever, learning is intimately linked with the wealth and well-being of nations. It has become the linchpin in planning for Canada's future.*[28]

The mania for standardized test scores and school and provincial league tables is an indication of the degree to which this competitive mindset has come to permeate the educational enterprise itself. These market mechanisms grease the wheels of an education system increas-

> An accountability system that rewards successful schools and teachers and incurs sanctions against poorly performing schools fosters a competitive approach yielding winners and losers.

ingly focused on securing and maintaining Canada's position in a fiercely competitive global economy. An accountability system that rewards successful schools and teachers (success as narrowly measured by improved test scores) and incurs sanctions against poorly performing schools fosters a competitive approach yielding winners and losers.

As democratic accountability for public education through elected local school boards has been systematically eroded, bureaucratic forms of accountability through the centralization of curriculum, assessment and funding decisions in ministries of education, in parallel with "market accountability" in the form of school choice and privatization, have gained currency.

In Canada, the Fraser Institute is one of the leading advocates of a market-based approach. Having asserted itself as an authority on all matters educational, the Fraser Institute's web site trumpets the virtues of an "educational market" in which "schools compete more freely for students," leading to "better educational results for more students" and an improved education system overall. Among the "market incentives" necessary to accomplish this are school choice, vouchers, charter schools, and school rankings – the latter being the mechanism that allows parents as consumers to pick the "winning" school of choice from among those on offer. This, in theory, is how accountability through market competition is supposed to work. In practice, school choice policies have led to increased stratification by race and social class as they provide greater choice only to more affluent families.[29]

> There needs to be wider recognition and appreciation of the fact that accountability for the delivery of high-quality, equitable public education is very much a *shared responsibility* among diverse education stakeholders.

The Fraser Institute's annual "report cards" ranking provincial high schools have been put out in B.C. since 1998, in Alberta since 1999, and more recently in Quebec and Ontario. Newfoundland's secondary schools are reportedly up next, and school ranking is even coming to elementary schools. Several ministers of education have criticized the rankings exercise, as have teachers' organizations, school boards, and other education groups – and with good reason. On the 2001 Ontario report card, which was publicly criticized for containing inaccurate data, Shaker observed that,

It is more than a little ironic that the Fraser Institute, a vocal proponent of greater choice in education, has designed a ranking that effectively penalizes schools that have made a commitment to offering students a wide range of choice in programs and areas of study in an attempt to meet the diversity of student needs and interests.[30]

Indeed, this is one of the criticisms levelled at the report by Philip Nagy, a researcher who specializes in educational assessment and evaluation. In his damning analysis of the Fraser Institute ranking of Ontario high schools, he bluntly concludes that:

The method of ranking can be criticized both conceptually and empirically. Conceptually, the rankings are based on a narrow set of values concerning what is important about a child's education, along with a misapplication of basic conceptions of gender equity. Empirically, the rankings capitalize on small differences, and, through the weighting system used, give unjustified importance to some of the criteria. The report, written from a particularly narrow value system, is seriously flawed and damaging to education. It should play no role in judging the quality of schools.[31]

Such pseudo-science casts serious doubt on all Fraser rankings of provincial high schools and needs to be exposed.

In addition to their conceptual and empirical shortcomings, accountability policies such as ranking schools on the basis of test scores are simply unethical. Reminding us that they ignore family socioeconomic status and other conditions outside the control of schools, Leithwood says that

we have known for more than three decades that family background factors alone explain in excess of 50 percent of the variation in student achievement. This widespread and unnecessary practice [school rankings] demeans the work of schools serving less advantaged students, masks the significant contributions made by many of these schools to the growth of their students, and lionizes the work of schools serving exceptionally advantaged students, even if they are not adding much of value.[32]

Others such as Corson have remarked on the unethical nature of many of the Ontario government's education policies, manipulating as they do students and teachers in the pursuit of ideological goals.[33]

Rethinking educational accountability

A rethinking of the concept and practice of educational accountability is clearly in order. The starting point for this much-needed discussion is a recognition of public accountability as a fundamental underlying principle of public education, coupled with the fact that "the consequences flowing from the current slate of educational accountability *policies* ... are wreaking havoc on the quality of public education."[34] This section will attempt to provide the broad brush strokes for an alternative framework to move us closer to true accountability.

Workable alternatives to standardized testing have existed for some time and must be part of any reconceptualization of educational accountability. This would include, but not be limited to, some combination of the following practices:

- continuous observation of children by their teachers, the outcomes of which are relayed by teachers in writing to and/or in discussion with parents; Kohn notes that the "best way to judge schools is by visiting them and looking for evidence of learning and interest in learning"[35];
- parent-teacher or student-led conferences;
- performance-based assessments such as science experiments, class presentations, debates, and dance and musical performances;
- portfolio assessment – rather than an unfocused snapshot at a specific moment in time (yielded via the standardized testing approach), a portfolio provides an ongoing means for students to effectively demonstrate both what they know and can do; it is developed over a period of time; contains multiple examples of student learning (some chosen by the student, others by the teacher in conjunction with the student); may be conceptually organized on the basis of multiple intelligences; and can be presented by the student to the parent and teacher at a student-led conference.

"Our counselor said our class score is one standard divination above average!

All of these have the potential to demonstrate a more accurate expression of accountability on the part of the teacher and the school toward the student and parent than any single standardized test.

At the same time, we need to place more confidence in, and reliance on, teachers' professional judgment of how students are doing. Teachers, after all, are experts in pedagogy. Teachers in turn require the necessary professional training in the development and use of meaningful classroom-based assessment that is integrated with curriculum and instruction.

Alternatives to standardized testing, however, are necessary but not sufficient, as they have been shown to be corruptible within a high-stakes environment.[36] Authentic forms of student assessment must be developed and integrated within a comprehensive accountability framework.

Such a framework would need to incorporate a number of other elements. As high-stakes testing and narrow academic standards go hand in hand, it would be necessary to critique the standards-based reform movement in which testing is firmly embedded. Kohn describes standardized testing as "the enforcement mechanism of the standards".[37] He suggests evaluating learning standards on the basis of several criteria including whether they are broadly conceived guidelines for thinking, or mandates driven by what is easy to measure rather than by what actually makes sense for child learning and development. As noted earlier, standards-based reform is also working its way into the very youngest classrooms.[38]

There needs to be wider recognition and appreciation of the fact that accountability for the delivery of high-quality, equitable public education is very much a *shared responsibility* among diverse education stakeholders. This is often expressed as establishing who is accountable, to whom, for what, and by what means. Equally important is the need for coherence of accountability policies at these different levels.

As one of the major players in the system, teachers are most directly accountable to students and their parents. The concept of *professional accountability* – that is, accountability through a strong teaching profession – recognizes the important link between teacher quality and student achievement, and hence the need to provide teachers with ongoing access to the knowledge and support necessary to make sound decisions in the classroom in order to improve student learning.[39] As Darling-Hammond explains it,

> *the major reason for seeking to create a profession of teaching is that it will increase the probability that **all students will be***

well educated because they are well taught – that profes-
sionalism seeks to heighten accountability by investing
in knowledge and its responsible use. [emphasis added][40]

It should come as no surprise that student learning is highly dependent on continual teacher learning and growth.

In looking at the evidence on the negative impact of high-stakes testing on minority students, Madaus and Clarke add another important dimension to the accountability debate, one made conspicuous by its absence – the need for public oversight of test use in order to guard against its unintended negative effects. They reason that:

> *Testing is a powerful, but often blunt, tool. Like a medication,*
> *it may fail or have diverse, unintended negative consequences.*
> *A testing program, for example, may unfairly or unreasonably*
> *deny opportunities to certain classes of people. It may reward or*
> *punish the wrong individuals or institutions, or it may under-*
> *mine the performance of institutions it is intended to strengthen*
> *…. Policymakers and test users have been able to turn to exten-*
> *sive commercial, not-for-profit, and governmental infrastruc-*
> *tures that have evolved over the past ninety years to assist them*
> *in test development, administration, scoring, and reporting.*
> ***However, there has been no analogous infrastructure for***
> ***independently evaluating a testing program before or af-***
> ***ter implementation or for monitoring test use and im-***
> ***pact.*** [emphasis added][41]

Public oversight takes on added urgency when one considers that the enormous testing industry is largely unregulated. Madaus and Clarke go on to emphasize that:

> *The effects of testing are now so diverse, widespread, and seri-*
> *ous that it is necessary to establish … mechanisms for catalyzing*
> *inquiry about, and systematic independent scrutiny of, them.*[42]

Lest we forget, genuine accountability in education also extends to politicians and other decision-makers who must be held to account for their own "performance." This means, in part, holding them accountable for basing their policy decisions on sound research evidence if these decisions are to have any validity at all (implementing the "policy flavour of the month" seems to be the preferred course of action). It also means calling them to account for using problematic test results as the basis for policy-making because, as Popham states,

> *if education policy makers are arriving at flawed conclusions*
> *about school quality by using the wrong evidence [i.e. gleaned*

from standardized test results], then those conclusions are likely to produce unsound policies. Truly successful schools may be regarded as ineffective; truly unsuccessful schools may be regarded as effective. When education policy makers are guided by the wrong measurement data, it is a certainty that misguided policies will follow.[43]

As they say in the vernacular, this would seem to be a "no-brainer."

Decision-makers are also accountable for addressing broader social and economic conditions, including poverty and unemployment, that impact on schools' and school systems' capacity to do their job.

Another piece of the accountability puzzle is the importance of accountable governance in education. The public interest in education is not well served when democratically elected school boards give way to volunteer-based parent councils whose concerns may not necessarily extend beyond the current year's student body. Also, Pan-Canadian and international bodies such as the Council of Ministers of Education and the Organisation for Economic Cooperation and Development, not accountable to any electorate, have a significant influence on the direction of education policy through, for example, their large-scale assessment programs (the School Achievement Indicators Program [SAIP] and Program for International Student Assessment [PISA], respectively).

> The response to the question "accountability for what?" must be informed by a desire on the part of all players to ensure that *all* schools are good schools which value and promote student learning and which provide learning opportunities for *all* students, especially those with the greatest needs.

The response to the question "accountability for what?" must be informed by a desire on the part of all players to ensure that *all* schools are good schools which value and promote student learning and which provide learning opportunities for *all* students, especially those with the greatest needs. There is obviously no standard formula for creating a good school. Good schools are as complex and multi-faceted as the students, teachers and administrators within them, and as the communities and societies in which they are embedded.

That being said, the research evidence on what constitutes a good or effective school consistently focuses on the same factors[44]: high quality early childhood education, small class sizes (particularly at the primary level), small school size, resources for curriculum support and school libraries, additional resources and programs for poor and special needs students, support for principals as instructional leaders, well-trained experienced teachers, support for ongoing high quality professional development, parental involvement in education, and strong ties between public schools and the community.

Many of these things could be provided or strengthened using funds currently allocated to testing budgets. All of these things contribute to creating the proper conditions for teaching and learning; they all require adequate and appropriate "inputs" – people, material resources, infrastructure, and dollars; and there must be accountability for their provision. This focus on inputs is a necessary counterbalance to what often seems to be an exclusive emphasis on accountability for narrowly defined "outputs." The B.C. Teachers' Federation believes that measures of student achievement need to be balanced with "measures of the resources used and required to improve student learning. In other words, the onus is on the opportunities students have to learn and our responsibility to provide them."[45]

It goes without saying that an accountability framework must be firmly grounded in the overarching goals and objectives of education. More specifically, it must be driven by a strong vision of the role of public education in forging a democratic society, a vision equally informed by the principles of equity, accessibility, universality, and quality.

In the end, if what we want is an education system narrowly conceived to meet the utilitarian demands of a competitive global marketplace and which blurs the fundamental distinction between education and training, then perhaps we have the form of accountability we deserve (e.g., collecting, ranking, and reporting standardized test scores), although even this is debatable.

Mass standardized testing is well suited to an education system increasingly driven by an economic agenda and shaped by market principles of efficiency, competition, deregulation and privatization. Metcalf echoes this idea with regard to the "No Child Left Behind" Act, observing that the

> *reauthorization of the Elementary and Secondary Education Act is widely regarded as the most ambitious federal overhaul of public schools since the 1960s ... The new Bush testing regime emphasizes minimal competence along a narrow range of skills, with an eye toward satisfying the low end of the labor market. All this sits well with a business community whose first*

preoccupation is "global competitiveness": a community most comfortable thinking in terms of inputs (dollars spent on public schools) in relation to outputs (test scores).[46]

If, on the other hand, the intent is to create good schools which foster the capacity for critical and creative thinking and which prepare students to become thoughtful, responsible and active citizens, then we need to carefully craft a system of genuine educational accountability with these goals uppermost in our minds. A lofty objective, to be sure, but anyone concerned about the future of Canadian public education should expect no less. ◖◗

Bernie Froese-Germain is a researcher with the Canadian Teachers' Federation and author of Standardized Testing: Undermining Equity in Education. Ottawa, Canadian Teachers' Federation, 1999.

Endnotes

[1] Linn, R. L. (2000, Mar.). "Assessments and Accountability." *Educational Researcher*, 29(2), p. 14.

[2] Bracey, G. W. (2001, Oct.). "The 11th Bracey Report on The Condition of Public Education." *Phi Delta Kappan*, 83(2), p. 158.

[3] Amrein, A. L., & Berliner, D. C. (2002, Mar. 28). "High-Stakes Testing, Uncertainty, and Student Learning." *Education Policy Analysis Archives*, 10(18), Arizona State University. URL: http://epaa.asu.edu/epaa/v10n18/

[4] Ibid.

[5] Ontario English Catholic Teachers' Association (2002, Mar.). *Weighing In: A Discussion Paper on Provincial Assessment Policy.* Toronto, pp. 3-4. URL: http://www.oecta.on.ca./news/nr2002/nr020311.htm

[6] See for example:

Amrein & Berliner, 2002, op. cit.

Froese-Germain, B. (2001). "Standardized Testing + High-Stakes Decisions = Educational Inequity." *Interchange*, 32(2), pp. 111-130.

Kohn, A. (2000). *The Case Against Standardized Testing: Raising the Scores, Ruining the Schools.* Portsmouth, NH: Heinemann.

[7] Bartlett, L. (2001). "The Tyranny of the Test: The Social Implications of North Carolina's Accountability Program." pp. 8-9. URL: http://www.unc.edu/depts/anthro/talks/bartlett.pdf

[8] Kohn, 2000, *The Case Against Standardized Testing*, op. cit., pp. 26-29.

[9] Alliance for Childhood (2001, April 25). "High-Stakes Testing: A Statement of Concern and Call to Action." Washington, DC. URL: http://www.allianceforchildhood.net/news/histakes_test_position_statement.htm

[10] Ibid.

[11] Karp, S. (2002, Summer). "Let Them Eat Tests." *Rethinking Schools*, 16(4). URL: http://www.rethinkingschools.org/Archives/16_04/Eat164.htm

[12] McVety, J. (2002, Feb. 7). "ESEA Boosts Potential for K-12 Private Sector." *The Education Industry Reports* (Pre-K-12 issue). Eduventures.com, Inc., p. 1.

[13] Ibid., p. 1.

[14] Ibid., p. 2.

[15] Ontario Teachers' Federation (2001, April 12). *Teaching for Success. Presentation to the Task Force on Effective Schools*. URL: http://www.otffeo.on.ca/news/inter/teachingdocument.pdf

[16] Bracey, 2001, op. cit., p. 159.

[17] Ibid., p. 159.

[18] The new "No Child Left Behind" Act mandating testing in Grades 3 through 8 may well put an end to that practice as the untested grades disappear (the name of the Act may be more than a little ironic if it has the effect of increasing testing exclusion rates for students considered to be 'liabilities').

[19] Kohn, A. (2000, Dec.). "High-Stakes Testing as Educational Ethnic Cleansing." *The Education Digest*, 66(4), p. 15.

[20] Ontario Teachers' Federation, 2001, op. cit.

[21] Canadian Teachers' Federation (2001, June). *Workplace Survey*. URL: http://www.ctf-fce.ca/e/press/2001/workplc.htm

[22] Hargreaves, A. (1998, Nov.). "The Emotional Practice of Teaching." *Teaching and Teacher Education*, 14(8), pp. 835-854.

[23] Leithwood, K. (2001). "Five Reasons Most Accountability Policies Don't Work (and What You Can Do About It)." *Orbit*, 32(1), p. 4.

[24] Froese-Germain, B., & Moll, M. (2001, Fall). "Teacher Testing FAQ." *PD & Research News* (Canadian Teachers' Federation), 1(4), pp. 1, 6-8.

[25] Hatch, J. A. (2002, Feb.). "Accountability Shovedown: Resisting the Standards Movement in Early Childhood Education." *Phi Delta Kappan*, 83(6), p. 459.

[26] Brawdy, P., & Egan, R. (2001, Winter). "The Ersatz Phenomenon: Reclaiming Authenticity in the Mirrored Halls of Accountability." *Educational Studies*, 32(4), pp. 438-452.

[27] Kohn, 2000, *The Case Against Standardized Testing*, op. cit., p. 39.

[28] Industry Canada (2001, April). "The Canadian Education and Training Industry – Service Industries Overview Series." URL: http://strategis.ic.gc.ca/SSG/bp00416e.html. This document on the "Canadian Education and Training Industry" proudly claims that our "education and training industry is well positioned to compete in the international marketplace" given the "diversity of players", among which are public schools and universities.

[29] Leithwood, 2001, op. cit.

[30] Shaker, E. (2001, Summer). "How to Score High in School Rankings." *PD & Research News* (Canadian Teachers' Federation), 1(3), p. 3.

[31] Nagy, P. (2001, Dec.). "An Analysis of the Fraser Institute Rankings of Ontario High Schools." [Draft] Ontario Institute for Studies in Education/ University of Toronto, p. 1.

[32] Leithwood, op. cit., p. 2.

[33] Corson, D. (2001, July). "Ontario Students as a Means to the Government's Ends." *Our Schools/Our Selves*, 10(4), #64, pp. 57-80.

[34] Leithwood, op. cit., p. 1.

[35] Kohn, 2000, *The Case Against Standardized Testing*, op. cit., p. 47.

[36] Froese-Germain, 2001, op. cit.

[37] Kohn, A. (2001, Sept. 26). "Beware of the Standards, Not Just the Tests." *Education Week on the Web*, 21(4), Editorial Projects in Education. URL: http://www.edweek.org/ew/newstory.cfm?slug=04kohn.h21

[38] Hatch, 2002, op. cit.

[39] Darling-Hammond, L., & Berry, B. (1998, May 27). "Investing in Teaching." *Education Week on the Web*, Editorial Projects in Education. URL: http://www.edweek.org/ew/1998/37darlin.h17

[40] Darling-Hammond, L. (1988, Winter). "Accountability and Teacher Professionalism." *American Educator*, p. 8.

[41] Madaus, G., & Clarke, M. (2001). "The Adverse Impact of High-Stakes Testing on Minority Students: Evidence from One Hundred Years of Test Data." In G. Orfield & M. L. Kornhaber (eds.), *Raising Standards or Raising Barriers? Inequality and High-Stakes Testing in Public Education*. New York, NY: The Century Foundation Press, p. 104.

[42] Ibid., p. 105.

[43] Popham, W. J. (2002, Feb.). "Right Task, Wrong Tool." *American School Board Journal*, 189(2), p. 19.

[44] See for example:

Elementary Teachers' Federation of Ontario (2001, April 12). *Brief to the Task Force on Effective Schools*. Toronto, ON. URL: http://www.etfo.ca/ display_document.htm?ETFO_token=6AS06&id=1422&isdoc=1&catid=273

Greenwald, R., Hedges, L. V., & Laine, R. D. (1996, Fall). "The Effect of School Resources on Student Achievement." *Review of Educational Research*, 66(3), pp. 361-396.

Molnar, A. (ed.). (2002, Jan.). *School Reform Proposals: The Research Evidence*. Tempe, AZ: Education Policy Research Unit (EPRU), Education Policy Studies Laboratory, Arizona State University. URL: http://www.asu.edu/educ/epsl/EPRU/documents/EPRU%202002-101/epru-2002-101.htm

[45] B.C. Teachers' Federation (1997, June). *Opportunities to Learn: Accountability in Education in British Columbia*. A Brief to the Minister of Education, Skills and Training from the British Columbia Teachers' Federation. URL: http:// www.bctf.ca/publications/briefs/ocg/

[46] Metcalf, S. (2002, Jan. 28). "Reading Between the Lines." *The Nation*, p. 18. URL: http://www.thenation.com/issue.mhtml?i=20020128

Fighting the tests

A practical guide
to rescuing our schools

by Alfie Kohn

D on't let anyone tell you that standardized tests are not accurate measures. The truth of the matter is they offer a remarkably precise method for gauging the size of the houses near the school where the test was administered. Every empirical investigation of this question has found that socioeconomic status (SES) in all its particulars accounts for an overwhelming proportion of the variance in test scores when different schools, towns, or states are compared. Thus ignorance would be the most charitable explanation for why charts are published that rank schools (or towns or states) by these scores – or why anyone would use those rankings to draw conclusions about classroom quality.

However, if this were the only problem with standardized tests, we probably would not have sufficient reason to work for their elimination. After all, one could factor in SES in evaluating test results to determine the "true" score. And one could track a given school's (or district's) results over time; assuming no major demographic changes, a statistically significant shift in scores would then seem to be meaningful.

But here's the problem: even results corrected for SES are not very useful because the tests themselves are inherently flawed.[2] This assessment is borne out by research finding a statistical association between high scores on standardized tests and relatively shallow thinking. One such study classified elementary school students as "actively" engaged in learning if they went back over things they didn't understand, asked questions of themselves as they read, and tried to connect what they were doing to what they had already learned. Students were classified as "superficially" engaged if they just copied down answers, guessed a lot, and skipped the hard parts. It turned out that the superficial style was positively correlated with high scores on the Comprehensive Tests of Basic Skills (CTBS) and the Metropolitan Achievement Test (MAT).[3] Similar findings have emerged from studies of middle school and high school students.[4] These are only statistical relationships, of course – significant correlations, but not absolute correspondences. Many students think deeply and score well on tests, while many others do neither. But, as a rule, better standardized exam results are more likely to go hand-in-hand with a shallow approach to learning than with deep understanding.

What is true of a student's thinking is also true of a teacher's instruction. A rise in scores may be worse than meaningless: it may actually be reason for concern. What matters is how that change was brought about and what had to be sacrificed to make it happen. Across the nation, schools under intense pressure to show better test results have allowed those tests to cannibalize the curriculum. Administrators have cut back or even eliminated vital parts of schooling: programs in the arts, recess for young children, electives for high schoolers, class meetings (and other activities intended to promote social and moral learning), discussions about current events (since that material will not appear on the test), the use of literature in the early grades (if the tests are focused narrowly on decoding skills), and entire subject areas such as science (if the tests cover only language arts and math). When students will be judged on the basis of a multiple-choice test, teachers may use multiple-choice exercises and in-class tests beforehand. (This has aptly been called the "dumbing down" of instruction, although curiously not by the conservative critics with whom that phrase is normally associated.) Teachers may even place all instruction on hold and spend time administering and reviewing practice tests.

In my experience, the people who work most closely with kids are the most likely to understand how harmful standardized testing is. Many teachers – particularly those who are very talented – have what might be described as a dislike/hate relationship with these exams. Support for testing seems to grow as you move away from the students, going from teacher to principal to central office administrator to school board member to state board member, state legislator, and governor. Those for whom classroom visits are occasional photo opportunities are most likely to be big fans of testing and to offer self-congratulatory sound bites about the need for "tougher standards" and "accountability." The more that parents and other members of the community learn about these tests, the more critical of them – if not appalled by them – they tend to become.[5]

There is much more to be said about how standardized tests measure what matters least, about their psychometric deficiencies and pedagogical consequences. But a good deal of this has already been said – by me[6] and by others.[7] Kappan readers may have come to the same conclusions based on their own experience.

Even someone who does not have to be convinced of the merit of the arguments, however, may need to be reminded of their cumulative significance. It is this: As the year 2001 begins, we are facing an educational emergency in this country. The intellectual life is being squeezed out of schools as they are transformed into what are essentially giant test-prep centers. The situation is most egregious, and the damage most pronounced, where high stakes are attached to the tests – for example, where money is dangled in front of teachers, principals, and schools if they manage to raise the scores, or where students are actually forced to repeat a grade or denied a diploma on the basis of their performance of a single test.

Most of us have pet projects, favorite causes, practices and policies about which we care deeply. These include such issues as multiple intelligences, multiage classrooms, or multicultural curricula; cooperative learning, character education, or the creation of caring communities in schools; teaching for understanding, developmentally appropriate practice, or alternative assessment; the integration of writing or the arts into the curriculum; project- or problem-based learning, discovery-oriented science, or whole language; giving teachers or students more autonomy, or working with administrators to help them make lasting change. But every one of these priorities is gravely threatened by the top-down, heavy-handed, corporate-style, standardized version of school reform that is driven by testing. That's why all of us, despite our disparate agendas, need to make common cause. We must make the fight against standardized tests our top priority because, until we have chased this monster from the schools, it will be difficult, perhaps even impossible, to pursue the kinds of reforms that can truly improve teaching and learning.

WHENEVER SOMETHING IN THE SCHOOLS IS AMISS, it makes sense for us to work on two tracks at once. We must do our best in the short term to protect students from the worst effects of a given policy, but we must also work to change or eliminate that policy. If we overlook the former – the need to minimize the harm of what is currently taking place, to devise effective coping strategies – then we do a disservice to children in the here and now. But (and this is by far the more common error) if we overlook the latter – the need to alter the current reality – then we are condemning our children's children to having to make the best of the same unacceptable situation because it will still exist.

Standardized testing being a case in point, let me begin by offering these short-term responses:

First, if you are a teacher, you should do what is necessary to prepare students for the tests – and then get back to the real learning. Never forget the difference between these two objectives. Be clear about it in your own mind, and whenever possible, help others to understand that the distinction. For example, you might send a letter to parents explaining what you are doing and why. ("Before we can design rigorous and exciting experiments in class, which I hope will have the effect of helping your child learn to think like a scientist, we're going to have to spend some time getting ready for the standardized tests being given next month. Hopefully we'll be able to return before too long to what research suggests is a more effective kind of instruction.") If you're lucky, parents will call you, indignantly demanding to know why their kids aren't able to pursue the more effective kind of instruction all the time. "Excellent question!" you'll reply, as you hand over a sheet containing the addresses and phone numbers of the local school board, state board of education, legislators, and the governor.

Second, do no more test preparation than is absolutely necessary. Some experts have argued that a relatively short period of introducing students to the content and format of the tests is sufficient to produce scores equivalent to those obtained by students who have spent the entire year in test-prep mode. "You don't need to study only the test and distort your entire curriculum eight hours a day, 180 days a year, for 12 years," says Harvey Daniels, who specializes in literacy education. "We've got very interesting studies where teachers do 35 or 38 weeks of what they think is best for kids, and then they'll give them three weeks of test cramming just before the test. And the kids do just as well as kids who have 40 weeks of test-driven curriculum."[8] This is corroborated by some research that found a one-hour intensive reading readiness tutorial for young children produced test results equivalent to two years of skills-oriented direct instruction.[9] (Of course, this will vary depending on the child and the nature of the test.) Or consider compromises such as this:

One first-grade teacher in Kentucky helped her students develop their own reading program, which moves them faster and more effectively through (and beyond) the district's reading program objectives than the basal. Even so, she is required by her school's administration to put her class through a basal reader program on a prescribed weekly schedule. The solution, quickly evolved by the class: They do each week's work in the basal on Monday, with little effort, then work on the meaningful curriculum – theirs – Tuesday through Friday.[10]

Third, whatever time is spent on test preparation should be as creative and worthwhile as possible. Avoid traditional drilling whenever you can. Several educators have figured out how to turn some of these tests into a kind of puzzle that children can play an active role in solving. The idea is to help students become adept at the particular skill called test-taking so they will be able to show what they already know.[11]

Fourth, administrators and other school officials should never brag about high (or rising) scores. To do so is not only misleading; it serves to legitimate the tests. In fact, people associated with high-scoring schools or districts have a unique opportunity to make an impact. It's easy for critics to be dismissed with a "sour grapes" argument: You're just opposed to standardized testing because it makes you look bad. But administrators and school board members in high-scoring areas can say, "Actually our students happen to do well on these tests, but that's nothing to be proud of. We value great teaching and learning, which is precisely what suffers when people become preoccupied with scores. Please join us in phasing them out."

Finally, whatever your position on the food chain of American education, one of your primary obligations is to be a buffer – to absorb as much pressure as possible from those above you without passing it on to those below. If you are a superintendent or assistant superintendent facing school board members who want to see higher test scores, the most constructive thing you can do is protect principals from these ill-conceived demands to the best of your ability (without losing your job in the process). If you are a building administrator, on the receiving end of test-related missives from the central office, your challenge is to shield teachers from this pressure – and, indeed, to help them pursue meaningful learning in their classrooms. If you are a teacher unlucky enough to work for an administrator who hasn't read this paragraph, your job is to minimize the impact on students. Try to educate those above you whenever it seems possible to do so, but cushion those below you every day. Otherwise you become part of the problem.

AS IMPORTANT AS I BELIEVE THESE SUGGESTIONS TO BE, it is also critical to recognize their limits. There is only so much creativity that can be infused into preparing students for bad tests. There is only so much buffering that can be done in a high-stakes environment. These recommendations merely try to make the best of a bad thing. Ultimately we need to work to end that bad thing, to move beyond stopgap measures and take on the system itself.

Unfortunately, even some well-intentioned educators who understand the threat posed by testing never get to that point. Here are some of the justifications they offer for their inaction:

- "Just teach well and the tests will take care of themselves." This may be true in some subject areas, or in some states, or in some neighborhoods. But it is often a convenient delusion. Especially in science and social studies, to prepare students for the tests in the most effective way may well be to teach badly – to fill them full of dates and definitions and cover a huge amount of material in a superficial fashion. Conversely, to teach in a way that helps students understand (and become enthusiastic about) ideas may actually lower their scores. Linda McNeil's description of the choice faced by Texas educators will be instantly and painfully familiar to teachers across the country – but may come as news to some parents, school board members, politicians, and reporters:

    The myth of the proficiencies [that is, the standards] was that because they were aimed at minimum skills, they would change only the weakest teaching. The "good" teachers would as a matter of course "already be covering" this material and so would not have to make adjustments. In fact, the transformation of the curriculum into received knowledge, to be assessed by students' selection of one answer among four provided on a computer-scored test, undermined both the quality and quantity that "good teachers" could present to their students. . . . [Thus,] teachers faced serious ethical dilemmas. They could teach to the proficiencies and assure high test scores for their students. Or they could teach the curricula they had been developing (and

wanted to continue to develop) and teach not only a richer sub-
ject matter but also one that was aimed at students' under-
standing and their long-term learning, not the short-term goals
inherent in the district testing of memorized fragments. This
was not an easy choice.[12]

Nor is the dilemma likely to be painlessly resolved by consultants who tell us we need only adopt a specific instructional reform to have the best of both worlds: an intellectually impressive classroom that will help students meet the state standards. The degree of standardization in most accountability-based systems is so high, and the quality of the tests is so low, that the proposed reform either (a) will not raise the scores or (b) isn't particularly impressive after all. That's why we should react with caution, if not alarm, to the word alignment. The dictates to which we are supposed to be aligning the curriculum are often pedagogically suspect, and the motive for doing so may have more to do with compliance than with what is in the best interest of children. Moreover, even if their objectives and our motives were defensible, the process of alignment typically requires a degree of uniformity – and is undertaken with a degree of rigidity – that ought to raise concerns about the whole enterprise.

- "This too shall pass." Education has its fads, and standards on steroids may be one of them, but there is no guarantee that it will fade away on its own. Too much is invested by now; too many powerful interest groups are backing high-stakes testing for us to assume it will simply fall of its own weight. In any case, too many children will be sacrificed in the meantime if we don't take action to expedite its demise.

- "My job is to teach, not to get involved in political disputes." When seven-year-olds can't read good books because they are being drilled on what Jonathan Kozol calls "those obsessively enumerated particles of amputated skill associated with upcoming state exams,"[13] the schools have already been politicized. The only question is whether we will become involved on the other side – that is, on the side of real learning. In particular, much depends on whether those teachers and administrators who already harbor (and privately acknowledge) concerns about testing are willing to go public, to take a stand, to say, "This is bad for kids." To paraphrase a famous quotation, all that is necessary for the triumph of damaging educational policies is that good educators keep silent.

- "The standards and tests are here to stay; we might as well get used to them." Here we have a sentiment diametrically opposed to "This too shall pass," yet one that paradoxically leads to the identical inaction. Real children in real classrooms suffer from this kind of defeatism, which can quickly become a self-fulfilling prophecy: assume something is inevitable and it becomes so precisely because we have decided not to challenge it. The fact of the matter is that standardized tests are not like the weather, something to which we must resign ourselves. They haven't always existed and they don't exist in most parts of the world. What we are facing is not a force of nature but a force of politics, and political decisions can be questioned, challenged, and ultimately reversed.

HOW WE TAKE ON THE TESTS MAY DEPEND PARTLY ON practical considerations such as where we can have the greatest impact. Those of us who see little benefit at all from standardized tests in their current forms need to remember that this is not an all-or-nothing crusade but a movement that can proceed incrementally. One way to begin is by fighting for the principles most likely to generate widespread support.

For example, even Education Week, known for its relentless advocacy of the standards-and-testing agenda, has acknowledged that there is "virtually unanimous agreement among experts that no single measure should decide a student's academic fate."[14] This is true: the prestigious National Research Council came to that conclusion,[15] as have most other professional organizations (such as the American Educational Research Association and the American Psychological Association), the generally protesting American Federation of Teachers and even the companies that manufacture and sell the tests. To make students repeat a grade or deny them diplomas on the basis of a single exam is unconscionable – yet about half the states, at this writing, are either doing so or planning to do so. This issue is not a bad point of entry for potential activists. It may be persuasive even to politicians who have not thought much about these issues and otherwise accept the slogans of standards and accountability.[16]

Similarly, even people who are unwilling to dispense with standardized testing altogether may be open to persuasion that these tests

- should not be the only means by which students or schools are evaluated, inasmuch as they miss (or misrepresent) many aspects of student learning that ought to be assessed some other way;

- should not, in any case, be imposed by fiat on all schools in the state, with the result that communities are prevented from making their own decisions;[17]
- should not be administered too often;
- are inappropriate for young children; and
- should be used only to rate, never to rank (since the goal is to derive useful information, not to create winners and losers and thereby discourage schools from working together).

This is not to say that we shouldn't also be inviting people to question ideological assumptions that are harder to dislodge – to consider, for example, that a preoccupation with results and achievement can in itself interfere with learning,[18] or that educational progress need not (and, to some extent, cannot) be reduced to numbers. But even someone who resists those ideas may agree that it is wrong to make a student's future hinge on a standardized test. (Needless to say, allowing students several chances to retake the same test does little address the problem. Besides, many students are likely to give up and drop out after the first or second failure.)

Some of the ideas that follow can be pursued individually, but most depend on working with others. Thus, the first suggestion is to organize. Find people in your area who share your concerns so you can have a more powerful impact together. You are not alone in opposing standardized testing, but without collective action, you might as well be. So work with friends, neighbors, and colleagues to set up study groups, committees, phone trees, websites, and listservs. Give yourselves an organizational name, print up some letterhead, and you instantly gain more credibility. (Now you're not just a bunch of rebels. You're the "[name of area] Educators Opposing Excessive Testing.") Every person who seems interested in becoming involved should be asked to find ten more potential recruits, and each of those recruits should be asked to do the same. Even as you engage in the activities listed below, you should be continuing to fold others into the effort.[19]

There is no reason, however, to waste time duplicating someone else's efforts. You may want to begin by checking out and joining an existing network if one is already active in your area, such as the one accessible on my website (go to www.alfiekohn.org, click on "Standards and Testing," and follow the links) or that of the nation's leading organization challenging standardized testing, FairTest (www.fairtest.org). This group also has a quarterly newsletter, a storehouse of useful documents, and a listserv called the Assessment Reform Network (ARN).

Whether you join an existing organization or help to form a new one, begin by learning all you can about the tests used in your state as well as more generic testing issues. Then:

1. Talk to friends and neighbors at every opportunity: in line at the supermarket, in the dentist's waiting room, on airplanes, at the hairdresser's and the playground, at dinner parties and children's birthday parties. Help people in your community understand that if a local official boasts about rising test scores, they should consider responding, "You know, if that's what you're mostly concerned about, then I'm worried about the quality of my child's schooling."

2. Get in the habit of attending – and speaking out at – school board meetings and other events dealing with educational policy.

3. Let parents know they can write a letter to school administrators or board members expressing concern that test preparation is eclipsing more important learning activities. Here is a sample, provided by James Popham:[20]

> Dear _____:
>
> *I want to register my concern that there seems to be an excessive emphasis in our school on getting students ready for the standardized achievement tests scheduled for administration during (give the month of the upcoming test-administration). The reason I'm concerned is that I'm fearful the teaching staff's preoccupation with raising scores on those tests may be preventing the teachers from covering other important skills and knowledge that the school's students need.*
>
> *I realize that you and your teaching staff are under considerable pressure to "raise test scores" because it is widely believed that students' scores on standardized achievement tests reflect the quality of a teaching staff and, by implication, the quality of the school's principal.*
>
> *I've been doing some reading on that topic, and I understand why it is that students' standardized test scores do not provide an appropriate indication of a teaching staff's competence. Scores on those tests are more a reflection of the student population served by a school than an indication of the skill of the school's educators.*
>
> *I hope that you and your staff will address this test-preparation issue in the near future. Parents want the school's children to*

get the very best education possible. I'm sure you do too. That will not happen, however, if our school's heavy emphasis on test-preparation deflects the school's teachers from dealing with the curricular content our children need.

Sincerely,

[Your Name]

4. Write to – or, better yet, pull together a delegation of concerned citizens and then visit – your state legislators and other public officials. (This is the sort of familiar and predictable recommendation that you may be tempted to skip over, but it really ought to be taken seriously. Politicians respond to pointed and persistent lobbying, and, as a rule, they haven't heard nearly enough from those of us who feel strongly about this issue.) Your goal may be simply to educate policy makers about the effects of testing, or it may be to encourage them to oppose (or support) specific policies and legislation.

5. Write letters to the editor – or, better yet, op-ed articles – for your local newspaper.

6. Organize a delegation of educators and/or parents and request a meeting with the education reporter and top editors of your paper. Help them to see how problematic it is to cite rising or falling test scores as an indication of educational quality. Explain to them that most experts in the field oppose high-stakes testing in particular. And tell them: "Every time you publish a chart that ranks schools on the basis of test scores, our kids' learning suffers. Here's why…"

7. Sponsor a forum or teach-in on testing. Invite the media. Sign up new volunteers. Such a meeting might carry a provocative title to attract those already on your side (e.g., "Standardized Testing: Waste of Time Or Menace to Children?"), but then again it might be promoted in more neutral terms ("Rethinking Standardized Testing") to attract more people. Those responsible for the tests can be invited to appear and respond to questions.

8. Print some bumper stickers with slogans such as STANDARDIZED TESTING IS DUMBING DOWN OUR SCHOOLS. (Here, it is definitely appropriate to be provocative.)[21]

9. Participate in – and ensure press coverage of – some form of protest. This can include marches and demonstrations, as well as other, more

targeted activities, such as those already taking place in some areas, described below.

10. For every workshop on in-service event offered by educational service agencies, universities, and administrators that provide advice on raising test scores and teaching to the standards, three should be offered that encourage teachers to challenge the standards and tests – or at least help them think about how to protect their students from the damaging effects.

11. Invite researchers in the area to commission a survey. When it's completed, release the results at a press conference. One group of investigators suggested including these questions:

Do the tests improve students' motivation? Do parents understand the results? Do teachers think that the tests measure the curriculum fairly? Do administrators use the results wisely? How much money is spent on assessment and related services? How much time do teachers spend preparing students for various tests? Do the media report the data accurately and thoroughly? Our surveys suggest that many districts will be shocked to discover the degree of dissatisfaction among stakeholders.[22]

12. Challenge politicians, corporate executives, and others who talk piously about the need to "raise the bar," impose "tougher standards," ensure "accountability," etc., etc., to take the tests themselves. This is especially important in the case of high-stakes exit exams, which are increasingly being used to deny diplomas to students who don't pass them. In many states, the reality is that few adults could pass these tests.

There are two ways to issue such an invitation to decision makers: as a private opportunity for them to learn more about (and, perhaps, understand the absurdity of) the exam, or as a public challenge for them to take the test and agree to have their scores published in the newspaper. The first approach was used in West Bend, Wisconsin, where about 30 business leaders took a short version of the state's proposed graduation exam. They "had so much trouble with it that some wonder[ed] whether it truly will measure the quality of future employees." One bank executive – presumably a supporter of testing in the abstract until he encountered the actual test – remarked, "I think it's good to challenge students, but not like this."[23]

The second approach was taken by the St. Petersburg Times when it "challenged several top elected officials to join 735,000 Florida schoolchildren . . . by taking the rigorous Florida Comprehensive Assessment Test. They declined. Some did so with a sense of humor. Some admitted the math might give them fits. Others were unamused by the entire exercise. All said no."[24] Educators and parents might consider holding a press conference to issue such a public challenge, arguing that if officials fear they won't be able to pass the test, they should be prepared to justify requiring teenagers to do something that they, themselves, cannot. And if they refuse the challenge, they should be called on to defend their refusal.

13. Consider filing a lawsuit against the tests, which are potentially vulnerable in many ways. They may be inherently discriminatory. They may be used despite the absence of evidence that they are statistically valid measurement instruments. They may be inconsistent with the state's own standards – or require students to know that which hasn't yet been taught.

14. Investigate whether your state has an "opt-out" clause that allows parents to exempt their children from testing just by notifying the authorities. These are not widely known – indeed, even some activists are not always aware of their existence in their own states – but they ought to be publicized if they are on the books where you live.

15. Perhaps the most extreme – but, in the opinion of a growing number of people, well justified – strategy is to boycott the tests even where there is no opt-out provision. If that suggestion seems drastic, I can only respond that desperate circumstances call for drastic action. Punitive consequences are being meted out on the basis of manifestly inadequate and inappropriate exams. Children are literally becoming sick with fear over their scores. We are facing the prospect that massive numbers of students – particularly low-income and minority students – will be pushed out of school altogether.[25]

   In short, more and more people believe that writing letters to the editor isn't enough, that a line has been crossed such that we can no longer justify our participation in – and tacit support of – these testing programs. One kind of boycott involves students who, on their own or at their parents' behest, refuse to show up for tests and make it clear why they are doing so. There are various ways in which educators can support such an action: by making sure that students and parents know that boycotts already are taking place elsewhere, by speaking out in support of those who decide to do this, by teaching students about the theory and practice of civil disobedience, by suggesting alternative educational activities in which prospective boycotters can participate on test day, and by lobbying local officials to make sure that these students are not punished. (Of course, educators who are also parents can invite their own children to consider being part of such a protest.)

In another kind of boycott, teachers and administrators themselves refuse to be part of the testing program. Like Bartleby in Melville's short story, who created an uproar when, "in a singularly mild, firm voice, [he] replied, 'I would prefer not to,'" they declare that they simply cannot in good conscience break the shrink-wrap on those exams and thereby become part of something they believe is bad for children. It takes considerable courage to put one's job on the line. Yet that courage has already been displayed, with striking results, in other countries. "Elementary [school] achievement is high" in Japan, for example, partly because teachers in that country "are free from the pressure to teach to standardized tests." It is important to understand why there are no such tests in that country (with the exception of an infamous university admission exam): it is because Japanese teachers collectively refused to administer them. For many years now, they have successfully prevented the government from doing to their children what our government is doing to our children.[26] Similarly, in the early 1990s, teachers in England and Wales basically stopped the new national testing program in its tracks, at least for a while, by a comparable act of civil disobedience. What began there "as an unfocused mishmash of voices became a united boycott involving all teacher unions, a large number of governing bodies, and mass parental support." Teachers made it clear that their action was taken in behalf of students, based on their recognition that "to teach well for the tests was in effect to teach badly."[27]

In 1999, Jim Bougas, a middle school teacher in a small town in Massachusetts, noticed that the history portion of the state's MCAS exam required students to answer questions about the Civil War even though the state's own guidelines called for that topic to be covered at the end of the year, after the test was administered. For him, this was the last straw with respect to a testing system that was already geared toward memorization and was forcing instruction to become more superficial. The teacher, a soft-spoken man who had been teaching for 28 years, informed his principal that he would not administer the test. He was reassigned to the library during that period, and a stern letter of reprimand was placed in his file along with a warning not to repeat his protest. The next year, following a denial of his request to be reassigned to other duties when the test was to be administered, he agonized about what to do. Finally, he decided that if the test was just as unfair and destructive in 2000 as it had been in 1999, his response could not be any different – even at the risk of suspension or dismissal. Besides, as he told a reporter, "if the MCAS continues, I have no job because they've taken it away from me as long as I have to spend my time teaching to the test. I can't do that anymore. So I have nothing to lose."[28]

Such a protest is not only inspirational to many of us but an invitation to ponder the infinitely greater impact of collective action. Imagine, for example, that a teacher at any given school in your area quietly approached each person on the staff in turn and asked: "If ___ percent of the teachers at this school pledged to boycott the next round of testing, would you join them?" (The specific percentage would depend on what seemed realistic and yet signified sufficient participation to offer some protection for those involved.) Then, if the designated number was reached, each teacher would be invited to take part in what would be a powerful act of civil disobedience. Press coverage would likely be substantial, and despairing-but-cowed teachers in other schools might be encouraged to follow suit.

Without question, this is a risky undertaking. Theoretically, even an entire school faculty could be fired. But the more who participate, and the more careful they are about soliciting support from parents and other members of the community beforehand, the more difficult it would be for administrators to respond harshly. (Of course, some administrators are as frustrated with the testing as teachers are.) Participants would have to be politically savvy, building alliances and offering a coherent, quotable rationale for their action. They would need to make it clear – at a press conference and in other forums – that they were taking this action not because they are unwilling to do more work or are afraid of being held accountable, but because these tests lower the quality of learning and do a serious injustice to the children in our community.

The bottom line is that standardized testing can continue only with the consent and cooperation of the educators who allow those tests to be distributed in their schools – and the parents who permit their children to take them. If we withhold that consent, if we refuse to cooperate, then the testing process grinds to a halt. That is what happened in Japan. That is what can happen in the United States if we understand the urgency of the situation. Discuss it with your university students, your staff, your colleagues: What if they gave a test and nobody came?

MOST OF THESE SUGGESTIONS – ALONG WITH OTHER ACTS
of resistance – spring not from someone's imagination but from real
activities being undertaken around the country. Parents in Wisconsin
successfully lobbied their state legislators to prevent a high-school exit
exam from being the sole determinant of whether students are permit-
ted to graduate – a stinging defeat for Gov. Tommy Thompson. In
Florida, where schools are graded on the basis of test scores, with successful schools receiving more money and the neediest schools threatened with a loss of funding, a group of teachers and their principal at an
"A" school (Gulf Gate Elementary) publicly refused to accept their bo-
nuses. In a similar protest in North Carolina, teachers (at East Chapel
Hill High School) pooled their state bonus checks and formed a foundation to send grants to the state's poorer schools.

Parents and teachers have taken to the streets in Colorado and Ohio.
Lawsuits have been filed in Louisiana, Indiana, and Nevada to challenge the legality of high-stakes tests. (The first case to go to trial, in
Texas, was decided in favor of the state.) Petitions are being circulated,
locally and nationally; legislators are being lobbied; websites are being
set up in several states to help testing opponents coordinate their efforts.[29] And individuals are courageously challenging the system in a
variety of ways. In early 1999, George Schmidt, a veteran Chicago high
school teacher, published some of that city's tests (after students had
already taken them) in a small independent newspaper so that the public could evaluate the validity and value of the questions. He was promptly
charged with "gross disruption of the educational process," suspended
without pay, and sued for $1.4 million.

Eugene Garcia, dean of the school of education at the University of
California, Berkeley, resigned his position on an advisory committee to
the State Board of Education. He did so to protest – and draw attention
to – the Board's decision to subject students with limited English proficiency to tests on which they are certain to do poorly just because they
don't speak the language. He then called for parents of such students to
decline to participate in the testing program, thereby increasing the
number of English-speaking students who would score below the median (since the state's high-stakes test, incredibly, is norm-referenced).
These results, he speculated, might shock some of these families into
opposing the tests.

Most impressive, and most dramatic, has been the growing number
of boycotts all across the nation. Parents have said, in effect, "Not with
my child you don't!" and refused to allow their children to take the

tests. At first in scattered fashion – reflecting the lack of coordination among people who had independently decided the tests were destructive – students either declined to take them or failed them on purpose. This happened as long ago as 1989 in Torrance, Calif. and two years later in a parent-led protest involving several Colorado districts. Then, in 1998-99, parents across Michigan exempted 22.5 percent of students from the high school proficiency portion of the Michigan Educational Assessment Program (MEAP). Some districts had up to 90 percent of their students waived from taking the test, suggesting a "grassroots revolt by parents and students."[30] The following year, high school students walked out on a test in Marin County, Calif., calling it unjust that non-English-speaking students would have to take an English-language test, while students at the Whitney Young Magnet School in Chicago deliberately flunked the Illinois exam, saying they "refused to feed this test-taking frenzy." That same year, there were protests in Danvers, Cambridge, and Newton, Mass. and in Merton, Wisc. Last spring, a genuine boycott movement spread across Massachusetts, with hundreds of students sitting out that state's required tests as the result of a student-led campaign, with something similar happening in Illinois.

Boycotters and other protesters are disturbed not only by the tests themselves but by the profoundly undemocratic nature of what passes for school reform today: a one-size-fits-all set of standards and assessments handed down from the state capital and imposed with the force of law. Thus, individual schools or districts may devise thoughtful criteria for awarding a high school diploma, perhaps using what the Coalition of Essential Schools calls "exhibitions" of mastery – only to have the state's education czar brush aside such alternatives and declare that nothing will count except a student's score on a uniform set of pencil-and-paper tests. This is precisely what has happened in New York, and it has recently led to an intriguing and constructive form of rebellion. A group of superintendents in Monroe County (whose students happen to do quite well on the state's Regents exams) are in the early stages of creating an independent local board that will issue a diploma to students "who meet a set of validated criteria based on multiple assessments and multiple forms of assessment," according to William Cala, the superintendent of Fairport Schools. Representatives of business and higher education will help to formulate these criteria and then oversee administration of the diplomas. The participation of these groups will ensure that receiving a county rather than state-sanctioned diploma will not put students at a disadvantage. Indeed, a document that certifies the ability to think deeply in different ways, using a variety of formats – and to apply knowledge in realistic situations – ultimately may be worth more than a diploma certifying the ability to take standardized tests well. Moreover, the schooling that precedes graduation may be far more worthwhile than the sort held hostage to conventional exit exams. In any event, the idea of creating a legally valid, practically useful, locally devised diploma neatly neutralizes the standards-and-accountability autocracy. What state authorities are doing already lacks logic and the support of research. Now it may be stripped of the one thing it does possess: the power to compel compliance.

Less because of such protests than because decision makers are starting to realize the catastrophic effects of high-stakes testing, there has been some tinkering with the tests. It appears that more states will step back from the brink, particularly when it becomes clear that affluent, white students may be affected. Some test backers grudgingly concede that they may have moved a little too quickly, and now we are witnessing a delay of implementation here, a lower passing grade there, some sanctions waived and some expectations softened. This tentative response has already begun to generate a counter-reaction from hard-core pundits and politicians who affect a macho tone and taunt those responsible for watering down the tests and giving in to pressure groups (such as alarmed parents). As a harsh, punitive approach begins to reveal itself as counterproductive, this contingent has responded by demanding an even harsher, more punitive response.

In fact, though, the problem with this back-pedalling is that it doesn't go nearly far enough. Those who understand the weaknesses of standardized tests – and, indeed, the deficiencies of the whole tougher standards sensibility – will derive scant comfort from efforts to adjust the scores required for passing or to tinker with the applications of rewards and punishments. These minor repairs don't address the underlying problems with using such exams to judge students and educators, much less to bully them into higher scores. We are not quibbling about how high or how fast; we are calling the whole enterprise into question. We are not proposing to make school easier, but to make it better – and that requires rethinking standardized testing, per se. ♥

Alfie Kohn is a writer on human behaviour, education and social theory, living in the Boston area of the United States. He is the author of eight books, including The Schools Our Children Deserve: Moving Beyond Traditional Classrooms *and* 'Tougher Standards' *(Houghton Mifflin, 1999) and* The Case Against Standardized Testing: Raising the Scores,

Ruining the Schools (Heinemann, 2000), from which this article is adapted."

Copyright 2001 by Alfie Kohn. Reprinted from Phi Delta Kappan with the author's permission. For more information, please see www.alfiekohn.org."

Notes

[1] A study of math scores on the 1992 National Assessment of Educational Progress found that the combination of four variables unrelated to instruction (number of parents living at home, parents' educational background, type of community [e.g., "disadvantaged urban," "extreme rural"], and state poverty rate) explained a whopping 89 percent of the differences in state scores. In fact, one of those variables, the number of students who had one parent living at home, accounted for 71 percent of the variance all by itself. See Glen E. Robinson and David P. Brandon, NAEP Test Scores: Should They Be Used to Compare and Rank State Educational Quality? (Arlington, Va.: Educational Research Service, 1994). The same pattern holds within states. In Massachusetts, five factors explained 90 percent of the variance in scores on the Massachusetts Comprehensive Assessment System (MCAS) exam, leading a researcher to conclude that students' performance "has almost everything to do with parental socioeconomic backgrounds and less to do with teachers, curricula, or what the children learned in the classroom. " See Kevin J. Clancy, "Making More Sense of MCAS Scores," Boston Globe , 24 April 2000, p. A19. Another study looked just at the poverty level in each of 593 districts in Ohio and found a .80 correlation with 1997 scores on that state's proficiency test, meaning that this measure alone explained nearly two-thirds of the differences in test results. See Randy L. Hoover, "Forces and Factors Affecting Ohio Proficiency Test Performance," available at http://cc.ysu.edu/~rlhoover/OPT. Even a quick look at the grades given to Florida schools under that state's new rating system found that "no school where less than 10% of the students qualify for free lunch scored below a C, and no school where more than 80% of the students qualify scored above a C." See Jodi Wilgoren, "Florida's Vouchers a Spur to Two Schools Left Behind," New York Times, 14 March 2000, p. A18. Then there is the SAT, which, far from being a measure of merit (sometimes pointedly contrasted with affirmative action criteria), is largely a measure of family income. Break down the test takers by income, measured in $10,000 increments, and without exception the scores rise with each jump in parents' earnings. See "1999 College Bound Seniors' Test Scores: SAT," FairTest Examiner, Fall 1999, p. 13; the information is also available at www.collegeboard.org.

[2] The nature and extent of those flaws vary with the nature of the testing program, of course. Exams that are norm-referenced, timed, composed largely of multiple-choice questions, given to young children, or designed to measure the short-term acquisition of isolated facts and skills are particularly unhelpful.

[3] See Judith L. Meece, Phyllis C. Blumenfeld, and Rick H. Hoyle, "Students' Goal Orientations and Cognitive Engagement in Classroom Activities, Journal of Educational Psychology vol. 80, 1988, pp. 514-23. The correlation was .28, significant at p<.001.

[4] The middle school students "who value literacy activities and who are task-focused toward literacy activities" got lower scores on the CTBS reading test. See Eric M. Anderman, "Motivation and Cognitive Strategy Use in Reading and Writing." Paper presented at the National Reading Conference, San Antonio, Tex., December 1992. The same pattern showed up with high schoolers taking the SAT: researchers classified students' approaches to studying as "surface" (doing as little as possible and sticking to rote memorization), "deep" (understanding ideas and connecting new material to existing knowledge), or "achieving" (trying to get good grades and beat everyone else, without interest in what was being learned). It turned out that those who adopted a surface or achieving style did the best on the SAT. Scores were negatively correlated with a deep approach to learning. See Cathy W. Hall, Larry M. Bolen, and Robert H. Gupton, Jr., "Predictive Validity of the Study Process Questionnaire for Undergraduate Students," College Student Journal, vol. 29, 1995, pp. 234-39.

[5] It would be instructive to see a poll that measured familiarity with the tests as well as attitudes about testing, and then looked at the interaction between the two. But we do not have to speculate about the effect of becoming familiar with alternatives to standardized tests. A survey of parents of third graders in an ethnically diverse, working-class district near Denver found higher levels of support for performance assessments than for standardized tests once the former option was presented and explained. Parents in this study were shown examples of standardized test questions such as "How much change will you get if you have $6.55 and spend $4.32? [a] $2.23 [b] $2.43 [c] $3.23 [d] $10.87" as well as performance assessment questions such as "Suppose you couldn't remember what 8 x 7 is. How could you figure it out?" A large majority of respondents preferred performance assessments. Indeed, many remarked that the latter were more challenging and gave teachers more insight into what the students understood and where they were struggling. The researchers admitted being "surprised that parents rated informal sources of information – talking to the teacher and seeing graded samples of their child's work – as more useful than standardized tests for learning about their 'child's progress in school' and even for judging the 'quality of education provided at their child's school.'" Clearly, they concluded, "parents' favorable ratings of standardized national tests do not imply a preference for such measures over other less formal sources of information." See Lorrie A. Shepard and Carribeth L. Bliem, "Parents' Thinking About Standardized Tests and Performance Assessments," Educational Researcher, November 1995, pp. 25-32.)

[6] See Alfie Kohn, The Case Against Standardized Testing: Raising the Scores, Ruining the Schools (Portsmouth, N.H.: Heinemann, 2000) or chapter 4 of The Schools Our Children Deserve (Boston: Houghton Mifflin, 1999), from which much of the former book was adapted.

⁷ See, for example, Peter Sacks, Standardized Minds (Cambridge, Mass.: Perseus, 1999); and Kathy Swope and Barbara Miner, eds., Failing Our Kids: Why the Testing Craze Won't Fix Our Schools (Milwaukee: Rethinking Schools, 2000). For background information about these tests, see Gerald W. Bracey, Put to the Test: An Educator's and Consumer's Guide to Standardized Testing (Bloomington, Ind.: Phi Delta Kappa, 1998); and any of several publications by W. James Popham.

⁸ Harvey Daniels, "Whole Language: What's the Fuss?" Rethinking Schools, Winter 1993, p. 5

⁹ See Merle B. Karnes, Allan M. Shwedel, and Mark B. Williams, "A Comparison of Five Approaches for Educating Young Children from Low-Income Homes." In As the Twig Is Bent . . .: Lasting Effects of Preschool Programs, edited by The Consortium for Longitudinal Studies (Hillsdale, N.J.: Erlbaum, 1983), pp. 133-69.

¹⁰ See Hilton Smith, "Foxfire Teachers' Networks," in John M. Novak, ed., Democratic Teacher Education: Programs, Processes, Problems, and Prospects (Albany: State University of New York Press, 1994), p. 29.

¹¹ See Kathe Taylor and Sherry Walton, Children at the Center: A Workshop Approach to Standardized Test Preparation, K-8 (Portsmouth, N.H.: Heinemann, 1998); and Lucy Calkins, Kate Montgomery, and Donna Santman, A Teacher's Guide to Standardized Reading Tests: Knowledge Is Power (Portsmouth, N.H.: Heinemann, 1998). Several articles in the December 1996 / January 1997 issue of Educational Leadership are also relevant.

¹² Linda M. McNeil, Contradictions of School Reform: Educational Costs of Standardized Testing (New York: Routledge, 2000) , pp. 204, 203.

¹³ Jonathan Kozol, Foreword to Will Standards Save Public Education? by Deborah Meier (Boston: Beacon, 2000), p. x.

¹⁴ Lynn Olson, "Worries of a Standards 'Backlash' Grow," Education Week, 5 April 2000, p. 12. Note that even the headline of this article assumes that a backlash against the standards-and-testing movement is something one should worry about rather than welcome – a bias reflected in most coverage of the issue.

¹⁵ "No single test score can be considered a definitive measure of a student's knowledge," so "an educational decision that will have a major impact on a test taker should not be made solely or automatically on the basis of a single test score. Other relevant information about the student's knowledge and skills should also be taken into account," according to Jay P. Heubert and Robert M. Hauser, eds. High Stakes: Testing for Tracking, Promotion, and Graduation (Washington, D.C.: National Academy Press, 1999).

¹⁶ For example, one Republican state legislator in Delaware announced: "I cannot support, under any circumstances, a test that will be the be-all and end-all of a student's [getting a diploma]. So why don't we just remove that? How have we ever got to the point where we allow one test to determine our children's future?" At that point in the debate, according to a newspa-

per account, "several in the chamber spoke of how they had successfully moved from high school through college to even advanced degrees without having to pass a single, difficult, standardized test. Others recalled conversations with teachers who admitted they would not be successful taking the tests themselves. 'It seems like we're trying to treat the symptom instead of the disease,'" remarked another Republican representative, adding, "The problem is the testing." See Tom Eldred, "Education Bill Passes Delaware House," Delaware State News, 17 March 2000. Similarly, Pennsylvania's state board of education ruled out a test to determine whether students would receive a diploma, with one board member commenting, "I couldn't sit here in this seat and take that kind of decision out of the hands of teachers who had worked hard with the students for 13 years." See Christopher Newton, "State Education Board Rules Out High School Test," Philadelphia Inquirer, 20 April 2000.

[17] This argument in particular resonates with people across the political spectrum.

[18] For more on this point, see The Schools Our Children Deserve, chap. 2.

[19] For further thoughts on helping educators to become more adept at political organizing, see Ellen H. Brinkley and Constance Weaver, "Organizing for Political Action: Suggestions from Experience," in Kenneth S. Goodman, ed., In Defense of Good Teaching: What Teachers Need to Know About the "Reading Wars" (Portsmouth, N.H.: Heinemann, 1998), pp. 183-90.

[20] This letter appears in W. James Popham, Testing! Testing!: What Every Parent Should Know About School Tests (Boston: Allyn and Bacon, 2000), p. 284.

[21] One bumper sticker now being circulated asks, IS STANDARDIZED TESTING HURTING OUR KIDS? Another, more decisive one features the initials of the state's test in a circle with a red diagonal slash running through them, followed by: THESE TESTS HURT KIDS! Meanwhile, some educators have printed up t-shirts that read, HIGH STAKES ARE FOR TOMATOES.

[22] Scott G. Paris, Theresa A. Lawton, Julianne C. Turner, and Jodie L. Roth, "A Developmental Perspective on Standardized Achievement Testing," Educational Researcher, June-July 1991, p. 17.

[23] Anne Davis, "Executives in West Bend Struggle with Sample of State Graduation Test," Milwaukee Journal Sentinel, 20 January 1999.

[24] Stephen Hegarty, "Officials Dodge FCAT Dare," St. Petersburg Times, 13 February 2000.

[25] On the respects in which standardized testing is most damaging to low-income and minority students, see Alfie Kohn, The Case Against Standardized Testing, chap. 4; Kohn, "Standardized Testing and Its Victims," Education Week, 27 September 2000, pp. 60, 46, 47; Swope and Miner; and McNeil.

[26] See Catherine C. Lewis, Educating Hearts and Minds: Reflections on Japanese Preschool and Elementary Education (Cambridge, England: Cambridge University Press, 1995), pp. 201, 16.

[27] Jane Coles, "Enough Was Enough: The Teachers' Boycott of National Curriculum Testing," Changing English (published by the University of London's Institute of Education), vol. 1, no. 2, 1994, pp. 16, 23.

[28] This account is based on Robin Lord, "Harwich Teacher Refused to Hand Out MCAS Test," Cape Cod Times, 3 June 1999; Ed Hayward, "MCAS Opponents Hold Rally in Hub," Boston Herald, 16 May 2000; and personal communications. Bougas received a two-week suspension without pay in May 2000 but, at this writing, still has his job. Several other Massachusetts teachers have also refused to administer the MCAS, so far without repercussions.

[29] For example, www.stopopts.org in Ohio, http://personal.cfw.com/~dday/VASOLs.html in Virginia, www.xfcat.com in Florida, www.geocities.com/nccds/index.html in North Carolina, www.taasblues.com in Texas, www.castausa.com in Nevada, www.cpog.org in Georgia, www.fairtest.org/arn/masspage.html in Massachusetts, www.pipeline.com/~rgibson/meap.html in Michigan, and www.stopAIMSnow.org.

[30] Tracy Van Moorlehem, "Students, Parents Rebel Against State Test," Detroit Free Press, 29 April 1998, p. 1-A. Overall, "those opting out of the test tend to be average or above-average students," some of whom wore t-shirts that urged their peers to "just say no" to the test, Moorlehem reports. In response, state officials did not reconsider the value of the tests but began offering students substantial scholarships for high scores.